# THEOLOGICAL REFLECTION AND THE PURSUIT OF IDEALS

# Theological Reflection and the Pursuit of Ideals

## Theology, Human Flourishing and Freedom

*Edited by*

DAVID JASPER
*University of Glasgow, UK*

*and*

DALE WRIGHT
*Occidental College, Los Angeles, USA*

*with Maria Antonaccio and William Schweiker*

ASHGATE

Published by
Ashgate Publishing Limited
Wey Court East
Union Road
Farnham
Surrey, GU9 7PT
England

Ashgate Publishing Company
110 Cherry Street
Suite 3-1
Burlington, VT 05401-3818
USA

www.ashgate.com

**British Library Cataloguing in Publication Data**
Theological reflection and the pursuit of ideals :
    theology, human flourishing and freedom.
    1. Religious thought. 2. Philosophical theology.
    3. Religion and sociology. 4. Ideals (Philosophy)
    I. Jasper, David.
    201.7-dc23

**The Library of Congress has cataloged the printed edition as follows:**
Theological reflection and the pursuit of ideals : theology, human flourishing, and freedom /
edited by David Jasper and Dale Wright, with Maria Antonaccio and William Schweiker.
    pages cm
  Includes bibliographical references and index.
  ISBN 978-1-4094-5239-3 (hardcover) -- ISBN 978-1-4094-5240-9 (ebook) --
ISBN 978-1-4724-0055-0 (epub) 1. Philosophy and religion. 2. Theology.
3. Philosophical theology. I. Jasper, David. II. Wright, Dale Stuart. III. Antonaccio,
Maria. IV. Schweiker, William.

  BL51.T423 2013
  210--dc23

                                                                              2012040653
ISBN 9781409452393 (hbk)
ISBN 9781409452409 (ebk – pdf)
ISBN 9781472400550 (ebk – ePUB)

Printed and bound in Great Britain
by MPG PRINTGROUP

# Contents

# List of Contributors

**Thomas J. J. Altizer** was Associate Professor of Bible and Religion at Emory University from 1956–1968, and is now Emeritus Professor of the State University of New York, Stony Brook. In 1965 and 1966 he published two articles in *Time* Magazine on the Death of God, drawing on Hegel, Blake and Eliade. The author of numerous books, his memoir, *Living the Death of God*, was published in 2006.

**Pamela Sue Anderson** is Reader in Philosophy of Religion at the University of Oxford and Tutorial Fellow in Philosophy at Regent's Park College, Oxford. Well known for her work in the feminist philosophy of religion she has recently published *Re-visioning Gender in Philosophy of Religion: Reason, Love and Epistemic Locatedness* (Ashgate, 2012).

**Maria Antonaccio** is a Professor in the Religion Department at Bucknell University. She is the author of *Picturing the Human: The Moral Thought of Iris Murdoch* (Oxford University Press, 2000) and numerous articles on topics in religious ethics and moral theory. Her current research focuses on contemporary expressions and appropriations of ascetic discourse and practice, as well as issues related to the ethics of consumption.

**Daniel Boscaljon** received his doctoral degree in Religious Studies from the University of Iowa in 2009, and is working on a second doctoral degree, also from Iowa, in English with a focus on dwelling as a theme in 19th century American Literature. His first book, *Skeptical Faith and the Need for Vigilance*, is currently under review.

**Forrest Clingerman** is Associate Professor of Philosophy and Religion at Ohio Northern University. His research focuses on the relationship between hermeneutics and environmental thought. He is co-editor of *Placing Nature on the Borders of Religion, Philosophy and Ethics* (Ashgate, 2011) and a forthcoming volume on environmental hermeneutics. His work has also appeared in journals such as *Environmental Philosophy*; *Worldviews*; *Ethics, Place and Environment*; and *Environmental Values*.

**W. David Hall** is NEH Associate Professor of Religion and Philosophy at Centre College. His work explores the intersection of theology, hermeneutics, and phenomenology. He has authored two books on the thought of Paul Ricoeur and numerous articles in theology and philosophy of religion.

**Andrew W. Hass** lectures in Religion at the University of Stirling, Scotland. He has authored and edited several books on the crossover between religion, philosophy and the arts, including *Auden's O: The Loss of One's Sovereignty in the Making of Nothing* (under consideration), *The Oxford Handbook of English Literature and Theology* (co-eds. Jasper and Jay, Oxford University Press, 2007), and *Poetics of Critique: The Interdisciplinarity of Textuality* (Ashgate, 2002). Since 2004, he has been the General Executive Editor of OUP's journal *Literature and Theology*. Currently, he is writing a book for I.B. Tauris entitled *Hegel and the Art of Negation*.

**David Jasper** is Professor of Theology and Literature at the University of Glasgow and Changyiang Chair Professor at Renmin University of China, Beijing. The founding editor of the journal *Literature and Theology*, he is the authors of eight monographs and the co-editor of the *Oxford Handbook of English Literature and Theology* (Oxford University Press, 2007). He holds an honorary doctorate in Theology from the University of Uppsala, Sweden.

**William Klink** is Professor Emeritus in the Department of Physics and Astronomy at the University of Iowa. His research specialty is the study of symmetry, with emphasis on applications to relativistic nuclear and particle physics. He has published over 100 papers in mathematics and physics journals and book chapters, and was supported in his research by the nuclear division of the Department of Energy. He continues to have active collaborations with nuclear theorists, and in particular with members of the Institute for Physics in Graz, Austria.

**Julia A. Lamm** is Associate Professor of Theology at Georgetown University in Washington, D.C. She is author of *The Living God: Schleiermacher's Theological Appropriation of Spinoza* (Penn State University Press, 1996), as well as several articles on Schleiermacher, and is editor of *The Blackwell Companion to Christian Mysticism* (J. Wiley, 2013). She is also bringing to completion *Schleiermacher's Christmas Eve Dialogue and Other Works*, co-edited with Dawn DeVries, for *The Classics of Western Spirituality Series* (Paulist Press), and a monograph entitled *Julian of Norwich on Revelation and Grace*.

**William Schweiker** is the Edward L. Ryerson Distinguished Service Professor of Theological Ethics at the University of Chicago and also the Director of the Martin Marty Center for the Advanced Study of Religion. He is the author of several books, including, most recently, *Theological Ethics and Global Dynamics: In the Time of Many Worlds* (Blackwell Pub., 2004), *Religion and the Human Future: An Essay on Theological Humanism* (Blackwell Pub., 2008) written with David E. Klemm, and also *Dust That Breathes: Christian Faith and the New Humanisms* (Wiley-Blackwell, 2010) as well as many articles and edited volumes. Besides teaching at Chicago, Schweiker has been guest professor at Uppsala University and the University of Heidelberg.

**Glenn Whitehouse** is Assistant Dean of Arts and Sciences and Associate Professor of philosophy and religion at Florida Gulf Coast University, where he was a founding faculty member. His scholarly work is interdisciplinary in scope, focusing on religion and film, religion and humanism, and the philosophy of Paul Ricoeur. He has presented his scholarship at venues such as the AAR, SPEP, and the ACLA, and has published in *Literature and Theology* and *Modern Theology*, among other journals.

**Dale S. Wright** is the Gamble Distinguished Professor of Religious Studies and Asian Studies and Chair of the Department of Religious Studies at Occidental College in Los Angeles. Among his publications are *Philosophical Meditations on Zen Buddhism* (Cambridge University Press, 1998), *The Six Perfections: Buddhism and the Cultivation of Character* (Oxford University Press, 2009), and a series of five books on Zen Buddhism, co-edited with Steven Heine.

# Preface

David Jasper and Dale S. Wright

Contemporary thought is marked by heated debates about the character, purpose, and form of religious thinking and its relation to a range of ideals: spiritual, moral, aesthetic, political, and ecological, to name just the most obvious. This book addresses the interrelation between theological thinking and the complex and diverse realm of human ideals. What are the ideals appropriate to our moment in human history, and how do these ideals derive from or relate to theological reflection in our time? Written by internationally renowned thinkers from a range of disciplines (physics, art, literary studies, ethics, comparative religion, history of ideas, and theology), the chapters in this volume engage this crucial question with the intention of articulating a new and historically appropriate vision of theological reflection and the pursuit of ideals for our global times.

Well aware of the ambiguous character of religion in the contemporary world and religion's historic role in the generation of cultural ideals, the scholars represented in this book have gathered at conferences over the past five years in an attempt to articulate a distinctively theological contribution to the pursuit of ideals in contemporary culture. The chapters contained in this volume reflect this long-standing conversation and share an orientation to contemporary thought that is both humanistic and theological. They focus, therefore, on the flourishing of human culture and on what transcends the human sphere, the larger and more comprehensive context upon which and within which human life is grounded. The shared norm reflected in these chapters has come to be called "the integrity of life," the ground of human life and what is transcendent to humanity. While reflecting the integrity of life theologically, the chapters continue the humanistic tradition of celebrating human freedom, creativity, and autonomous critical thinking, seeking to encourage a love of life rooted in the wholeness and integrity of life.

The culmination of conversations between the authors in this volume occurred on the campus of the University of Chicago in early May 2011 when each of the authors presented the final form of their work. The editors extend their sincere appreciation to William Schweiker, Edward L. Ryerson Distinguished Service Professor of Theological Ethics and Director of The Martin Marty Center, for hosting what all participants agreed was an exceptionally productive intellectual convergence. Moreover, authors William Schweiker and Maria Antonaccio shared in the initial conception and ongoing structuring of this volume, and the editors extend their utmost appreciation.

This book is dedicated to David E. Klemm whose innovative and transformative work in the field of philosophical theology has inspired the variety of historical, philosophical, and religious thinking found in this volume. Each of the authors owes much to David and we offer these chapters in gratitude and with heartfelt affection.

# Chapter 1

# Freedom and Matter

William H. Klink and David E. Klemm

## Introduction

What do we mean by "theological reflection" and "the pursuit of ideals"? We can construct a simple model of these activities—and how they are related—by focusing on our most basic, pre-reflective modes of thinking. In our inner world of thinking, we oscillate between *trusting what reveals itself to us* and *understanding what something is*. "Trusting" refers to the manifold of events in which we *respond* to something or someone who presents itself. For our purposes, seeing a tree or listening to someone speak are acts of trusting. "Understanding" refers to all of the times in which we actively *grasp* what something is or what some language means by applying concepts. Both trusting and understanding are free acts of the singular subjectivity that is the "I," in that "I" trust and "I" understand.

Whether we are aware of it or not, trusting and understanding are in some sense grounded in the acts of theological reflection and the pursuit of ideals, respectively. Ordinarily we understand everyday things or states of affairs when we know what to do with them, and we understand other people when we grasp how their expressions and deeds freely embody another "I" (as a "you" for me) in a shared world. For example, I understand that the budget is tight so I must be frugal and that my sister's birthday next month is important to her. When we understand anything at all, we reduce a set of possible meanings to an actual meaning. That is to say, when we think about something, we connect it with a set of (universal) concepts. When we undertake to understand what we understand when we understand anything at all, we are engaged in the pursuit of ideals. The ultimate norm of understanding is "being," which we can provisionally define as the real connection in something, which is reflected in thought, between the particular entity and its defining universal characteristics.[1] In theoretical judgments, being appears as truth; in practical decisions, being appears as goodness; in aesthetic awareness, being appears as beauty or meaningfulness.

Likewise, we typically trust both the world around us and many of the people in it. For example, I trust that the ground will support me when I walk and that the one whom I call "Mother" really is my mother. When we trust anyone or anything at all, we choose to assent to the word or presence of another person or thing, rather than to doubt it, deny it, or otherwise question it. When we trust or believe someone or something present to us, we let it be, or allow it to be, what it presents itself to be. However, when I ask "Whom do I trust in trusting anyone and anything at all?" then I have begun theological reflection. I trust my own trusting in naming the One in the Many, who is also the One beyond the Many, "God." The ultimate norm of trusting is "God," in the sense that Martin Buber gave when he defined God as the "eternal You," the one you that appears in every immediate relationship I have with a finite you, or in the sense that Paul Tillich gave in defining God as the symbol of "being-itself."[2] Theological reflection is thinking about what it means to respond to God. Just as the pursuit of ideals arises from understanding, so also theological reflection reciprocally arises from the free act of trusting—yet the pursuit of ideals and theological reflection concern the ultimate norms of understanding and trusting, respectively.

Our simple model of thinking now has the following basic elements— namely, 1) the acts of understanding and trusting as the active and responsive poles of thinking, respectively; 2) the "I" who thinks; 3) theological reflection and the pursuit of ideals as reflexive acts of thinking about thinking in its two modes; and 4) "Being" and "God" as the ultimate principles of the pursuit of ideals and theological reflection, respectively. The pursuit of ideals arises from understanding, and theological reflection is grounded in trusting. Even this highly simplified model requires one more principle, however. Intermediate between the reflexive acts of theological reflection and the pursuit of ideals, on one hand, and the ultimate principles of "Being" and "God," on the other hand, is *freedom*.

---

[1]   See Robert P. Scharlemann, *The Reason of Following* (Chicago: University of Chicago Press, 1991), pp. 38–61.

[2]   Martin Buber, *I and Thou*, trans. Walter Kaufmann (New York: Charles Scribner's Sons, 1970), p. 123. Paul Tillich, *Systematic Theology*, vol. I (Chicago: University of Chicago Press, 1951), p. 239.

Theological reflection and the pursuit of ideals are both grounded on the idea of freedom, for freedom is presupposed by these intellectual activities. Freedom, we say, is the capacity to actualize one among several possibilities—or, conversely, to open up what is actual to a new set of possibilities. An act of freedom transforms a mode of *possible being*, in which several alternatives present themselves within being, into a mode of *actual being*, in which one of the alternatives is chosen, enacted, and becomes real. Without freedom, neither trusting nor understanding would be possible, because freedom is the capacity to cross from the "I can" to the "I do," and back again. The pursuit of ideals, and theological reflection, therefore, both require freedom, as the condition of their possibility.

The Western philosophical tradition has typically assigned the capacity of freedom to what we might call, with Schleiermacher, the *intellectual* faculty of human being (thinking by means of reason, the ideal)—as opposed to the *organic* faculty (bodily sensing what is material, the real).[3] The intellectual faculty provides the form of things, while the organic faculty responds to the material aspect of things. The presumption of freedom is commonly taken to be evidence that there is a spiritual aspect of human being, in addition to its material side. The basis of this belief is that the idea of freedom implies a causal agency of the will that is spiritual rather than material. We hold ourselves, and others, to be responsible for our intentions, decisions, and deeds, because we assume that the faculty of will is not determined by any natural or material cause, but is free to determine itself. The power of freedom, we assume, is the power to initiate a causal series from ourselves and on our own, quite independently of any physical sensations or bodily feelings.

In the history of Western philosophy, Kant clarified the meaning of freedom in a pivotal way by relating it to the idea of causality. Kant held that all experience is subject to the law of causality—the law that a thing given in experience must itself be caused by another thing. He argued, however, that there are two kinds of causality, and that only two kinds are conceivable by us: "causality is either according to *nature* or arises from *freedom*."[4] Natural causality is "the connection in

---

[3] *Friedrich Schleiermachers Dialektik*, ed. Rudolf Odebrecht (Darmstadt: Wissenschaftliche Buchgesellschaft, 1988), pp. 38–44.

[4] Immanuel Kant, *Critique of Pure Reason*, trans. Norman Kemp Smith (New York: St. Martin's Press, 1965), A532/B560, p. 464.

the sensible world of one state with a preceding state on which it follows according to a rule." For example, April showers bring May flowers. By contrast, freedom in its "cosmological" meaning is "the power of beginning a state *spontaneously*."[5] Here we are presented with a causality that is utterly different than the causality of nature, because a free cause does not itself "stand under another cause determining it in time, as required by the law of nature." For example, I am now reading these words, but I could be doing something else.

Freedom, in the sense of absolute spontaneity, is "a pure transcendental idea," rather than an empirical idea, according to Kant, because it signifies the invariant structure within which we become acquainted with any causal series whose origin is different than the causation of nature. An empirical idea would refer us to an empirical object, and freedom is not an object of sense perception. As a transcendental idea, freedom is a necessary condition of our thinking. It alone accounts for our ability to initiate an event, such as the activity of our own thinking. But we cannot know that freedom exists—not in the strict sense of knowing, that is, the subsuming of sense perceptions under a concept. Rather, we recognize and acknowledge freedom in those cases when events happen through causes that are distinct from natural causes—such as cases of causal agency.

Kant continues. Freedom also has a distinct *practical* meaning in its application to ethics, where the concept of freedom means the self-legislation of a rational will, or the power of the will to be a law unto itself.[6] What we will as laws for ourselves, in Kant's view, are maxims, by which he means rules that take the form of "Do this act for the sake of that purpose."[7] Here, practical freedom is the capacity of rational self-determination—or, otherwise named, autonomy—in which the agent constitutes his or her own identity in its integrity, or lack of it, by how well he or she makes maxims for himself or herself. A morally "good" maxim is one that can function as a universal law for all agents facing the same moral

---

[5]     Kant, *Critique of Pure Reason*, A533/B561. See also Martin Heidegger, *The Essence of Human Freedom: An Introduction to Philosophy*, trans. Ted Sadler (London: Continuum, 2002), pp. 15–22.

[6]     Immanuel Kant, *Groundwork of the Metaphysics of Morals*, ed. Mary Gregor, intro. Christine M. Korsgaard (Cambridge: Cambridge University Press, 1997), p. 52.

[7]     For a helpful discussion of maxims in Kant, see Christine M. Korsgaard, *Self-Constitution: Agency, Identity, and Integrity* (Oxford: Oxford University Press, 2009), p. 11.

situation. Adopting good maxims makes the agent, as author of the maxims, into a good, unified, and whole person.

There is a relationship between the cosmological idea of freedom and the practical concept of freedom that is significant for the argument of this chapter. Heidegger points it out: "Absolute spontaneity (transcendental freedom) is not a matter of will and the law of the will but of the self-origination of a state; autonomy, on the other hand, concerns a particular being to which there belongs willing."[8] Autonomy is therefore a certain *kind* of absolute spontaneity. Absolute spontaneity determines the invariant structure of autonomy. If absolute spontaneity did not exist, then autonomy could not exist. "The possibility of autonomy is *grounded* in spontaneity," or, put differently, "practical freedom is grounded in transcendental freedom."[9] According to Kant, therefore, transcendental freedom—the freedom of absolute spontaneity—has a far wider application than does practical freedom. Kant does not tell us, however, what else, if anything, belongs under the idea of transcendental freedom in addition to rational self-determination (autonomy). In this chapter, we will propose a kind of transcendental freedom in matter that is indeed different than autonomy. Before we turn to our argument, however, let us reflect on the split between mind and matter that is the inheritance of modern philosophy, for it is that split which we hope to overcome within a revived dualism.

The foremost of Kant's contemporary interpreters, Johann Gottlieb Fichte, one of the most rigorous of all systematic thinkers, was highly aware of the problem. As we said earlier, for Kant, the idea of freedom is not something for which we have empirical evidence. Its status is that of a necessity for thinking. Consequently, from the empirical standpoint, one can say that the principle of sufficient reason (or natural causality) governs all of the activities of theoretical reason, and that this fact is incompatible with the existence of freedom.[10] Conversely, from the transcendental standpoint (that is, the standpoint from which we think about what we *must think* in order to make sense of our moral experience), one can say that moral law applies to all activities of practical reason, and that this fact is incompatible with determinism. Therefore, Fichte argued, systematic philosophy

---

[8]  Heidegger, *The Essence of Freedom*, p. 18.

[9]  Heidegger, *The Essence of Freedom*, p. 18.

[10]  The principle of sufficient reason was formulated as such by Leibniz, but it was known well before him. It is the principle that whatever is so must have a reason, which came to mean a natural causal explanation.

necessarily divides into two fundamental types, which he somewhat pejoratively called dogmatism and idealism. Dogmatism and idealism, he claimed, are equally valid (that is, logically self-consistent) systems of thought. Both systems can claim that they express the truth of things, and neither one can successfully refute the other, "for their quarrel is about the first principle, which admits of no derivation from anything beyond it."[11] The first principle articulates a certainty for knowing, which explains how our experience of the external world is possible.

For dogmatism, the first principle is the "thing-in-itself," which is "transcendent" to consciousness. In other words, we experience the world as we do, because objects, or things-in-themselves, present themselves to human consciousness, which in turn reflects these things as they are in themselves. Dogmatism treats consciousness, the "I think," like any other object—that is, as a finite, material reality. Dogmatism is the philosophical approach that is consistent with the natural sciences from Newton to the present. It is necessarily a rigorous determinism that must deny freedom, because for dogmatism all objects obey the causal law of nature. Idealism, on the other hand, explains experience on the basis of its first principle, the self-in-itself, which is "immanent" within consciousness. According to idealism, we experience the world as we do, because consciousness constitutes all objects of experience in the activity of thinking, even though the material out of which objects are composed is simply given to our senses. The transcendental "I," or self-in-itself, is a certainty for thought, because its original thinking activity *is* its own being; in positing its own being in thinking, it defines what objects are according to the laws of reason. Idealism is the philosophical stance that is compatible with Romanticism in poetry and the arts, as well as with political and legal theories that ascribe individual responsibility to free citizens.

According to Fichte, one must choose between the two rival systems, and "reason provides no principle of choice," because each one claims to be true, and there is no neutral standpoint from which to settle the dispute.[12] A dualism between mind and matter, such as Descartes bequeathed us, was ruled out by Fichte, because

---

[11]    Johann Gottlieb Fichte, *Science of Knowledge (Wissenschaftslehre)*, ed. and trans. Peter Heath and John Lachs (New York: Appleton-Century-Crofts, 1970), "First Introduction" (I, 425–429), pp. 8–28.

[12]    Fichte, *Science of Knowledge* (I, 433), p. 14, and Frederick C. Beiser, *German Idealism: The Struggle Against Subjectivism, 1781–1801* (Cambridge, MA: Harvard University Press, 2008), pp. 261–2.

it fails to explain how mind and matter are interrelated, while presupposing that there is some necessary continuity between them. Fichte believed that the choice between idealism and dogmatism is made on the basis of inclination and interest—on what sort of person one is. The dogmatist analyzes things, and how laws of nature explain observed regularities among them. The idealist reflects on the workings of mind, and how freedom and imagination combine to create meanings in art and language.

Things have not really changed much in the past two centuries. Today, philosophy is divided between successor-forms of dogmatism and idealism. Freedom or determinism—are these still the only options? In this chapter, we argue that there is another option. What would happen if freedom were conceived as embedded in matter itself—not as practical freedom, but as an instance of absolute spontaneity nonetheless? What if there is a material appearance of transcendental freedom that is different than the causal agency of the will? If so—if freedom is ingredient in matter—then, among other things, new life would be breathed into dualism, because we would then have the missing point of continuity between mind and matter. Other consequences for the pursuit of ideals and theological reflection would also follow, because the domain of freedom would extend to the entire universe. In this chapter, we propose precisely this: a dualist model of freedom in matter, by which we mean an appearance of transcendental freedom as absolute spontaneity that is ontologically an element in matter itself. We begin with a discussion of matter.

**The Argument**

From observing such things as rocks and tables, we tend to think of matter as being inert. But plants and animals (including human beings) are also composed of matter, and they are not inert. A common viewpoint is to say that rocks and tables are made of more fundamental forms of matter, such as atoms and molecules, and, since atoms and molecules are inert, this explains why rocks and tables also are. But then it is necessary to give an explanation as to how freedom could arise in animate things. This is the problem that has to be solved in a materialist perspective. In this chapter we start from a different perspective, namely that matter at the level of atoms and molecules is not inert, but exhibits primitive manifestations of freedom by virtue of having the property of being able to opt from sets of alternatives.

To make such a viewpoint plausible, we start from a common intuition, namely that human beings live in two disparate worlds, the world of mind and thinking, which we will call the transcendent order, and the world of matter. Planning a hike for tomorrow is mental activity, while actually hiking is physical activity. Writing about the difficulties of the hike after having hiked is different from hiking. Theories such as quantum theory, which purport to describe the material world, are not themselves material. Such examples are so commonplace as to make it easy to forget how mysterious it is that there should be two such utterly disparate worlds.

For disparate these two worlds actually are. The body, as an example of matter more generally, is limited in space and time, subject to physical and biological laws, and bounded by birth and death. In contrast, the thinking mind is able to transcend space and time, as often occurs in daydreams or flights of fancy. In the imagination, it is possible to ignore physical laws such as gravity, and to imagine living indefinitely. Further, while matter seems constrained by finiteness, the mind is able to reach to infinity, to think, for example, of infinite sets of numbers, such as the set of all integers, or all fractions.

What is perhaps even more astounding is that in human beings these two worlds intersect in very complicated and often mysterious ways; the mental world influences the physical world and vice versa. When I have an unsettling thought my palms get sweaty. Conversely, drinking too much wine can greatly influence my ability to think. To understand how these two disparate worlds intersect in human beings constitutes one of the very deepest puzzles of our time.

One of the most important early modern thinkers to grapple with the problem of how these two disparate worlds might interact was Descartes. In his work, *Meditations on First Philosophy*, he clearly states the problem, and yet is at a loss as to how to make sense of the interaction, finally resorting to locating the seat of the interaction in the pineal gland.[13] The problem of how mind or spirit is related to the brain, or more generally to the body, continues to challenge many thinkers

---

[13]    Descartes' letter to Mersenne, 21 April 1641, quoted in René Descartes, *Meditations on First Philosophy* (86), in *The Philosophical Writings of Descartes*, vol. II, trans. John Cottingham et al. (Cambridge: Cambridge University Press, 1984), p. 59.

today, and has resulted in a number of different viewpoints as to how the problem might be resolved.

The extreme positions are clear enough. On one side are realists or materialists—descendants of Fichte's dogmatists—who argue that the universe consists only of matter, and that the existence of mind or spirit is simply a manifestation of complex forms of matter, such as the brain produces, and has no independent existence. On the other side is the viewpoint of the idealists, that mind and spirit are primary, and that matter, in all its complex manifestations, is composed of ideas or representations that are known only by the mind.

Both realists and idealists propose to eliminate one side of the mystery by claiming to explain it on their own terms. But then they run into trouble. Materialists have great difficulty accounting for both the existence of the world of mathematics and other manifestations of the universal transcendent order and also the first-person experience of the thinking "I." Conversely, the idealist has the problem of accounting for properties of matter that are universal and seemingly independent of this or that mind. A dualist position, in contrast to both idealism and materialism, maintains the integrity of both worlds—the material world and the transcendent order—in its difference from the other. Our dualist position, in other words, grants to each world its own structure and independence. Our dualism also posits an inter-dependence of the material world and the transcendent order.

In this chapter, we want to argue that the interdependence of these two worlds is already present in matter at the level of quantum systems. That is, quantum systems manifest in their very nature properties that indicate the presence of freedom as well as material properties. It is our thesis that quantum systems exhibit elements of transcendental freedom, that is, absolute spontaneity, alongside their material aspects, because quantum systems can opt out of a set of alternatives presented to them in a measurement process. Moreover, the opting of quantum systems results in material changes in the quantum system, so that elements in the transcendent order influence the material properties of the quantum system. In order to develop this thesis, we will begin with a quick overview of Newtonian theory, where freedom and mind are superfluous, and use this overview to contrast how different is the case with quantum theory.

## Newtonian Theory

The starting point for Newtonian theory, as applied to point particles, is the notion of a trajectory. The trajectory of a thrown ball is a specification of its position and velocity as a function of time. The trajectory describes how the object moves in time through space. Thus, at some specific time, the ball (taken for simplicity to be a point particle) is located somewhere in space (relative to an observer) and is moving with a known velocity. The object is also assumed to have a definite mass. Newton's second law says that if the force on the object is known, the trajectory can be calculated as the solution of a differential equation (assuming known initial conditions).

Newton's equations are examples of elements in the transcendent order. They are not themselves material, but describe the behavior of material systems. Sending a rocket with a payload to Jupiter involves solving complicated differential equations in accelerating reference frames. The calculated trajectory is then used to predict what the initial speed and direction of the rocket should be so that the rocket eventually gets to Jupiter. The material system, the rocket and payload, is manipulated from knowledge of the solutions of equations that themselves are not material. More generally, the transcendent order includes all ideas, and in particular the theorems of mathematics, and the notions of logical thinking that go into making mathematics possible. Further, all physical theories, true and false, reside in the transcendent order; thus, quantum theory as a theory of matter, to be discussed subsequently, exists in the transcendent order.

The trajectory of a Newtonian object is always given relative to an observer. But there may be many observers, and for each, the trajectory of the object will look different. Yet it must be possible to have agreement between different observers, since there is only one object. Thus, Newton's second law must have a further property of providing agreement between different observers. If a person on a moving train throws a ball straight up in the air, the trajectory is that of the ball moving upwards to its highest point and then accelerating downwards until the ball is caught. However, for the person standing on the earth as the train moves by, the trajectory of the ball will appear parabolic.

Newton's equations have the property of being covariant with respect to different observers. That is, their form is unchanged relative to observers in different reference frames, which means that the differential equations can be formulated in any frame of reference. This has the consequence of not only guaranteeing that all observers will agree on the trajectory of the ball, but also leads to the famous conservation laws of energy, momentum, and angular momentum. That is, if the Newtonian equations are not only covariant, but are also invariant under transformations from one observer to another, then a conservation law follows. For example, if an equation is rotationally invariant (that is unchanged under a rotation of reference frames), it follows that angular momentum is conserved. A practical application of such a conservation law occurs when a diver goes from a straight body position to a tuck position; the spin velocity increases, as required by the conservation of angular momentum.

Newtonian theory was originally applied to systems of "particles" such as planets in the solar system, or objects moving on the earth. But very quickly it was also applied to fluids and gases, from which developed theories of hydrodynamics and fluid mechanics. It is striking how successful the many generalizations of the original Newtonian particle mechanics were, and how it seemed as though one was in possession of an entirely new way of understanding the structure of the universe. But what is even more striking about this picture is that mind and freedom as experienced by human beings seem to play no role whatsoever. Though "observers" could be taken to mean human beings with mind and consciousness, it could equally well mean devices equipped with cameras that record the trajectory of objects. Thus, freedom arises only with the choice of reference frame. I may choose the earth frame of reference while you choose a frame of reference tied to the moon. But the Newtonian equations are indifferent to these choices, as they are covariant with respect to any frame of reference. Moreover, any property of the system (or subsystem) that an observer chooses to measure can be extracted from the trajectories of the system. A measurement simply confirms properties that the system has by virtue of its trajectories.

If observers are taken to mean human beings, then the relation between the physical observables, obtained from trajectories, and experience, as felt by a self, is totally bypassed. Precisely the ontological difference between the inner world of a person, even that person as an observer, and the outside material world, is made irrelevant in Newtonian theory. Newtonian theory is therefore a form of materialistic and mechanistic determinism. For it, real things are material, they behave according to necessary causal laws in a mechanical fashion, and whatever happens in the world of real things must necessarily happen in precisely that way. However, though Newtonian theory makes no use of subjectivity, Newtonian theory is a theory, which exists in what we have called the transcendent order. Its success as a theory hinges on the correlations set up between predictions of the theory and the actual behavior of material systems. In this very restricted sense, there is use made of a world outside the material world, in that to have a theory at all, even one which makes no use of mind and self, is to presuppose some notion of a transcendent order. Elements in the theory, such as notions of space and time, mass and spin, substance and properties, potentia and actuality, and so on, are ideas that are necessary to formulating a physical theory, yet all these notions belong to the transcendent order.

At the beginning of the twentieth century, Newtonian theory reigned supreme. There were a few problems, such as what is known as Olber's paradox, which stated that if the universe as a whole is homogeneous and isotropic, there should be no difference between day and night. But it was felt that these sorts of problems could successfully be resolved into the Newtonian framework. In particular, it was felt that a new "quantum" domain, dealing with atoms and molecules, though challenging, could also be understood in the Newtonian framework. It was not so, however. Newtonian theory showed its limitations by breaking down in dealing with atoms and molecules, and even lower levels on the material hierarchy. There is also a breakdown in Newtonian theory at much higher levels of the inorganic hierarchy dealing with galaxies and massive star systems. Here the general theory of relativity, enunciated by Einstein in 1916 as a theory of gravitation and space-time, replaces the Newtonian framework. Unlike quantum theory, this newer theory of gravitation and space-time is deterministic and has an ontology similar to Newtonian theory.

**Quantum Theory**

Between 1900 and 1925, there was intense competition between the more conservative adherents of Newtonian theory and those willing to give up parts of the Newtonian ontology. The domain of the struggle was that of atoms and molecules, where the first successful quantum models were created. In fact, in the newly developed quantum theory, some parts of Newtonian ontology remained—such as the claim that mass (and also spin) characterize material objects. But more importantly, there were radical differences—such as quantum objects, like atoms, no longer have trajectories. The content of the famous Heisenberg uncertainty relations is that while it is possible to measure the position of an atom, or to measure the velocity of an atom, it is impossible to simultaneously measure both, so that the notion of a trajectory does not exist. What is even stranger is that the act of measurement brings certain properties of quantum systems into being.

Such features of quantum theory are so strange that it is worthwhile presenting a simple example to illustrate the differences between Newtonian theory and quantum theory. The example we choose makes use of the quantum theory of angular momentum; in Newtonian theory, angular momentum is never quantized, in quantum theory it is always quantized. Consider a spinning atom; it is characterized by its velocity and spin (we neglect the mass for simplicity). In the classic Stern-Gerlach experiment, which first demonstrated the quantization of angular momentum, an oven produces a horizontal beam of atoms that pass through a non-homogeneous (that is, not constant spatially) magnetic field whose axis is in the vertical direction.[14] The magnetic field produces forces on the spinning atoms that cause them to deviate from their original direction, which we call the forward direction.

A Newtonian model might picture the spinning atom as a tiny ball of charge spinning about its axis as it moves in the forward direction. Since spinning charge constitutes a current, when the spinning atom moves through the magnetic field, a force between the magnetic field and the spinning charge causes the axis of the spinning charge to change, as well as causing a change in the direction of motion from the forward direction. After the atom has left the magnetic field, it thus has a new axis of spin as well as a new direction of motion. Given knowledge of the magnetic field and the axis of spin before entering the magnetic field, the Newtonian equations are supposed to predict what the axis and direction of motion will be after the atom leaves the magnetic field.

---

[14]   See any book on quantum theory, such as J. Sakurai, *Modern Quantum Mechanics* (New York: Addison Wesley, 1985). There is also a short discussion on Wikipedia: "Stern-Gerlch Experiment."

What Stern and Gerlach found was that the Newtonian predictions were not only wrong, they rested on entirely invalid assumptions about the nature of a spinning atom. First, they discovered that only two spin axes were observed; one possibility was the axis pointing vertically upwards, the other pointing vertically downwards. Further, they found that the amount of spinning was always proportional to a new constant called Planck's constant. What would have been expected of the Newtonian spinning atom is that, depending on the original spin axis before entering the magnetic field, atoms exiting the magnetic field would have some new spin axis, which was not necessarily either vertically up or down. The important point here is that Newtonian theory says properties of the atom, after exiting the magnetic field, should be functions solely of the trajectory and interactions, properties that are causally related to the initial properties of the atoms.

To understand the behavior of spinning atoms requires ideas from quantum theory that are completely different than Newtonian theory. To begin, in contrast to Newtonian theory, spin in quantum theory is always quantized. Being quantized means, first, that the total amount of spin is an invariant quantity, which, along with its mass, characterizes the atom. Being a silver atom in its ground state means having a specific mass and a spin of ½ (in units of Planck's constant). Invariant means that every silver atom has the same mass and spin, no matter who the observer might be and what the state of motion of the atom relative to the observer might be. Second, the component of the spin along an arbitrarily chosen axis is also always quantized, and the possible values of the spin along this axis are determined by the total spin. In the case of the silver atom, which has a total spin of ½, the values of the spin along some axis can only be plus or minus ½.

Consider again the Stern-Gerlach experiment, only now assume that the spins of all atoms leaving the oven have the value ½ along the vertical axis. When they enter the magnetic field, there is again an interaction between the spinning atom and the magnetic field. Now the exiting atoms continue to have spin value ½ along the vertical axis, as would also be predicted by Newtonian theory. Similarly, an atom with spin value minus ½ along the vertical axis will continue to have spin value minus ½ along the vertical axis after exiting the magnetic field. As we will see in our dualist model, the atom in this case has no alternatives open to it. It must remain in the same state after exiting the magnetic field.

Next consider atoms leaving the oven with spin axis perpendicular to both the vertical magnetic field axis and the direction of motion. The Stern-Gerlach experiment showed that the outcomes after exiting the magnetic field were: 50 percent of the time the outcome is plus ½ along the vertical axis, and 50 percent of the time the outcome is minus ½ along the vertical axis. But why any given atom so prepared has either a plus or minus outcome is not explained. Put in more quantum mechanical terms, the atom with spin axis perpendicular to the vertical and forward direction has no spin value that is either vertical plus ½ or vertical minus ½; rather, it is a superposition of the two. But in the act of interacting with the magnetic field, the outcome is reduced to one or the other; this is the origin of the term "reduction of the wave packet."

In the dualistic model we are proposing, the atom has open to it two alternatives, either plus ½ or minus ½, and it opts for one or the other. In interacting with the measuring apparatus (in this case the magnetic field with a further device recording the changed direction of motion), the atom opts for one or the other of the alternatives open to it. In opting for one or the other, the atom is manifesting a property not seen in Newtonian matter, namely, the expression of a primitive sort of freedom.

This sort of language can be generalized to any system that exhibits quantum behavior. Quantum systems are characterized by states (in spaces called Hilbert spaces, unrelated to space in the usual sense). All the properties of the system can be extracted from the state of the system. Some properties, such as mass and spin, are invariants of the system. They remain unchanged under interactions with other systems and identify the type of system being investigated. Other properties of the system are available only potentially. When the system interacts with a device measuring a certain observable, such as the spin along a given axis, the system has a set of alternatives open to it, and it opts for one alternative out of the manifold of possibilities. After opting for one alternative, the new state of the system is given by what is called the eigenvector of the observable, correlated to the alternative that has been opted. What is striking in this language is that the observable being measured is brought into being in the act of measurement. It did not exist as a unique property of the system before measurement.

In the Stern-Gerlach experiment, the atom with spin axis perpendicular to the vertical and forward directions did not have a definite vertical spin value. Only the act of measurement brought it into a definite vertical spin value, and that value, in our dualistic model, was freely opted. After having opted for, say, the plus ½ value, the atom has the property of having spin value along the vertical axis of plus ½. If a subsequent measurement is made using a Stern-Gerlach apparatus with the magnetic field tilted away from the vertical axis, upon measurement the new possible outcomes are plus or minus along the new axis defined by the direction of the magnetic field. The atom does not have a definite value of spin along the new magnetic field axis until the measurement is made. When the measurement is made, the atom opts for one specific alternative out of the two possibilities, so that one particular spin value is actualized out of a set of potential outcomes. This is what Heisenberg meant when he said that potentia has been converted to actuality.[15] And potentia exists in the transcendent order while the actualized value of the spin exists in the material world.

Moreover, if many atoms pass through the magnetic field, the outcomes resulting from opting give a probability distribution, which is not in general 50 percent along the plus axis and 50 percent along the minus axis; rather, the probability depends on the angle of the magnetic field relative to the vertical axis. Though freely opting, the atoms have a propensity, which is manifested in the probability distributions predicted by quantum theory.

Thus we see that a measuring device provides the means by which the quantum system opts for one out of a manifold of possibilities. A measuring device is so called if, when the quantum system encounters it, it provides a range of alternatives relative to a specified observable such as energy or spin projection, out of which the quantum system then opts for one alternative, which is actualized. One of the great successes of quantum theory is that for a vast variety of different systems, it has always correctly predicted the correct set of alternatives corresponding to a given observable. Sometimes the observable has a continuous set of alternatives, as is the case with the observable called momentum (related to velocity). Sometimes the observable has only a discrete set of alternatives, as is the case with spin and angular momentum. More often, the set of alternatives is a combination of both. The hydrogen atom has both discrete and continuous energy alternatives open to it; the discrete alternatives are called

---

[15]    Werner Heisenberg, *Physics and Philosophy: The Revolution in Modern Science* (New York: Harper & Row, 1958), p. 54.

the bound states, while the continuous ones give the alternatives for ionization, when the electron and proton break apart. But in all cases, quantum theory predicts a constrained and well-defined set of alternatives. Measuring devices are then actual physical devices that make possible opting for one out of a set of alternatives of a given observable open to a quantum system, and converting the opted alternative to macroscopic readings that can be suitably recorded.

## Reception of Quantum Theory

Given this short overview of quantum theory, we turn to the question of interpretations of the theory. We want to show that our dualist interpretation is able to deal with aspects of quantum theory that are inexplicable in other interpretations. We will deal with three well-known interpretations, the Copenhagen, realist, and idealist interpretations, before sketching our own model.

The first interpretation to emerge from the newly developed quantum theory was the Copenhagen interpretation, so called because it was largely developed at the institute in Copenhagen founded by Nils Bohr in the mid 1920s.[16] It developed from intense discussions between the primary creators of quantum theory, in an effort to make sense of the strange features of the quantum world.

In the Copenhagen interpretation, there is a sharp split between the quantum and classical worlds. A quantum system with its incompatible observables and lack of trajectories interacts with a measuring device, which is necessarily a classical device, obeying the dictates of Newtonian theory. Though the boundary between the quantum system and classical measuring device is not always sharp, the split must inevitably be drawn somewhere. In the Stern-Gerlach experiment, the quantum system is usually taken to be the beam of atoms, and the measuring device is the magnetic field and the detector for recording the deviated beam. But the quantum system could also include parts of the magnetic field, which would then change the nature of the measuring device.

Further, the nature of the interaction between quantum system and measuring device is not itself taken from quantum theory. Rather, the quantum system is prepared in certain states, and the measuring device is calibrated relative to these

---

[16] See, for example, Heisenberg, *Physics and Philosophy*, Chapter III.

states; thus, in the Stern-Gerlach experiment, if the beam of atoms has spin axis along the vertical direction and the magnetic field also points along the vertical direction, the measuring device is properly calibrated if the exiting atoms continue to have spin axis along the vertical direction.

The state of the system is given by a wave function, which provides all the information that can be known about the quantum system. But the Copenhagen interpretation makes no ontological claims. In the Copenhagen interpretation, quantum theory is an epistemological theory, which deals only with our knowledge of the system, and not with the system itself. As the system evolves in time according to the Schroedinger equation, knowledge about properties of the system changes. It also changes when a measurement is made, resulting in new knowledge of the system as recorded by the classical measuring device, as well as obtaining new information about the state of the system after measurement, as encoded in the appropriate eigenvector.

The Copenhagen interpretation has been criticized on a number of grounds. The invariant characterization of quantum systems by their mass and spin is an ontological claim, yet the Copenhagen interpretation purports to make no ontological claims. Further, measuring devices, although behaving classically, are made of atoms, and therefore should themselves be understood in quantum-theoretic terms. And the interactions between the quantum system and measuring device should also be understood in quantum-theoretic terms.

Such criticisms led to a different interpretation of quantum theory, developed in the early 1930s by von Neumann, and then more fully elaborated by London and Bauer.[17,18] In the von Neumann interpretation, there are two distinct processes by which quantum systems evolve, through the time evolution given by the Schroedinger equation, and in the measuring process, which is not governed by the Schroedinger equation. Even though the measurement process is not governed by the Schroedinger equation, both quantum system and measuring device are to be understood in terms of quantum theory. But if the reduction of the wave function is outside of quantum theory, what then actually produces a measurement? The

---

[17]   J. von Neumann, *Mathematical Foundations of Quantum Mechanics* (Princeton: Princeton University Press, 1955), Chapter VI.

[18]   F. London and E. Bauer, in *Quantum Theory and Measurement*, ed. J.A. Wheeler and W. Zurek (Princeton: Princeton University Press, 1983), p. 217.

answer alluded to by von Neumann and stated directly by London and Bauer was that only something outside the material universe, such as consciousness, could complete a measurement.

Needless to say, this conclusion was and continues to be disputed. Unlike the Copenhagen interpretation, the von Neumann interpretation makes ontological claims. But the logic of the interpretation seems to lead inevitably to the introduction of mind into the measuring process, a result that is anathema to a realist interpretation of quantum theory.

So over the years a number of quantum theorists have tried to construct a realist interpretation of quantum theory that is faithful to the actual structure of the theory.[19] In particular, a goal of a realist interpretation of quantum theory is to understand the measurement process solely in quantum-theoretic terms. One possibility for doing this would be to modify the Schroedinger equation so as to incorporate directly the measurement process. A number of models have been suggested, but they all invoke processes,which have not been seen experimentally.[20]

Another possibility in a realist interpretation is to enlarge the domain of quantum system and measuring device to include the surrounding environment. In a process called decoherence, it is the interaction between the quantum system and the environment that makes it possible to understand how the potentia contained in wave functions are converted to probability distributions.[21] But in spite of these and other advances in the understanding of quantum theory, the goal of a comprehensive realist interpretation of quantum theory has not yet been achieved.

And while any alleged realist interpretation does make ontological claims, it has not been possible to eliminate the observer from the measuring process. If the Schroedinger equation is not modified, there seems to be no way in which the strong objectivity of Newtonian theory can also hold for quantum theory. A simple way to see this is to recall that a measuring device measures an observable quantity. The experimenter freely chooses which observable to measure. When the measurement is made, the outcome is one out of the set of alternatives as prescribed by the observable. The property in question is not already inherent in

---

[19]    B. d'Espagnet, *In Search of Reality* (New York: Springer-Verlag, 1983).

[20]    See, for example, G.C. Ghirardi, A. Rimini, and T. Weber, "Unified Dynamics for Microscopic and Macroscopic Systems," *Physical Review D*, vol. 34 (1986), p. 470.

[21]    See, for example, E.D. Zeh, in *Decoherence and the Appearance of a Classical World in Quantum Theory*, ed. D. Giulini et al. (New York: Springer-Verlag, 1996).

the system, as would be the case for a Newtonian system, but comes into being as a result of the experiment. Mind and intention are intrinsically present in quantum theory—both in selecting which observable to measure and in the appearance of the observable itself.

Moreover, there is no attempt made in the Copenhagen and realist interpretations to account for the puzzling fact that measurements made on individual quantum systems always result in a definite outcome. When such outcomes of individual systems are averaged over an ensemble of identically prepared systems, the results can be understood through the probability predictions of quantum theory. The inability of these interpretations to account for the behavior of individual systems having definite outcomes in a measurement process was famously expressed by Dirac as "Nature chooses." But this is taken to mean that these interpretations simply cannot deal with individual quantum systems.

The upshot of these considerations is that both the Copenhagen and realist interpretations of quantum theory have significant shortcomings. Since these shortcomings have to do both with the intrusion of mind into quantum theory and the inability to deal with individual systems, is it possible to give an idealist interpretation of quantum theory? In this case the transcendent order introduced earlier plays a fundamental role, and the existence of a material world is gained through perception. How is the measuring process to be understood in such an interpretation? These questions have been discussed in an article by Goswami, who understands the wave function describing a quantum system as an element in the transcendent order.[22] The wave function evolves in time according to the Schroedinger equation, as is conventionally the case. When a measurement is made, the wave function collapses to the eigenvector wave function, which is correlated to the outcome of the measurement. This collapse, as in the von Neumann interpretation, is not described by the Schroedinger equation. According to the idealist interpretation, what collapses the wave function is the consciousness of the observer; more significantly, the consciousness of the observer chooses the outcome out of the set of alternatives that becomes actualized for the quantum system. In this idealist interpretation, the material aspects are all subsumed under

---

[22]   A. Goswami, "The Idealistic Interpretation of Quantum Mechanics," *Physics Essays*, vol. 2 (1989), p. 385.

the transcendent order. Further, such an interpretation is able to account for the outcomes of individual systems, by invoking the consciousness of the observer.

There are again significant problems with such an interpretation. As with most idealist views of the world, there is the problem of multiple observers seeing the same material world. In quantum mechanical terms, why should there be invariant characterizations of quantum particles such as mass and spin that are wholly independent of the perception of these particles? And in a quantum experiment, how does the consciousness of the observer choose the outcome that is actualized by the quantum system from the set of alternatives open to the quantum system?

## A Dualist Interpretation: Freedom in Matter

In our dualist interpretation of quantum theory, knowledge of quantum systems such as electrons or hydrogen atoms is encoded in the wave function, an element in the Hilbert space pertaining to the given system and existing in the transcendent order. After an observable is (freely) chosen, a measuring device is constructed (in the material world) to interact with the quantum system (also in the material world). Quantum theory predicts the range of alternatives open to the quantum system for a given observable. The wave function can then be thought of as a form of potentia, indicating the possible values of the observable from which the quantum system can opt, as well as predicting the propensity for the quantum system to opt for one alternative over another. At this point, we hold that the quantum system spontaneously opts for one alternative on its own accord. A measurement is a specific outcome resulting from the opting of the quantum system and recorded by the measuring device.

When the system has opted, it finds itself in a new state, called the eigenstate relative to the recorded outcome. In this interpretation, the free opting of the quantum system influences material objects, both itself and the measuring device. Thus, our dualist interpretation, in agreement with a realist interpretation, claims there are features of quantum systems that are independent of observers; mass and spin (and other features such as charge and magnetic moment) characterize a quantum system. But, with the idealist interpretation, we claim that the free choice of the observer or experimenter to measure a given observable, and bring into existence a property of the quantum system connected with that observable, indicates the necessary presence of the transcendent order. Where we disagree with the idealist interpretation is in the opting; in our model, the quantum system itself does the opting and not the observer.

Accompanying the different interpretations of quantum theory, there are also different ways of explaining the fact of individual outcomes. As stated previously, Dirac said, "Nature chooses"; this could be taken to mean that the process is inherently random, and it simply is not possible to give a further explanation. On the other hand, it is possible to give a theological interpretation for the mysterious character of definite outcomes; the physicist and theologian William Pollard says, "God chooses."[23] Robert Russell has taken up this suggestion more recently, in his claim that some sort of divine agency is at work in quantum events.[24] Finally, as stated previously, in an idealist interpretation, the consciousness of the experimenter chooses. All of these suggestions are in contrast to our dualist model, which we offer as an alternative.

In our model the quantum system itself displays the property of transcendental freedom, that is, the capacity of absolute spontaneity. In other words, the quantum system has the ability to initiate an outcome on its own accord. Quantum opting is an event of freedom and not a random happening, in which the occurrence is caused by external factors acting on some system. When quantum systems opt, and the potential encoded in a wave function is actualized in one way or another, a new material state of being is brought into existence by the opting, and there are no external causal factors that make the event happen. We can call it a primordial event of "cosmological" freedom, using Kant's term. It is primordial, because we are talking about the most elementary constituents of matter. It is cosmological, because the idea of causality contains the idea of a series of finite antecedent conditions that either has a spontaneous, free, and absolutely first cause outside the series or it does not. Those who say, "God chooses," or "nature chooses," represent the former, and the realists represent the latter.

[23]    W. Pollard, *Chance and Providence: God's Action in a World Governed by Scientific Law* (New York: Faber & Faber, 1968).

[24]    Robert John Russell, *Cosmology: From Alpha to Omega* (Minneapolis: Fortress Press, 2008), pp. 151–211, esp. p. 186.

In our dualist model, it is the quantum system that opts, and the transcendental freedom that it exhibits is the ground for the notion of freedom as it appears in higher organizations of matter in sentient beings, all the way up to human beings, where we find practical freedom. The difference between freedom in quantum systems and freedom as manifested in human beings is to be found mainly in the reflexive structure of human consciousness in which the self as "I" is aware of its own freedom, as well as in the huge increase in the number of alternatives that are open to human beings.

Our interpretation potentially solves two problems that have always plagued dualism. First, by claiming that under certain circumstances quantum systems can opt, we introduce a notion of freedom into the very foundations of matter. What has always been inexplicable in other interpretations, namely what the mechanism is that determines the outcome for an individual system, we explain by introducing a new element into the notion of matter, namely a capacity of freedom as absolute spontaneity. And, second, by claiming that opting leads to changes in the state of matter, we are able to show how elements from the transcendent order, in this case the potentia encoded in wave functions, influence matter. Our model exhibits, in other words, the element that plays the role of the necessary continuity between mind and matter.

With regard to the topic of theological reflection and the pursuit of ideals, our dualist model sets before us an agenda of thinking in this direction. When interpreted theologically, our model suggests an idea of God not as the theistic agent of otherwise indeterministic quantum events, but as the a/theistic ground of being whose absolute act of self-instantiation manifests itself as the dualistic presence of freedom in matter. Just as human beings instantiate themselves as a free "I" in "this one here" of their bodies in the world, so God instantiates itself as the decentered presence of freedom in the material world. This world, in its dualistic yet manifold structure, is the embodiment of God.

The pursuit of ideals likewise faces a reorientation of sorts through our dualistic model. Ideals, we know, belong to the transcendent order. In extending our model to its theological depths, we want to think the existence of the transcendent order as ultimately grounded in the self-instantiation of God. Just as when humans think in any language, they embody some ideas from the transcendent order, which then affect what they think and do, so God instantiates itself in the ideas

of the transcendent order, which we think of as existing in the mind of God. Because freedom is a necessary condition of the possibility for the pursuit of ideals and theological reflection, and freedom is present in the very structure of matter, these activities, while directing us to the transcendent order, nonetheless also and simultaneously direct us to the material world, where freedom equally resides. Theological reflection and the pursuit of ideals, insofar as they are self-conscious and reflexive activities, do not sever us from the material world or from science, as the disciplined way of reflecting on the material world. They join us to the material world as the home of freedom and to science as thinking that can in principle reach into the divine grounding principle of both the material world and the transcendent order.

### Selected Bibliography

Buber, Martin, *I and Thou*. Trans. Walter Kaufmann (New York: Charles Scribner's Sons, 1970).

Heidegger, Martin, *The Essence of Human Freedom: An Introduction to Philosophy*. Trans. Ted Sadler (London: Continuum, 2002).

Neumann, J. van, *Mathematical Foundations of Quantum Mechanics* (Princeton: Princeton University Press, 1955).

Scharlemann, Robert P., *The Reason of Following* (Chicago: University of Chicago Press, 1991).

Conceptual
ideas and theology.

# Chapter 2

# The Call of Conscience

## William Schweiker

### Introduction

Whether our age and culture—rife with wanton consumption but blind to the scourge of poverty, self-righteous in its pretensions and yet violently killing children, decadent and yet also broken—has an easier conscience than other places and times is something I cannot answer. But if it is at least partly true that conscience is self-knowledge about what one has done or failed to do, then an easy conscience is distorted, false, deceptive knowledge of self. Are we unknown to ourselves? And what does Christian theological reflection have to say to this condition? Martin Luther put it this way: "[O]ur conscience is bound to the law in its former state of the old sinful self. But when this self is put to death by the spirit, our conscience is set at liberty, and each is released from the other ... [F]or the first time it can really cling to Christ ... and bring forth the fruit of life."[1] Conscience, it would seem, is knowing and avowing oneself as an acting being bound to a sense of the goodness or blameworthiness of one's conduct, intentions, and character together with a feeling of obligation to do right or be good. It testifies to shared dignity and capacities of human beings. Theologically construed, the old self bound to law pants, strives, and strains for an active righteousness, the avowal of the self attaining an ideal of perfection. The new self is righteous in Christ and freed from the tyranny of moral perfection and empowered to love others. What could these philosophical and theological claims about conscience mean in our time and place?

Of course, there is a long line of criticism of attempts to relate reflection on self and moral claims. Sigmund Freud, for instance, worried about the super-ego and the psychological damage morality can do. Friedrich Nietzsche sought

---

[1] Martin Luther, "Preface to Romans," in J. Dillenberger (ed.), *Martin Luther: Selections from his Writings* (Garden City, NY, 1961), p. 30.

to demolish Western morality and its stunting of the will-to-life. Conscience—the bad conscience—is the drive for self-mastery in which inclinations, natural vitalities, our instincts are damned, taken as evil. It is a form of cruelty.[2] And there are accounts of self-consciousness that have no reference to conscience. Iris Murdoch wrote: "Man is a creature who makes a picture of himself and then comes to resemble the picture. This is the process which moral philosophy must attempt to describe and analyse."[3] What is neglected, and what marks the arena of my reflections, is how to understand the claim or call, the hold on us of what is right and good with and for others, despite the "pictures" we fashion, our ideals. What form of self-mastery does that entail? How is it, in other words, that the good and right can make a claim on the self despite our self-understandings, forms of identity, or, theologically speaking, our sinful selves? This seems to denote a specific kind of self-mastery.

The critics and the neglectors of conscience present paradigmatic accounts of self-mastery. The distinction between these accounts is crucial for my interpretation of conscience. One account, an *ascetic* one, defines the project of being a self as attaining some ideal of perfection by engaging in various spiritual practices that aim to overcome weakness or resistance to that ideal. Murdoch, for example, understands it as the ascetics of consciousness through loving attention to others and the idea of perfection, the Good. That is a decidedly different account than a Nietzschean type of artistry of the self. That picture of self-mastery is an *aesthetic* project, that is, the self giving form to instincts, desires, the will-to-power. Both accounts of self-mastery see it as a kind of spiritual practice that aims to form the self. Conscience attests to another project of self-determination contrasting with these ascetical and aesthetic ones. In the reflections to follow, I aim to clarify that difference.

That being said, we still confront yet another problem. A dominant theme of contemporary theological and philosophical thought has been that modes of reflection that begin with or are grounded in the thinking, feeling, and willing self—even those modes of thought seeking to understand the meaning of being—never,

---

[2]   See Friedrich Nietzsche, *The Birth of Tragedy and the Genealogy of Morals*, trans. F. Gilffing (New York, 1956).

[3]   Iris Murdoch, "Metaphysics and Ethics," in M. Antonaccio and W. Schweiker (eds), *Iris Murdoch and the Search for Human Goodness* (Chicago, 1996), p. 252.

finally, escape the totalizing drive of the self. If that is so, then the thinking self can never actually encounter the other as other or the disclosure of the divine other than in terms of the self. Because of this problem, some thinkers, like Emmanuel Levinas, try to think the constitution of the self from the encounter with the face of the other.[4] Others, such as Jürgen Habermas, turn to the dynamics of inter-subjective communicative action to ground moral norms. And among theologians and philosophers there are attempts to articulate phenomena that exceed the condition of their appearance as well as onto-theological ideas of revelation. Is an appeal to conscience beside the point, a virtual denial of the other?

The call of conscience, and any attempt to reclaim it in our time, provokes the debates just noted. It has been linked to the self-legislative power of practical reason and so questions about the proper form of self-mastery. Conscience is a form of subjectivity, but does it, as some worry, exclude a radical encounter with the other as other? And while it has been interpreted as the voice of God, perhaps that line of thought remains trapped in the clutches of the self and thus is, in truth, a denial of God. Conscience might bespeak the tenacious hold of onto-theological modes of thought on our very conceptions of the self and the labor of becoming a self.

Mindful of criticisms and counter-proposals, I want to reclaim and reconstruct a concept and experience for how it is that human beings can sense the claim of norms and ideals upon themselves. The theological and ethical potential and plausibility of conscience as an experience and concept is only possible, I contend, once it is articulated and understood in a way other than ascetic and aesthetic ideas of self-mastery. On that different conception, one escapes the entrapment of the self in itself and yet also reclaims a robust idea of human inwardness. At least that is my contention. My reflections, so defined, continue and extend previous work but now with special focus on modalities of subjectivity that come to light if we grasp conscience as a distinct form of self-mastery. In *Religion and the Human Future*, co-authored with David E. Klemm, we wrote this: "Conscience, the felt reality of the demand to respect and enhance the integrity of life tested by universality, finality, autonomy, and locality, is at one and the same moment an act of conformity

---

[4]    Emmanuel Levinas, *Otherwise than Being: Or, Beyond Essence*, trans. A. Lingis (Boston, 1981).

to a claim beyond the self and yet also the creative enactment of human powers."[5] In what follows I mean to advance that account of conscience with respect to other centrally important ones. The adequacy of my argument depends on its ability to answer problems in other accounts as well as its resonance with experience. With respect to other positions we will see two problems. Some distinguish conscience as a faculty of rule giving and action judging and thus fail to see how conscience is also a modality of self-relation. Others define conscience simply as a mode of self-relation yet, oddly, void of moral content or, more dangerously, without reference to the claim of others upon us. The constructive task of these reflections, then, is to provide an account of conscience that avoids those pitfalls. And I do so through a hermeneutics of conscience, that is, an interpretation of the metaphors and symbols packed into the concept and also the modalities of understanding they articulate. This hermeneutics seeks to present a distinct mode of self-understanding and what it means for the orientation of life.

However, at the outset I must admit that part of my struggle is to awaken an awareness of the call of conscience in a time when, for many reasons, we have lost this discourse and also deadened our moral and religious sensibilities. So, let me turn, first, to examples of the call of conscience in order to show their plausibility for us, how this symbol-concept (if I can call it that) still resonates. In a further step, I reconstruct thinking about conscience as a distinctive form of self-mastery, neither ascetical nor aesthetic, even if, as we will see, conscience has been interpreted in terms of those accounts. Here I aim to answer worries about the exclusion of the other on the plane of ethical reflection. My inquiry reaches its end by unfolding an account of the call of conscience that aims to show its theological meaning in the act of avowal. Thus, hermeneutics of conscience moves through registers of thinking: reclamation, reconstruction, and reorientation.

---

[5] David E. Klemm and William Schweiker, *Religion and the Human Future: An Essay on Theological Humanism* (Oxford, 2008), p. 86. Also see Willliam Schweiker, *Dust that Breathes: Christian Faith and the New Humanisms* (Oxford, 2010).

## Reclaiming Conscience

I assume, although in our age this might be a presumption rather than an assumption, that we all know—or at least know of people who can tell us—what it means to hear the call of conscience. There are examples within cultural memory, of course. Socrates is stopped in his tracks and rendered mute, because his "daemon" commands him to refrain from some act. An inviolable limit to action grips his existence. St. Paul insisted that the Gentiles have the law of God inscribed on their hearts. The law of freedom is accessible to those outside the discourse and practice of the Jews or early Christians. Martin Luther's terrified conscience nevertheless proclaimed before the Diet of Worms in 1521, "Hier stehe ich. Ich kann nicht weiter. Gott helfe mir. Amen." Recall Sir Thomas More and his fidelity to principle against the British Crown, a fidelity unto death. And remember countless numbers of people who have died imprisoned, abandoned, beaten, raped, and silenced because of fidelity to conviction. The old maxim is certainly right: conscience is a dangerous thing.[6] The call of conscience avows the integrity of self against self-betrayal, wrongful action, and tyranny. It is inscribed into cultural memory waiting reflection if we in easier times—or so we think—cannot or will not hear that call.

Is it that simple? Is the call only real in extreme situations and but a faint echo in our cultural memory? Actually, each of us has felt the claim of some principle or another person, say, honesty or friendship, rub raw against our desires betrayed in action, say, to get that job and thus to fudge credentials, to linger in a kiss with an illicit lover, to shield our vulnerability and misgivings before our children, to proclaim our faith knowing that it is, in truth, dead, or to chastise another's stupidity and faults while denying our own stupidity and faults. We too can sense, feel, that this rub, this rawness, betrays the inexplicable infusion of principle and claim of the other within our sense of self that punctures the pictures—vain, consoling, demeaning—we have made of ourselves. This infusion exposes a doubleness in identity which, if unheeded, threatens the disintegration of self. Is that not, too, the call of conscience, if less dramatically than the imprisoned or Socrates or Luther?

Typically in the history of ethics conscience denotes knowing oneself and one's deeds in, through, and with, *con-sciencia*, a principle or norm for the conduct of

---

[6]  See S. Fischer-Fabian, *Die Macht des Gewissens* (Munich, 1992).

life, and also the habit, as Thomas Aquinas put it, of reasoning about moral cases.[7] More technically, the idea names the supervening of a moral claim on the dynamics of self-consciousness without which the self would be dispersed into discrete acts, various intentions, desires and hopes without moral compass, limit, or purpose. And this is why a person without a "conscience" is humanly stunted or warped in their being and thus extremely dangerous. Put differently, conscience names how claims about what is right, just, and good in actions and relations supervene on self-understanding, if not reducible to self-understanding. Bishop Butler famously wrote in the Preface to the Sermons at Rolls Chapel, "Whereas in reality the very constitution of our nature requires that we bring our whole conduct before this superior faculty, wait its determination, enforce upon ourselves its authority, and make it the business of our lives, as it is absolutely the whole business of a moral agent to conform ourselves to it. This is the true meaning of the ancient precept, reverence thyself."[8]

Conscience thus exposes a double self-mastery.[9] There is a mastery of the self by principle or the claim of the other as essential to one's moral integrity even as one struggles for self-mastery, to heed the call of conscience, in one's self-understanding and conduct of life. Little wonder, then, that many thinkers, like Butler and Aquinas, have spoken about conscience as a "moral faculty" since it seems, in such moments of experience, to be distinct from capacities of desire, passion, and striving for ideals. However, thinking about conscience as a "faculty" is not quite right even if the sense of doubleness in self is experientially correct. What are we to make of this otherness or double mastery in self? Can the doubleness be an opening to what is other but through, not against, the inwardness we experience as selves? How is it that a principle or norm—otherwise a mute abstraction—or the existence of another person can be sensed as a "call" within ourselves?

The paradox that we are continuous and yet also discontinuous with ourselves, and so can feel the call of conscience as the integrity of self amid its dispersion,

---

7    St. Thomas Aquinas, *Summa Theologiae*, I–II, 90ff.

8    Joseph Butler, *Five Sermons*, ed. S. Darwall (Indianapolis, 1983), p. 17.

9    Georg Kateb recently notes, "Not two different persons, but one person capable of treating oneself as if one is two; one's flow of inwardness as it passes over one as one remains passive becomes an object confronting a subject who is self-consciously inward." Georg Kateb, *Human Dignity* (Cambridge, MA, 2011), p. 166.

has come to reflective interpretation in various ways. Consider a few accounts that will be important for my reconstruction of the call of conscience. Immanuel Kant writes in *The Metaphysics of Morals* that "this original intellectual, and (because it represents a duty) moral capacity called conscience (*Gewissen*), has this peculiarity in it, that although its business is man with himself, yet he finds himself compelled by his reason to transact it as if as the command of another person." And he adds: "The other may be an actual or simply ideal person, which reason (*Vernunft*) creates for itself."[10] Martin Heidegger, for his part, spoke of conscience as the call of *Dasein* to itself from its inauthenticity and to *Dasein*'s own most possibility in resoluteness in being-towards-death.[11] Paul Tillich explored the "transmoral conscience" as a mode of participation in the divine that transcends obedience to the moral law. "A conscience may be called 'transmoral'," he wrote, "if it judges not in obedience to a moral law, but according to its participation in a reality that transcends the sphere of moral commands. A transmoral conscience does not deny the moral realm, but is driven beyond it by the unbearable tensions of the sphere of the law."[12]

Broadly stated, there have been then two strands of thinking about conscience, as noted earlier. One strand sees it as the apprehension of norms and ideals, a kind of imprint of these in the self, given by God, reason or society, which practical reason deploys in guiding conduct. Call this model conscience as a moral faculty. Another strand of thought isolates it as a modality of self-relation in terms of a rationally constructed other (Kant), or fallen existence to authentic *Dasein* (Heidegger), or the transmoral conscience (Tillich). Call this model conscience as self-relation. Together, these strands of thought—these two models of conscience—complicate an account of self-mastery or the quest to govern one's own life. The aim is not simply to attain by ascetic practice an ideal end or artistically to fashion an identity, but, more radically, to integrate the self with itself in the avowal of being an agent who is claimed, called, by what is good and right. Not perfection or identity but integrity is the watchword for the self-mastery called conscience.

---

[10] Immanuel Kant, *Die Metaphysik der Sitten* Part II, par. 13 in *Werke 5* (Cologne, 1995), p. 528.

[11] Martin Heidegger, *Being and Time*, trans. J. Macquarrie and E. Robinson (New York, 1962).

[12] Paul Tillich, *Morality and Beyond* (Louisville, 1995), p. 77.

"Conscience" is then a thick symbol-concept, as I am calling it, that has packaged into it several meanings arising from experience and accrued through history. I have started to unfold these meanings embedded in the concept of conscience by thinking through exemplary figures, metaphoric constructs—a daemon, a "call," the capacity of reason to create ideal persons—and also its felt sense, say, in the betrayal of a lover or the dishonest fudging of a *curriculum vitae*. We have had experiences that give rise to this confusing array of discourses about conscience, or at least we can entertain their possibility as presented in the lives of real and fictional people and those who have brought the experience into reflective examination and articulation. If time allowed, these various meanings packaged in the concept of conscience could be further interrogated and interpreted. That would enable us a fuller grasp of the complexity of the idea but also the opacity of the experience of conscience. But now, I need to shift from reclaiming conscience to another register of inquiry. The task becomes reconstruction.

## Reconstructing Conscience

Within the discourse and experience of conscience there are, oddly, both over-determined and under-determined accounts that explain the complexity and opacity of discourse and experience. In each case, the self is finally entrapped within itself. Conscience is over-determined when it is thought to be the ground and source of specific and unambiguous rules of conduct. It is imagined to be not just the medium of moral norms but their source and subject. That can lead, as Freud knew, to a fastidious and rule-bound personality just as much as to amoralism and laxism. Nevertheless, conscience does have something to do with the self's determination of itself in and through binding moral norms which cannot be invalidated by desired ends. The ends I might seek cannot invalidate the claim of the other that supervenes on my very sense and labor of myself. The idea of conscience is also under-determined when one tries to articulate that self-relation qua self-relation without attention to norm or principle. In that move, conscience is ambiguous at best and vacuous at worse. This is seen in Heidegger's conception of conscience as authenticity or truthfulness to self, but also the claim that conscience is the voice of God in the soul or a spark of the divine, as the ancient Stoics put it. These are under-determined conceptions because of the vagaries of their content. What ethical work does the concept "conscience" do if it simply means truthfulness to self or it is imagined as the voice of God? In fact, the under-determination of the call of conscience is the root of the terrified conscience, it would seem. As Luther understood, the imagination can fill in any content for the voice of God, create idols and ideals of perfection, which then torment, aggrandize, or anesthetize the self. The insight is that conscience is a claim on self from within its freedom, fault, and fallenness. The challenge, then, is how to articulate experience by reconstructing an understanding of conscience in a way that avoids over- and under-determination, or, stated differently, avoids reducing the claim of the other—be it another person or God—simply to the self-legislation of moral norms or one's self-relation.

I have anticipated this reconstruction by briefly contrasting accounts of self-mastery or self-role. Recall, one account, an ascetic one, defines the project of being a self as the attaining of some ideal of perfection by engaging in various spiritual practices that aim to overcome weakness or resistance to that ideal. Murdoch's account of practices of attention, like prayer or mediation, in order to purify consciousness under the idea of the Good is an example. Nietzsche paradigmatically presents a picture of self-mastery as an aesthetic project, that is, the self as artist giving form to instinct, desires, will-to-power. Conscience attests to another project of self-determination contrasted with these ascetical and artistic ones. Self-mastery is in and through the call or sense of principles of right, the claim of others on self, and yet one's inmost integrity. Conscience is a symbol-concept for the demand to respect and enhance the integrity of self and other so that the aim of moral subjectivity—that is, responsible life with and for others—is experienced as the co-founding, the co-origin, of subjectivity. Conscience is not just the super-ego that punishes us for our wrongdoings and excites the experience of guilt, as Freud might argue; it is not simply the internalization of social mores that might give rise to guilt or shame, although these are important psychological and social dynamics. Rather, conscience must fundamentally mediate objective demands and the innermost felt integrative, free struggle that defines personal life. Albeit in different ways, what happens in the illicit kiss that betrays one's commitment to another no less than resistance to tyranny or coercion is a supervention of the integrity of one's life on consciousness so that any desired end or ideal is shown true or false and any act to seek that end right or wrong.

The call of conscience is the gathering of the self from its dispersion into projects, ideals, and relations in an avowal of its integrity. This call—as opposed to the work of conscience—is then the appearance of the integrity of oneself in the power to act as the necessary and also inviolable condition and purpose for envisioning and attaining ideals. I hasten to add that this is not all that conscience entails, as the reference to the "work" of conscience was meant to signal. The *work* of conscience is the labor of our moral existence carried out in the rough and tumble of daily personal and social life. That labor requires formation, attention to a variety of sources of moral knowledge, introspection and discernment, and also the making and assessment of judgments for actions. We might say that the work of conscience is simply the spiritual practice of a responsible life. However, my focus is on the *call* of conscience, that is, the avowal of our moral being as a project of self-determination.

It might seem that I have reformulated via hermeneutical reclamation and reconstruction Kant's position linking principle and subjectivity, Heidegger's claims about the call of *Dasein* to itself, or the idea of the transmoral conscience. Yet that is not the case, and for several reasons. Clarity about these reasons is central to showing the adequacy of my argument. So, remember that through the categorical imperative Kant formulated the co-originary nature of moral subjectivity as an end in itself, that is, rational freedom, with the legislation of a universal moral law against inclinations and desires. Of course, someone might say that with the categorical imperative, practical reason commands before the act whereas conscience is a retrospective judgment on the deed done and that shows its dependence on experience. But that is too narrow a conception of conscience and misses the deeper point that Kant saw about reason and desire. Heidegger for his part saw the gathering of the self in terms of resoluteness in being-towards-death as one's own most possibility. It is then a stance in and towards radical finitude, not the other or even moral principles. And the idea of the transmoral conscience is a participation in what exceeds the moral law, an ecstatic experience as Tillich calls it. What does that mean for the responsible life?

My strategy has been to dislodge conscience from its definition as a "faculty" of legislation and judgment or simply the call of the self to itself and to reconstruct it as a modality of self-mastery distinct from other accounts, the ascetic and the aesthetic. The crucial difference from the Kantian idea of autonomy, and so self-rule, is found in the idea of the "integrity" of life, one's own and others. And, further, integrity also denotes that which rightly and properly ought to master the self in an authentic act of genuine self-mastery. In that respect, it also designates a picture of human existence otherwise than the rubrics of "authenticity" or self-artistry. Explaining these points about integrity will complete the reconstruction of conscience. Yet it will also open onto another register of thinking.

Conscience, I have argued, is a kind of self-relation co-constituted through some norm about the treatment of human beings as agents who act and suffer and thus seek to realize envisioned ends and ideals. The question remains about the character of that self-relation. Here too the metaphors embedded in the concept beg for further interpretation: the weak conscience, the terrified or free conscience, the good or the bad conscience. These metaphors pick out different qualities or felt meanings of self-relation within the stream of on-going life. Yet once we see conscience as mode of self-mastery, its integrity can be further clarified by contrast to other conceptions already noted, namely, autonomy and authenticity. Autonomy in its Kantian expression is self-rule by acting on the dictate of practical reason in the form of the categorical imperative rather than being moved to act by inclination, habit, or desire. Autonomy thereby names, I contend, conscience interpreted in an ascetical mode. It seeks the ideal of rational self-rule against the pull and drag of desire. Authenticity, contrariwise, in Heidegger's or other accounts is truthfulness to one's own most possibility. It is under-determined since to be authentic is to live resolute before one's possibilities rather than in conformity to an ideal, a principle, or *Das Man*. Here, one might say, conscience is interpreted in aesthetic mode whether in a Nietzschean artistry of identity, or Heidegger's claims about *Dasein* as the Shepherd of Being. While conscience is central in these accounts, it is subsumed within the ascetical or aesthetic accounts of self-mastery. And these find expression in the rigorism of Kantian ethics as well as the vagary of claims about authenticity, the loss of the ethical into the artistry of self. And one might note, that a good deal of contemporary ethics has swung in favor of an aesthetic conception of the self against what is seen as the demands of moral autonomy.

I have tried to reconstruct conscience from within the meanings embedded in the symbol-concept and the experience of its call rather than typical accounts of self-mastery. In that light, integrity is a gathering of self from its dispersion into the needs and goods that must be integrated in order to stave off disintegration, that is, physical and existential death. Yet this gathering of self, this integration, as the call of conscience is also the avowal of the self in and through the claim of goods and norms to guide conduct with and for others. And this is the doubleness noted before: conscience gathers the self paradoxically through its own integrity such that a moral claim supervenes on the very flow of our inwardness. There are, then, limits on the artistry we can assume of and for ourselves, if our lives are to manifest integrity. We must respect and enhance the integration of a variety of goods in self and other.[13] Specification of those goods and the imperative to respect and enhance them avoids an under-determined conception of conscience. Yet the source of those limits is not pure practical reason, but rather the finite needs of others with their claims upon the self heard in the call of conscience. The demands upon us ushering from needs and goods that must be integrated in life against the force of disintegration nevertheless supervene on the integrity of our own lives and thereby are not reduced to self-consciousness, not over-determined in any rigorist way. Response to those needs and labor for the goods they require is not an ascetic practice of self-mastery but one creatively aimed at life's flourishing. The call of conscience as the claim of the integrity of life on the self marks out a distinctive conception and experience of self-mastery as the avowal of the self as acting being with others, on earth, and in time.

But this proposal now present is still incomplete because we need to clarify the double self-mastery and its relation to the act of avowal, as I have called it. One more turn in thinking is needed, a turn that will also be theological in character.

## Reorienting Conscience

I have reconstructed the meaning of the call of conscience as an avowal of the integrity of an acting being with others and for itself. This is a distinctive form of self-mastery, because conscience names the connection between avowal and

---

[13]     For this account of goods that must be integrated in life, see William Schweiker, *Responsibility and Christian Ethics* (Cambridge, 1995).

integrity and so the doubleness in self-mastery. Yet I have hitherto left unexamined the act of avowal and its theological meanings.

Avowal, from the Latin *ad-vocare* or to summon, means that in our acting and suffering, our response to or denial of the claims of conscience and so the demand of principle and the needs of others, one is summoned from within and yet beyond oneself. It is acknowledgment and confession of the integrity of one's own life from beyond one's self under the demand to respect and enhance the integrity of life with and for others. The fount of self-being is not only the act of attestation, which Paul Ricoeur has identified as the assurance of being oneself in acting and suffering.[14] The assurance we have of our active self-being is more radically the avowal of conscience which acknowledges the *integrity* of one's own life in and with the summons to respect and enhance the integrity of life with and for others. Not oneself *as* another in the act of attestation, but oneself *in* the other *through* the avowal of conscience. The doubleness in self is now between conscience as the felt sense and claim of the integrity of my life and that which summons me into the integrity of all life. When I feel the sting of conscience, or you feel it rubbed raw, or we sense ourselves over against ourselves in the call of conscience there is an avowal, a summoned acknowledgment, of the integrity of life in my, in your, in our acting being. This avowal is the mastery of the self and its projects by the integrity of life even as it is the appearance of the freedom of self-rule in responsible existence with and for others.

The call of conscience thereby discloses human beings as acting but also avowing creatures. That which we avow—acknowledge and confess—as the integrity of our lives, binds us to it and determines our existence, our life and death.[15] To avow and confess what binds the self without it freeing one for the fruit of life is a mode of death even while one is physically alive. In this light, theological reflection as St. Paul understood, is at its spiritual roots about deliverance from the law of sin and death into modes of life. Theologically, the call of conscience, its avowal, is nothing else than testimony against our bondage and

---

[14]   See Paul Ricoeur, *Oneself as Another*, trans. K. Blamey (Chicago, 1992). Also see W. David Hall, *Paul Ricoeur and the Poetic Imperative* (Albany, 2007) and John Wall, *Moral Creativity: Paul Ricoeur and the Poetics of Possibility* (Oxford, 2005).

[15]   It was one of the great insights of the Protestant Reformers, especially John Calvin, to grasp that human beings, whatever else they are, live as worshipping beings and thus always poised between idolatry and the worship of the true, living God.

death and a testimony to freedom and life. The Christian conscience is not the call to resoluteness in being-towards-death; it is a summons into real joy within finite, non-ideal life. And this reorients conscience towards the integrity of life.

The avowal of oneself as acting being discloses for Christian thought the integrity of one's life in another, in Christ, and also in others through responsible action. Theological reflection on the call of conscience thereby differs from ascetic and aesthetic conceptions of self-mastery. The call of conscience reorients one's existence through the awareness that one is called into life from the forms of death that threaten us with disintegration but without denial of death's presence in every finite thing. The work of conscience is to acknowledge, confess, avow that call in the midst of the turmoil of existence; it is responsible living as a spiritual practice. In this way, conscience is a testimony to the living God from within, not beyond as Tillich had it, our lives as acting and avowing beings. And, provocatively, we can say that Christ is the conscience of God. He is the testimony of the living God incarnate in the life of an acting and avowing human being who discloses the integrity of what is truly human and God as truly the integrity of life.

## Conclusion

I am now at the outer edge of these reflections. Certainly more could be said about the theological reorientation of conscience, and, for that matter, each step of these reflections. I have tried to rethink the call of conscience against other accounts and also ideas of self-mastery. This reconstruction of conscience has sought to avoid over and under-determination as the problems that haunt those positions. In this way, I argued for the greater adequacy on the one present in these all too brief reflections. Further inquiry is not possible at this time and place. So I will end by answering a possible objection and recalling a problem.

One might object that my theological reflections meant to reorient conscience are so thoroughly Christian that the entire argument of this chapter thereby falls into a confessional mode with little meaning or relevance for non-Christians. But, actually, one can accept the arguments I have forwarded about the call of conscience without being Christian. After all, I have undertaken a hermeneutics of a symbol-concept and the experience it articulates. That account of the meaning of conscience can be used in the moral life by anyone so claimed. What I have shown in the end about the Christian symbolics of conscience is how Christians can and ought to forge a humane and responsible ethics that insists on the dignity and inviolability of conscience. And that might require rethinking basic matters of doctrine and practice, as my claims about Christ as the conscience of God were meant to show. I can leave it to faithful people in other traditions to attempt the same for their communities while asking religious and non-religious people to affirm shared ethical insights.

So, the real challenge lies with the problem noted at the outset of these reflections. My struggle has been to awaken an awareness of the call of conscience in a time when we have lost this discourse and deadened our moral and religious sensibilities. I will have succeeded if in some measure within our lives there too is in fact an avowal of the integrity of life, the call of conscience, which summons one to struggle responsibly against forces of death that now plague our planet and for the sake of a humane and living future.

## Selected Bibliography

Hall, W. David, *Paul Ricoeur and the Poetic Imperative* (Albany, NY: SUNY Press, 2007).

Klemm, David E. and Schweiker, William, *Religion and the Human Future: An Essay on Theological Humanism* (Oxford: Wiley-Blackwell, 2008).

Ricoeur, Paul, *Oneself as Another*. Trans. K. Blamey (Chicago: Chicago University Press, 1992).

Schweiker, William, *Responsibility and Christian Ethics* (Cambridge: Cambridge University Press, 1995).

Tillich, Paul, *Morality and Beyond* (Louisville: Westminster John Knox Press, 1995).

# Chapter 3

# Spirituality and the "Humane Turn"

Maria Antonaccio

Spirituality has become something of a tainted concept within the field of religious studies. This is true in at least two respects. First, despite its long and distinguished history in Western theology and in religious thought more generally, spirituality is increasingly the default mode of a significant cohort in contemporary culture that is unbound or alienated from historic modes of religious belief and practice. Many people affirm being "spiritual but not religious" in order to signal their disavowal of institutional or tradition-bound forms of religious practice. The flight from religion to spirituality is driven by many factors, but among them is the notion that, while religion is bound up with forms of authority that demand obedience and inhibit the scope of individual freedom, spirituality allows for personal exploration and the unlocking of the self's full potential. Religion, in short, is perceived as dogmatic, moralistic, and exclusive, while spirituality is seen as experiential, open-minded, and inclusive. Whether such perceptions are valid or not, it is clear that in popular parlance the term spirituality often lacks any determinate content. For many people, that is precisely its attraction, but the category has become notoriously vacuous as a result.[1]

The notion of spirituality is tainted in a second sense as well. As John Dunne has noted, whereas spirituality was previously mapped on to "a conceptual space already densely marked by substantive ethical and religious traditions," it now tends to float free from such traditions and attaches itself to the consumerist and therapeutic mindset of contemporary culture.[2] At least in its popular "self-help"

---

[1] This is not to suggest that there has not been substantive academic work, particularly among sociologists of religion, on the resurgence of various forms of spirituality in contemporary culture. See, for example, the work of Robert Wuthnow and Robert Orsi.

[2] John Dunne, "After philosophy and religion: spirituality and its counterfeits," in David Carr and John Haldane (eds), *Spirituality, Philosophy and Education* (Routledge,

variants, contemporary forms of spirituality often seem intent on reducing the scope of human transformation to a checklist of carefully managed attitude adjustments. As Dunne puts it, "We can now speak of ... an entire culture that has absorbed and naturalized the therapeutic mode."[3] The fact that virtually every area of human activity—from health, exercise, and dietary regimens to interior design—can be marketed as a spiritual practice illustrates the extent to which consumer culture is capable of co-opting and often flattening human values. "If religion was once the opium of the impoverished proletariat," Dunne writes, "spirituality is now the opium of the affluent middle classes."[4]

Given the trends just noted, contemporary spirituality seems to be an easy target for ridicule, and academics have not flinched from doing so.[5] But to dismiss the turn to spirituality too quickly, or to avoid using the term because of its associations with consumerism, would be a mistake. For one thing, spirituality need not be defined by or limited to the shallow forms it often takes in popular culture. The spiritual practices associated with historic religious traditions—including prayer, meditation, confession, examination of conscience, practices of nonviolence and peacemaking, and so forth—continue to guide, sustain, and challenge the lives of millions of people around the world. At their best, such practices can encourage critical and engaged reflection on, rather than capitulation to, a culture's values, motivating human beings to live lives committed to compassion, justice, and integrity (among other virtues).

Moreover, the current attraction to spirituality suggests that the impulses that drive human beings to seek some outlet for their deepest questions and values have not abated, even if the religious context within which those impulses may have first come to articulation is in decline or is experienced as irrelevant.[6] Indeed, the flight from religion to spirituality may be understandable and even appropriate given the fact that religious traditions (as theologians from Paul Tillich to Michael

---

2003), pp. 97–111; the quotation is on p. 99.

    [3]   Ibid., p. 104.

    [4]   Ibid.

    [5]   As the editors of a recent volume on spirituality put it, "Much of what passes as contemporary spirituality seems an encouragement to indulgence and self-satisfaction ... couched in prose that lurches between psycho-babble and management-speak and generally [treating] the reader as witless or infantile." David Carr and John Haldane, "Introduction," in *Spirituality Philosophy and Education* (Routledge, 2003), p. 6.

    [6]   Dunne, "After philosophy," p. 102.

Fishbane have acknowledged) can so easily fall prey to the deadening effects of routinization and cease to convey their original animating impulse. As Fishbane notes, "Traditions [can] mask our thoughts, and glib pieties provide the hiding places where we crouch against the thunderous question: Where are you—just now in your life?"[7] The force and persistence of such questions suggests that the idea of spirituality remains a potential site of human flourishing and integrity, however vulnerable it may be either to distortion or deflation from wider cultural forces. Even in its popular forms, the vocabulary of spirituality may give voice to elemental questions that many persons find difficult to express in other terms.

Given the importance of the human concerns that spirituality addresses, the question is whether the concept can be rescued from the vacuousness that has been its fate in the sphere of popular religion and contemporary culture. Can the notion of spirituality regain a measure of integrity? What options for spiritual reflection are honestly available to those who find themselves alienated from historic traditions, such as those (in Raymond Gaita's phrase) "who cannot speak God's name in prayer or in worship"?[8]

The purpose of this chapter is to examine the recent "turn to spirituality" among Anglo-American philosophers and to ask what it might contribute to these questions. In the past decade, notable figures such as John Cottingham, John Haldane, Thomas Nagel, and Hilary Putnam have appropriated the notion of spirituality and spiritual exercises as a way to reconceive the idea of philosophy as a "lived practice."[9] Their interest is driven, in part, by a concern to save philosophy from the irrelevance and overspecialization into which they fear it has fallen by recovering a more capacious vision of the philosophical task. Nagel, for example, claims that modern philosophy has largely failed in its ancient task of providing "nourishment of the soul,"[10] a failure he lays at the doorstep of "the broad acceptance of scientific naturalism as a comprehensive world view."

---

[7] Michael Fishbane, *Sacred Attunement: A Jewish Theology* (University of Chicago Press, 2010), p. 3.

[8] Raymond Gaita, quoted in Dunne, "After philosophy," p. 107.

[9] John Cottingham, *The Spiritual Dimension* (Cambridge University Press, 2005); Thomas Nagel, *Secular Philosophy and the Religious Temperament* (Oxford University Press, 2010); John Haldane (ed.), *Spirituality, Philosophy and Education* (Routledge Falmer, 2003), and Hilary Putnam, *Jewish Philosophy as a Guide to Life* (Indiana University Press, 2008). In this chapter, I focus only on Cottingham and Pierre Hadot.

[10] Nagel, *Secular Philosophy*, p. 3.

Similarly, Cottingham proposes a "humane turn" in the philosophy of religion as a counterweight to the influence of scientific naturalism on philosophy for the last three decades.[11] He argues that it is time to help philosophy regain its original depth and insight by reclaiming its ancient role of addressing the spiritual longings of human beings.

The most influential figure in this context, of course, is Pierre Hadot, whose historical studies of the spiritual exercises of ancient philosophy, and especially his articulation of the idea that philosophy itself is "a way of life," seem to have emboldened many philosophers to affirm a set of convictions that they may have been quietly harboring all along.[12] Those convictions include one or more of the following: 1) that the practice of philosophy is not merely or even primarily a style of argumentation, but a mode of existence; 2) that the task of philosophy can be considered a broadly religious or spiritual one insofar as it is concerned with the transformation of the self according to an ideal of wisdom; and 3) that engaging in the spiritual exercises of philosophy may be preferable to what usually goes by the name of "religion" because it avoids any commitment to or complicity with the dogmatic encumbrances and dubious histories of *actual* traditions.

Can a so-called humane philosophy of religion centered on the idea of spiritual exercises help rescue the notion of spirituality from its indeterminacy? In this chapter, I argue that, although philosophers like Cottingham can be commended for recognizing that religion is not merely a set of propositions to be affirmed but a lived practice of self-transformation (i.e., an *askesis*), and for initiating a long overdue rapprochement between philosophy and religious studies, philosophical appropriations of spirituality may not entirely escape the problem of vacuousness noted earlier. Perhaps because some philosophers have so much at stake in reclaiming the fallen mantel of their discipline (i.e., as love of wisdom, or care of the soul), when it comes to spirituality they let down their critical guard, failing to press thinkers like Hadot, for example, on claims that deserve further scrutiny. If

---

[11]   Cottingham, *The Spiritual Dimension*, pp. viii–ix. Demonstrating his explicit debt to Hadot, Cottingham approaches philosophy as a lived practice rather than as a mode of conceptually precise argumentation, noting that that the general aim of the spiritual exercises of the Stoics, Descartes, and Ignatius Loyola, among others, "was not merely intellectual enlightenment, or the imparting of abstract theory, but a transformation of the whole person" (p. 5).

[12]   Pierre Hadot, *Philosophy as a Way of Life* (Blackwell, 1995).

spirituality has any hope of being reclaimed as an area of human flourishing and integrity, the spiritual turn in philosophy (and perhaps Hadot's work above all) requires a hermeneutics of suspicion.

This chapter, accordingly, has three modest aims: 1) to expose some of the submerged assumptions in some recent philosophical appropriations of the idea of spirituality or spiritual practices and to ask what interests are being served by the embrace of this terminology; 2) to question one of the central claims of the spiritual turn more generally and Hadot's work in particular, i.e., the notion of "the primacy of practice," which holds that spiritual exercises can be appropriated in the present apart from their original metaphysical presuppositions; and 3) to suggest some future directions for how the reconstruction of spirituality might proceed. I begin in Part I by briefly examining Cottingham's work as a recent example of the spiritual turn in philosophy. I contend that Cottingham's appeal to the category of spirituality may be suspect insofar as it does not adequately account for its own covert dependence on convictions associated with a particular religious and/or philosophical tradition. In Part II, I examine Hadot's strong claim for the primacy of practice and argue that it fails to provide criteria for distinguishing authentic spirituality from its counterfeits, even though Hadot himself believes such a distinction is critical.

## Part I: Constructing the Spiritual Dimension

As I noted earlier, Cottingham has called for a "humane turn" in philosophy as a response to what he sees as the increasing specialization and fragmentation of the discipline. Dismayed by the dominating influence of scientific naturalism, which holds that philosophy should adopt or emulate the methods of the natural sciences in order to meet criteria of objectivity and rationality, Cottingham seeks a mode of philosophical inquiry that can address itself to "questions about human self-understanding and self-discovery that will never be understood via the methods and resources that typify the naturalistic turn."[13] Such a philosophy would be "synthetic in its methods, synoptic in its scope, culturally and historically aware in its outlook, open to multiple resonances of meaning that come from the affective

---

[13]    Cottingham, *The Spiritual Dimension*, p. ix.

as well as the cognitive domains."[14] The animating impulse of Cottingham's humane philosophy is, therefore, an integrative or holistic one. His goal is to show "how a philosophical approach to religion needs to bring together the disparate areas of our human experience, emotional as well as intellectual, practical as well as theoretical, embracing the inner world of self-reflection as well as the outer world of empirical inquiry."[15] Accordingly, his book, *The Spiritual Dimension*, explores what the disciplines of science, ethics, psychoanalysis, research on the emotions, and the epistemology of belief can contribute to our understanding of human beings as spiritual beings.

Cottingham's initial preference for the language of spirituality over that of religion is largely a strategic one. He thinks spirituality is less likely to set off the kind of immediately polarizing reactions that religion does, and hence can smooth the way for a broadening of philosophy of religion to include a wider set of humanistic concerns.[16] Moreover, the admitted vagueness of the term "spirituality" has the advantage of identifying "activities and attitudes which command widespread appeal, irrespective of metaphysical commitment or doctrinal allegiance." "Even the most convinced atheist," Cottingham argues, "may be prepared to avow an interest in the 'spiritual' dimension of human existence, if that dimension is taken to cover forms of life that put a premium on certain kinds of intensely focused moral and aesthetic response, or on the search for deeper reflective awareness of the meaning of our lives and of our relationship to others and to the natural world."[17] In short, the language of spirituality is instrumental to Cottingham's larger purpose of expanding philosophical discourse about religion beyond the narrow agenda of analytic philosophy of religion, without engaging the more divisive issues associated with religious belief.

The second and more important reason that Cottingham appeals to the language of spirituality is its connection with practice. He writes: "Spirituality has long been understood to be a concept that is concerned in the first instance with activities rather than theories, with ways of living rather than doctrines subscribed to, with

---

[14]   Cottingham, "What is humane philosophy and why is it at risk?" Downloaded from http://www.johncottingham.co.uk.

[15]   Cottingham, *The Spiritual Dimension*, pp. ix–x.

[16]   Ibid., p. 3.

[17]   Ibid.

praxis rather than belief."[18] Demonstrating his clear debt to Hadot, Cottingham notes that in the history of philosophy, the term "spiritual" is more often associated with the term "exercises" rather than "beliefs," and he goes on to note examples of such exercises in the thought of Ignatius Loyola, Descartes, the Stoics, and others. In all of these cases, what we are dealing with is "a practical programme of training" aimed at "the art of living," the "ordering of the passions," or the cultivation of attention of presence of mind; in short, practices that are intended to induce a shift in mentality that is transformative of the whole person.[19]

Cottingham's emphasis on the practical dimension of spirituality allows him to recoup the notion of religion, which he had initially avoided as potentially divisive. At the level of practice, he suggests, there is essentially no difference between spirituality and religion: "What holds good for any plausible account of the tradition of spiritual exercises," he writes, "also holds good more generally for any true understanding of the place of religion in human life: we have to acknowledge what might be called the *primacy of praxis*, the vital importance that is placed on the individual's embarking on a path of practical self-transformation, rather than (say) simply engaging in intellectual debate or philosophical analysis."[20] The notion of self-transformation "is at the heart of the religious enterprise,"[21] and takes priority over rational disputations over the existence of God, or intellectual assent to the propositions of faith. As Cottingham puts it, "it is not as if one waits for a belief in God to somehow form itself in one's mind, and then decides, in the light of that belief, to join a Church or inquire about a possible program of spiritual *askesis*; rather the spiritual *askesis* is itself what sets the adherent on the long road" towards belief.[22]

Based on this brief summary, we can see why many scholars of religion welcomed Cottingham's "humane philosophy" as a helpful corrective to traditional and especially analytic philosophy of religion. In particular, Cottingham has been commended for "call[ing] attention to religion as a social practice" and for "criticiz[ing] narrowly fideistic and evidentialist approaches to the philosophy

---

[18]  Ibid.
[19]  Ibid., pp. 4–5.
[20]  Ibid., p. 5.
[21]  Ibid.
[22]  Ibid., p. 152.

of religion."[23] At the same time, critics have raised at least two questions about Cottingham's philosophical appropriation of spirituality.

First, as with any attempt to identify the defining characteristics of the general category like "spirituality" or "religion," questions can always be raised about whether those characteristics privilege some traditions over others. This is a familiar problem to scholars of religion, and it is one that may to a large extent be unavoidable. However, the problem is particularly obvious in Cottingham's case, given that the vocabulary, practices, and examples he refers to throughout *The Spiritual Dimension* are almost exclusively Christian. The question is whether Cottingham's construction of "the spiritual dimension" is simply his own version of Christianity given philosophical articulation. From this perspective, it hardly seems an accident that the form of spiritual praxis that Cottingham favors by the end of the book is a highly liturgical one built around "structures of organized ritual" that are "capable of expressing the mysteries of faith in a dignified and resonant way."[24] Cottingham recognizes that his position may be construed as "an essentially partisan commitment to a particular form of sacramentally based Christianity." However, he insists that his argument is not viciously circular. He rejects as problematic "any philosophical attempt to provide 'neutral' evaluations of any belief system from a supposed Olympian standpoint detached from cultural and historical particularities," arguing that "we can never achieve a 'sideways on' perspective on reality, from which we could pick out a certain set of practices or beliefs as somehow 'objectively' superior to others."[25] On this basis, he contends that his preference for a Christianly-informed spiritual praxis cannot be rejected on the grounds that it lacks "objectivity," since such a neutral or objective standpoint is not available anyway.

One can agree with Cottingham's rejection of a scientific model of neutrality, however, and still question whether his construction of spirituality smuggles Christian categories and premises into its definition under the cover of philosophical categories and arguments. The question is, what does Cottingham hope to gain by calling certain commitments "spiritual" or philosophical rather

---

[23]    Wayne Proudfoot, Review of Cottingham, *The Spiritual Dimension. Ethics*, Vol. 117, No. 3, 2007, pp. 549–552.

[24]    Cottingham, *The Spiritual Dimension*, p. 164.

[25]    Ibid., p. 165.

than more determinately religious (or Christian)? Is this simply a strategic move, intended to garner support for his "humane" philosophy without immediately alienating those who recoil from the symbolic language of historic traditions? This question speaks to the larger concerns of this chapter noted earlier: what resources are *honestly* available to those who call themselves spiritual but not religious? The demand for honesty suggests that we should be suspicious of the turn to an indeterminate "spirituality" if its intention is to provide an escape from the embarrassing dogmatic encumbrances of historic traditions, or to refurbish the reputation of philosophy as "care of the soul." The notion of spiritual integrity seems at the very least to require acknowledging the historical dependence of a conception of spirituality or *askesis* on the background beliefs of a particular tradition, even if one resists being fully bound to or committed to that tradition.

There is a second and related question that may be raised about Cottingham's turn to spirituality. Given his assertion of the primacy of praxis, on what basis can spiritual practices be assessed or subjected to rational reflection? Does the primacy of practice entail a non-cognitivist account of religion? In a review of *The Spiritual Dimension*, Wayne Proudfoot notes that Cottingham "sometimes gives the impression that he thinks that making spiritual practice central will silence skeptics and eliminate the need for critical reflection on and revisions of religious beliefs and doctrines."[26] Proudfoot argues that although Cottingham insists that "critical reflection can accompany the kind of receptivity that is generated by spiritual practice and that systems of such practices must be evaluated by critical moral judgment," he doesn't elaborate on either of these points.[27] At most, Cottingham suggests that only those systems of spiritual practice "whose insights are in harmony with our considered moral reflection" will meet the standards of rationality. He writes, "religious truth can only be accessed via faith, and faith can only be acquired via a living tradition of religious praxis," but "we can use our intuitions to assess the moral credentials of the systems of praxis on offer."[28] Cottingham wants to insist that religion is in no better or worse position in this regard than any other aspect of human judgment. "The primacy of praxis,"

---

[26]   Proudfoot, Review of Cottingham, p. 552.

[27]   Ibid.

[28]   Cottingham, *The Spiritual Dimension*, p. 16.

Cottingham argues, "is in some sense a feature of the whole human condition."[29] In every area of human life, we are formed by practices first, and learn to reflect on them only later, from within a perspective formed by the practices themselves.

As Proudfoot suggests, however, simply asserting the primacy of practice does not in itself justify them. Cottingham's affirmation of the priority of practice does not adequately address the need for criteria by which to critically evaluate the practices themselves, or to distinguish true or authentic versions of spiritual practices from their counterfeits. Without such criteria, it is hard to see how Cottingham can sustain the distinction between his own conception of spirituality and the "heterogeneous range of products and services, from magic crystals, scented candles and astrology, to alternative medicine, tai chi, and meditation courses" that he regards as baser examples of the phenomenon.[30]

On both of the critical points I have raised—the construction of the category of spirituality and the assertion of the primacy of practice—Cottingham's account leaves us with questions in need of further exploration: what is the philosophical appropriation of the language of spirituality really meant to achieve? What criteria, if any, do philosophers propose for assessing the aims and transformative efficacy of spiritual exercises? I want to press these questions further in the second part of the chapter by turning to the work of Hadot, to whom Cottingham's account is clearly indebted. In Hadot's work as well, the construction of the category of spirituality and the claim for the primacy of practice have the effect of suppressing questions regarding spirituality that are most in need of clarification.


## Part II: The Primacy of Practice

As I noted earlier, Hadot's work on the spiritual exercises of ancient philosophy has been remarkably influential in reclaiming an idea of philosophy not only as an academic discourse, but as a practice of spiritual formation whose aim is the transformation of perception and consciousness. If Cottingham's approach to

---

[29]   Ibid., p. 17.
[30]   Ibid., p. 3.

spiritual exercises can be considered a holistic or integrative one, Hadot's can be considered "existential," in two respects.[31]

First, Hadot insists on the terminology "spiritual" (as opposed to "moral" or "intellectual") in describing these exercises in order to emphasize what he refers to as their existential significance. No other term, he insists, captures their ability to effect a complete transformation of subjectivity.[32] The purpose of spirituality on the ancient model is to cultivate the vision of a universal or cosmic order that would provide a critical perspective on the disorder of the soul caused by the passions. Spiritual exercises correlate an ideal of wisdom defined by a universal order of nature, with an inner attitude of soul that attempts to conform itself to this order. The transformation thereby effected involves what Hadot calls a "universalization" of the self which transforms the self from an egoistic, passion-ridden individual to a transcendent, moral self, open to the universality and objectivity of thought: "This is a new way of being-in-the-world," Hadot writes, "which consists in becoming aware of oneself as a part of nature, and a portion of universal reason."[33]

In addition to the emphasis on the transformation of subjectivity just noted, Hadot's approach can be considered "existential" in a second respect as well, which signals his break with some of the assumptions of antiquity. This aspect of Hadot's account emerges in his somewhat surprising contention that ancient spiritual exercises can be retrieved in the present in abstraction from their original philosophical background. He writes, "I think modern man can practice the spiritual exercises of antiquity, at the same time separating them from the philosophical or mythic discourse which came along with them. It is therefore not necessary, in order to practice these exercises, to believe in the Stoics' nature or universal reason. Rather, as one practices them, one lives concretely according to reason."[34]

---

[31] Portions of this section of the paper were drawn from my essay "The return of spiritual exercises," in *A Philosophy to Live By: Engaging Iris Murdoch* (Oxford University Press, 2012).

[32] See Hadot, *Philosophy as a Way of Life*, p. 82 and also p. 127: "[T]hese exercises have as their goal the transformation of our vision of the world, and the metamorphosis of our being. They therefore have not merely a moral, but also an existential value. We are not just dealing here with a code of good moral conduct, but with a way of being, in the strongest sense of the term."

[33] Ibid., p. 211.

[34] Ibid.

Such statements suggest that Hadot embraces some version of noncognitivism, whereby concrete practices are prior to or separable from their philosophical or theoretical justification.[35] He contends that there is evidence for this view within ancient philosophy itself, which consistently held that "theory is never considered an end in itself; it is clearly and decidedly put in the service of practice."[36]

However, Hadot's assertion that spiritual practices are separable from their original theoretical background cannot, in my judgment, be accounted for solely by his appeal to the ancient philosophical evidence. Rather, it reveals the traces of his early training in existentialism, which exerted a strong influence on his conception of philosophy.[37] This influence can be seen at a crucial point, when Hadot characterizes the life of wisdom as a matter of choice rather than vision. The practice of spiritual exercises, he argues, represents an existential *choice* to follow a certain form of life, rather than an intellectual commitment to the dogmas of a philosophical system: "ethics—that is to say, choosing the good—is not the consequence of metaphysics, but metaphysics is the consequence of ethics ... [I]t is one's choice of life which precedes metaphysical theories, and ... we can make our choice of life, whether or not we justify it by improved or entirely new arguments."[38] In contrast to the cognitivist assumptions of the ancient model of spiritual exercises, which held that metaphysics (i.e., a vision of the cosmic order) is the condition for ethics, Hadot asserts that ethics is prior to any metaphysics.[39]

Hadot's claim that one can achieve the same universalizing perspective as, say, the Stoics, without buying into the metaphysical assumptions that undergird that

---

[35]   Hadot writes that "the same spiritual exercises can, in fact, be justified by extremely diverse philosophical discourses. These latter are nothing but clumsy attempts, coming after the fact, to describe and justify inner experiences whose existential density is not, in the last analysis, susceptible of any attempt at theorization or systematization." Ibid., p. 212.

[36]   Ibid., p. 61. Arnold Davidson places particular stress on this feature of Hadot's analysis. Quoting Hadot, in part, he notes that "the philosophers of antiquity were concerned not with ready-made knowledge, but with imparting that training and education that would allow their disciples to 'orient themselves in thought, in the life of the city, or in the world ... [T]he written philosophical work, precisely because it is a direct or indirect echo of oral teaching now appears to us as a set of exercises, intended to make one practice a method, rather than as a doctrinal exposition.'" See Davidson's introduction, ibid., p. 21.

[37]   See Hadot's remarks in the interview published as the "Postscript" to *Philosophy as a Way of Life*, esp. p. 278.

[38]   Ibid., p. 283.

[39]   Ibid.

perspective is, I would argue, one reason for the enormous popularity and influence of his work. In fact, it provides an exemplary justification for the way in which many forms of spirituality are appropriated not only in philosophy but in popular culture. The assumption is that one can practice spiritual exercises—and achieve the same results or benefits—without necessarily believing in the worldview from which they arose. I have already noted some reasons that we might be suspicious of this claim in Cottingham. At least two concerns can be raised about Hadot's claim for the primacy of practice as well.

First, Hadot argues that the efficacy of spiritual exercises lies in the transformation that results from the adoption of a cosmic perspective. Such a transformation, we noted, involves a "universalization" of the self's perception that permits a new way of being in the world. But how can the spiritual practices of ancient philosophy retain their transformative efficacy today in the absence of the theoretical grounds for this perspective? By asserting that one can choose the practices apart from the metaphysical worldview that informs them, Hadot seems to undercut the very thing that makes such practices transformative in the first place: their access to an "objective" or cosmic vision. This question is all the more pointed because Hadot himself criticized Foucault's appropriation of spiritual exercises for ignoring this crucial component of universalization. That is, he charged Foucault with neglecting or ignoring the cosmic dimension that Hadot insisted was essential to their transformative power. As Hadot writes, "The feeling of belonging to a whole is an essential element. Such a cosmic perspective radically transforms the feeling one has of oneself."[40] In contrast, Foucault's position seems to Hadot to promote an aesthetics of self-shaping, a mere stylistics of existence, precisely because it lacks the cosmic dimension. Arnold Davidson summarizes Hadot's criticism of Foucault as follows: "By not attending to that aspect of the care of the self that places the self within a cosmic dimension, whereby the self, in becoming aware of its belonging to the cosmic Whole, thus transforms itself, Foucault was not able to see the full scope of spiritual exercises."[41]

Hadot's critique of Foucault's appropriation of spiritual exercises is important because it suggests, contrary to what he claims, that the practices cannot be entirely severed from their background beliefs after all, since those beliefs provide

---

[40]    Ibid., p. 208.

[41]    See Davidson's introduction to *Philosophy as a Way of Life*, pp. 24–25.

the justificatory framework for the transformative efficacy of the practices. That is, one cannot simply choose the practices apart from their informing worldview and expect the same results. Without the framework, the practices will not have the same meaning or transformative efficacy. If that is not the case, it is hard to understand how Hadot can find fault with Foucault's appropriation of them.

This discussion helps us to identify two possible lines of response to Hadot's claim that spiritual practices can be severed from their metaphysical background. The first is voiced by John Haldane, who uses this issue to propose a return to religious traditions. Although Haldane is generally sympathetic to Hadot's work on the spiritual exercises of ancient philosophy, he directly challenges Hadot's claim that "spiritual formation may proceed independently of the truth of the accompanying metaphysical discourse."[42] Haldane's own view is that "the necessary condition for the possibility of spirituality is some religious truth."[43] Unlike Hadot, Haldane sees metaphysics and spirituality as "constituent components of a single enterprise, such that the content of spiritual formation depends upon its metaphysical complement."[44] Haldane finds it odd to suppose that no practical or spiritual consequences follow from adopting one fundamental view of reality rather than another. The content of the metaphysical belief makes a difference in the resulting disposition or demeanor with which one engages in spiritual practice. Without the proper metaphysical background, Haldane insists, one would lack the requisite disposition. He concludes that "Hadot is wrong to loosen the link between philosophy and philosophical discourse; spirituality and metaphysics go together."[45] Insisting on this link may have the added benefit, in Haldane's view, of provoking a rediscovery of religious traditions. If, as he insists (*contra* Hadot), spiritual practices make no sense apart from the religious truths from which they arose, practicing a form of spirituality might eventually lead towards a renewed engagement with the truths of that tradition. "If the need and possibility of spirituality should seem compelling," he asks, "might we have the beginnings of an argument for religion?"[46]

---

[42]   Haldane, "On the very idea of spiritual values," in A. O'Hear (ed.), *Philosophy, the Good, the True and the Beautiful* (Cambridge: Cambridge University Press, 2000), p. 23.

[43]   Ibid., p. 24.

[44]   Ibid., p. 23.

[45]   Ibid.

[46]   Ibid., p. 24.

Haldane's position will be attractive to those who insist that a certain notion of religious truth is authoritative or who harbor the hope that the flight to spirituality might give way to a return to historical religious traditions. However, there are other grounds on which one might object to Hadot's claim for the primacy of practice besides Haldane's insistence on a metaphysics of religious truth.

As an alternative, I suggest that we distinguish between stronger and weaker versions of the claim for the primacy of practice. For example, if what Hadot means by the priority of practice is simply that philosophical insight precedes the theoretical or systematic articulation of that insight in philosophical discourse, we can accept this weaker version of the claim. We also need not object to the claim that practices are "prior" to any theoretical or intellectual justification in the sense that the experience of spiritual practices precedes reflection in a temporal, psychological, or developmental sense. That is, in human life it is normally the case that one becomes acculturated in the practices of a tradition before one is exposed to (or capable of grasping) the intellectual underpinnings in which the practices are embedded. Therefore, we can agree to this extent with Cottingham's claim (noted earlier) that "we are formed by practices first, and learn to reflect on them only later, from within a perspective formed by the practices themselves."

Finally, we can also acknowledge that, insofar that many spiritual practices are intended to engage the senses and discipline the body and its desires, they have an immediacy of impact that the cognitive dimensions of a religious or spiritual tradition may lack. Indeed, emerging research in psychology and neuroscience suggests that some spiritual practices may produce physical benefits (i.e., the capacity to focus mental attention, calm the mind, quiet the passions, and so forth) even in the absence of any cognitive assent to their underlying worldview (as some have claimed for the physical and neurological benefits of meditation, whether or not one professes to be a Buddhist). So we might agree that practice is "primary" in the sense of the immediacy of physical or sensory experience.

However, even if we affirm the primacy of practice in any of these weaker senses, it still leaves open the question of whether the stronger claim for the primacy of practice can also be endorsed, namely, the claim that the practices *lose nothing* in the way of transformative efficacy when they are detached from their metaphysical or cognitive background. Hadot himself, as we saw earlier, gave us reason to be skeptical of this claim when he criticized Foucault's appropriation of spiritual exercises as overly "aesthetic," i.e., lacking the so-called cosmic dimension that Hadot considered crucial. Hadot's insistence that it is possible to detach spiritual practices from their background beliefs is a puzzling contradiction in this light.

What is missing from Hadot's retrieval of ancient spiritual exercises, in my judgment, is an explicit acknowledgment of the possibility that, when spiritual practices are loosened from their traditional moorings (as is so often the case with contemporary retrievals of practices such as Indian yoga, Buddhist meditation, or even Jewish Kabbalah), they may be put to instrumental ends quite different from the radical transformation of perspective which Hadot regards as their pre-eminent value. If one is seeking to regain some measure of integrity for the concept of spirituality today, the lack of criteria in Hadot's account for distinguishing true or genuine forms of spiritual practice from false or shallow forms of spirituality is worrisome. Although it is possible (as Haldane speculates) that Hadot recognizes that there are "limits to how wrong one can be at the speculative level while keeping on track in the practice of wisdom,"[47] he does not, as far as I can tell, acknowledge this point explicitly.

Proudfoot sheds valuable light on this issue when he points out that:

> Most traditions require a novice to practice under the guidance of a spiritual director or guru, and that guidance often continues even for experienced practitioners. Spiritual manuals, whether written or oral, include rules for both directors and practitioners. An important part of any such practice is concerned with criteria for discriminating the real from the counterfeit and from the merely apparent. Those criteria reflect the doctrine and beliefs that inform that particular tradition and practice.[48]

As an example, Proudfoot cites Jonathan Edwards' *Treatise Concerning Religious Affections*, written during the Great Awakening in the eighteenth century, which lays out the criteria for distinguishing genuine religious affection from their nearly indiscernible counterparts. Different criteria, Proudfoot notes, would be found in "an equally subtle and sophisticated manual for compassion meditation in Tibetan

---

[47]    Haldane, "On the very idea of spiritual values," p. 24.
[48]    Proudfoot, Review of Cottingham, pp. 551–552.

Buddhism."[49] Unlike Hadot, who claims that "the same spiritual exercises can, in fact, be justified by extremely diverse philosophical discourses," and that the latter "are nothing but clumsy attempts, coming after the fact, to describe and justify inner experiences whose existential density is not, in the last analysis, susceptible of any attempt at theorization or systematization,"[50] Proudfoot argues that beliefs of a tradition make a crucial difference in providing an explanatory and justificatory background for spiritual practices and their proper performance. In the absence of such guidance, spiritual practices can easily become instrumentalized in relation to a set of (personal or cultural) ideals that are quite foreign to their originating impulse, as is often the case in contemporary forms of spirituality in popular culture.

This should not be taken to mean that traditional beliefs offer the only possible justification for spiritual practices, or that such practices may not be adapted to new intellectual and cultural conditions that offer new forms of justification for them. As Proudfoot notes, spiritual practices "are parts of living traditions that develop over time. They are modified, as are the doctrines and beliefs of those traditions, in response to changes in ways of conceiving the world as well as in ways of evaluating persons and social institutions."[51] My point, rather, is that if the notion of spirituality is to remain a site of meaningful human aspiration, one that is capable of withstanding the distortions and deflations that assail every human pursuit of the good, then we should not assume that we can simply "use our intuitions to assess the moral credentials of the systems of praxis on offer" (as Cottingham suggests), or that the "existential density" of such practices is a sufficient mark of their authenticity (as Hadot argues). Although the background beliefs of a particular form of spiritual practice may lose credibility or require radical revision in response to changing historical, cultural, and intellectual conditions, the need for some explanatory framework seems essential if spirituality is to regain some measure of integrity.

---

[49]   Ibid., p. 552.

[50]   See n. 35.

[51]   Proudfoot, Review of Cottingham, p. 552. For an exemplary and persuasive attempt to reinterpret the spiritual practices of Buddhism in response to the challenges of modernity and globalization, see Dale S. Wright, *The Six Perfections: Buddhism and the Cultivation of Character* (Oxford University Press, 2009).

The question of what *type* of background is required is a question I address briefly in my concluding section.

## Conclusion: Spirituality and Metaphysics

In this chapter, I have argued that contemporary spirituality suffers from an indeterminacy that has diminished its integrity and value. Philosophers such as Hadot and Cottingham have been successful in renewing scholarly attention to spirituality and highlighting the value of spiritual exercises as a path of human transformation. However, in light of their insistence on the priority of practice, neither account has the resources needed to overcome the vacuousness that attends the concept of spirituality today. Although I cannot argue the point in detail here, I want to suggest in closing that the claim for the primacy of practice (at least in its stronger version, which stipulates the separability of "metaphysics" from "ethics") may actually undermine the aims of a humane philosophy.

If the goal of spiritual exercises, as Hadot notes, is "the transformation of our vision of the world, and the metamorphosis of our being," then the efficacy of such practices seems to depend on an account of human being that can make sense of why such a transformation is necessary and can articulate the human ideal that the practices are designed to achieve. But this is simply to say that an ethic necessarily entails a set of claims about the nature of reality and the being of the human—in short, a "metaphysics." To defend the necessity of metaphysics in this sense is simply to affirm that ethical reflection is carried out within a larger framework of assumptions about reality and human existence that gives the ethic its point and direction.[52] To suggest, as Hadot appears to do, that one can jettison the framework and rely on the practices themselves to have transformative effects opens the door to appropriations of spiritual practices that may depart significantly from the ideal of a "cosmic perspective" that Hadot considers essential to the idea of *askesis*.

Moreover, if the philosophical turn to spirituality is intended to recover a more capacious view of philosophy as care of the soul (i.e., a more "humane"

---

[52]   This account of metaphysics is indebted to the work of Iris Murdoch. For extensive analysis, see my *Picturing the Human: The Moral Thought of Iris Murdoch* (Oxford University Press, 2000) and *A Philosophy to Live By: Engaging Iris Murdoch* (Oxford University Press, 2012).

philosophy in Cottingham's sense), then one would expect it to offer a picture of the human as embedded in and responsive to a wider reality, rather than as making a choice to follow a particular form of life in seeming isolation from any such framework. What I referred to earlier as the existentialist flavor of Hadot's account of spiritual exercises seems far removed, in this respect, from the spirit of the Stoics' adherence to a cosmic vision. It is the *choice* that seems to matter most to him, not the belief in a cosmic logos. Yet as I have noted, this assertion of the primacy of the will over any metaphysical conception undercuts the very thing that makes such practices transformative on Hadot's account: their access to a "universalizing" perspective.

In *Sources of the Self*, Charles Taylor describes the modern condition in terms that seem to capture some of the reasons that it is so difficult to formulate an adequate notion of spirituality today. He argues that modern persons no longer understand themselves as participating in a universal order of reason that is thought to exist outside us in nature of the cosmos. Rather, any sense of an objective moral order is understood to depend on our own powers of construction or our own activity of willing. Taylor describes this development as a process of "internalization" whereby the moral sources which were previously understood as situated in the rational order of the cosmos are now sought within. As Taylor puts it, "We are now in an age in which the publicly accessible cosmic order of meanings is an impossibility. The only way we can explore the order in which we are set with an aim to defining moral sources is through ... personal resonance."[53] Contemporary forms of spirituality reflect this internalization of moral sources— so much so that they all too often remain caught up in the experience of "personal resonance" without any sense of the demand for transformation that a wider order of reality might entail. As Taylor notes, "the danger of a regression to subjectivism always exists" once we acknowledge that this wider order is only available through personal resonance.[54] Perhaps for this reason, many contemporary forms of spirituality seem to be little more than "a celebration of our creative powers."[55]

---

[53]   Charles Taylor, *Sources of the Self: The Making of the Modern Identity* (Harvard University Press, 1989), p. 512.

[54]   Ibid., p. 510.

[55]   Ibid.

Any contemporary reconstruction of spirituality will need to take into account the conditions Taylor identifies. Hadot and Cottingham recognize, in different ways, that the ground of spiritual exercises has shifted in modernity, and that the notion of a rational order of the cosmos is no longer directly available. Cottingham, for example, acknowledges that there is no "Olympian standpoint" (or cosmic perspective) from which to articulate a "neutral" or "objective" account of spirituality apart from the particular historical and cultural circumstances in which we are embedded. Similarly, Hadot's insistence that one can continue to practice ancient spiritual exercises without believing in the Stoics' idea of nature or universal reason is a concession to the demise of the ancient idea of an "ontic logos."

However, if Taylor's account is correct, what is required to overcome the vacuousness of spirituality today is a more sustained attempt than we find in either Cottingham or Hadot to specify how the practice of spiritual exercises can put us in touch with moral sources that make important human ideals come alive again, without collapsing the experience of *askesis* simply into an intensification of the self's own powers. An adequate philosophy of spirituality may depend, therefore, on a metaphysical background that acknowledges that, although access to moral sources today is only possible through "personal resonance," the practice of spirituality is incomplete if it allows us only to discover our own powers, without also heeding the demand for self-transformation. That demand, as Taylor notes, may be felt within, but "it emanates from the world."[56]

## Selected Bibliography

Carr, David, and Haldane, John (eds), *Spirituality, Philosophy and Education* (London and New York: Routledge, 2003).

Cottingham, John, *The Spiritual Dimension* (Cambridge: Cambridge University Press, 2005).

Hadot, Pierre, *Philosophy as a Way of Life* (Oxford: Blackwell, 1995).

---

[56]   Ibid., p. 513.

Chapter 4

# Tending the Garden of Humanism

Glenn Whitehouse

"Sustainability" has lately become a term one hears everywhere, from public policy, to the development of green technologies, to educational initiatives, among the many realms where the word has come into common use. Sustainability has obvious import for natural science and environmental studies; but if sustainability represents a norm for the relation between *human activity* and the processes of the natural world, then it would seem that the idea puts questions to humanism and to the humanities as well. In this chapter, I would like take up some of these questions: what challenges are placed to humanism by the idea of sustainability and by some of the ideologies that use the idea? What relation between the humanities disciplines and the natural sciences best fits the ideal of sustainability? What philosophical terms or ideas most adequately think the relation between humanity and nature? After pointing out problems with answers to these questions offered by some prominent advocates of sustainability, I will suggest that the idea of *integrity of life* as used in the theological humanism of David Klemm and William Schweiker may represent the most adequate way to think the ideal of sustainability broadly across the disciplines.

What then is sustainability? The phrase "sustainable development" entered wide public use following the so-called "Brundtland report" of the World Commission on Environment and Development in 1987, which proclaimed "Sustainable development is development that meets the needs of the present without compromising the ability of future generations to meet their own needs."[1] Understandably, many environmentalists have found this influential statement problematic, inasmuch as it stays entirely within the realm of human needs and

---

[1]    World Commission on Environment and Development, *Our Common Future* (Oxford: Oxford University Press, 1987), p. 43.

use values, and does not appear either to acknowledge any intrinsic value to the natural world, nor to conceive any bond between humanity and nature other than a utilitarian one.

The Earth Charter of 2000 attempted to remedy these defects by adopting a more broad and holistic approach to sustainability. Quoting from the Preamble:

> [W]e must recognize that in the midst of a magnificent diversity of cultures and life forms we are one human family and one earth community with a common destiny. We must join together to bring forth a sustainable global society ... We must decide to live with a sense of universal responsibility, identifying ourselves with the whole earth community as well as our local communities.[2]

The language of the Charter, then, attempts to think sustainability primarily in terms of bonds of solidarity between and among humans, and between humans and the natural world of which they are a part—bonds the document does not hesitate to identify as "sacred." The more mundane policy approach of the Brundtland report is not ignored in the Charter—it is present in substatements like: "II.5.a. Adopt at all levels sustainable development plans and regulations that make environmental conservation and rehabilitation integral to all development initiatives."[3] But for the Earth Charter, the policy initiatives are posited as *consequences* of a more broad ethical and spiritual stance.

It seems fair to identify the Earth Charter as a *humanist* document. This is so with regard to the invocation of "one human family" in the quote above, as well as in the emphasis on cultivating a more humane form of life within local human and biotic communities. The Earth Charter also follows the pattern of humanism in viewing sustainability as an ideal that can fully be realized only through the cultivation of different forms of humane learning, artistic creation, and political expression: "We must imaginatively develop and apply the vision of a sustainable way of life ... [T]he arts, religions, educational institutions, media, businesses, nongovernmental organizations and governments are all called to offer creative leadership."[4] For the

---

[2]   Earth Charter Initiative, *The Earth Charter*, http://www.earthcharterinaction.org: 2000 (accessed June 19, 2011).

[3]   Ibid.

[4]   Ibid.

Earth Charter, then, sustainability is at base something deeply human and spiritual, however much it may draw us into the realms of science or policy.

This brings us to consider Harvard biologist E.O. Wilson, who might be considered the foremost public intellectual of the sustainability movement, particularly regarding issues of biodiversity. Despite being a hard-nosed empirical scientist, Wilson often aims to inspire, and much of his writing appears to share the theme of common identity and common cause between humanity and nature. In *The Diversity of Life* Wilson writes, "Humanity is part of nature, a species that evolved among other species ... We do not understand ourselves yet and descend farther from heaven's air if we forget how much the natural world means to us. Signals abound that the loss of life's diversity endangers not just the body but the spirit."[5] Wilson also appears to share some of the humanist interest in the cultivation of scholarly inquiry, and not merely in that he studs his prose with literary allusions and rhetorical flourishes. Wilson conceives of sustainability as a broad goal that will call for the contributions of an array of scholarly disciplines: "The solution will require cooperation among professionals long separated by academic and professional tradition. Biology, anthropology, economics, agriculture and law will have to find a common voice."[6]

But the closer one gets to the writings of Wilson and others associated with him, the less hospitable the environment looks for humanists. Wilson, along with writers such as Daniel Dennett, Richard Dawkins and others who take inspiration from them, is engaged in the project of attempting a wholly naturalistic, scientific account of human culture; an account that at best has no use for and at worst exhibits open contempt for the humanities as traditionally practiced. Consider Wilson's assessment of the interpretive disciplines in his book *Consilience*:

> Interpretation has multiple dimensions, namely history, biography, linguistics and aesthetic judgment. At the foundation of them all lie the material processes of the human mind ... [Past interpretive approaches], which are guided largely by unaided intuition about the way the brain works, have fared badly. In the absence of a compass based on sound material knowledge, they make too many

---

[5] Edward O. Wilson, *The Diversity of Life* (Cambridge, MA: Harvard University Press, 1992), pp. 348–351.

[6] Ibid., p. 312.

wrong turns into blind ends. If the brain is ever charted, and an enduring theory of the arts created as part of the enterprise, it will be by stepwise and consilient contributions from the brain sciences, psychology, and evolutionary biology.[7]

The initial appearance that Wilson is sympathetic to the humanist project of cultivating diverse arts and scholarly disciplines as mirrors of humanity and nature, quickly dissipates as he begins to explain the need for what he calls "consilient" explanation:

> We already think of [different disciplinary domains] as closely connected, so that rational inquiry in one informs reasoning in the [others] … [Yet] each has its own practitioners, language, modes of analysis, and standards of validation. The result is confusion, and confusion was correctly identified by Francis Bacon four centuries ago as the most fatal of errors.[8]

One might have expected a humanist to say, "the result is *conversation*."

Wilson's "consilient" approach to interdisciplinary inquiry twists the humanist dictum that man is the measure of things, to propose that consciousness is the measure of all human things, and natural science is the royal road to measuring consciousness.[9] The basic idea of *Consilience* is that the astounding success of the natural sciences in producing causal explanations of natural phenomena is based primarily on the method of reduction, combined with the linkage of levels of explanation across different disciplines. Biological phenomena can be reduced to chemistry, and studied using the methods of chemistry; chemistry in turn can be reduced to physics and studied using *its* methods. The intellectual synthesis "consilience" is what takes place after the move of explanatory reduction, when scientists reconstitute knowledge of the individual organism by moving back up

---

[7]   Edward O. Wilson, *Consilience: The Unity of Knowledge* (New York: Knopf, 1998), p. 216.

[8]   Ibid., p. 9.

[9]   A version of this paragraph and the next appeared in Glenn Whitehouse, "Yes Richard, Theology is a Subject: Tillich's System of the Sciences vs. the Disciplinary Encroachments of the New Atheism," *Bulletin of the North American Paul Tillich Society* 36:4 (2010): pp. 10–11.

the chain of reduction.[10] This reconstitution depends on linked inter-scientific inquiry, whereby scientists whose objects lie further up the chain receive help from scientists whose objects are more "basic." But *Consilience* the *book* is not principally concerned with the traditional objects of scientific inquiry, but with extending consilient inquiry into the realm of the social sciences and humanities. Now, Wilson claims, advances in biology, genetics, cognitive psychology and evolutionary psychology have finally made the mind accessible to scientific inquiry. And if consciousness can be treated scientifically, so can the products of consciousness—art, music, customs, morality, religion; in short, what we call culture.[11] For Wilson, consilience opens the door for natural science to be the discourse that unifies knowledge—*all knowledge*—to the great benefit of science, which becomes comprehensive, and the greater benefit of the humanities, which at last become scientific.

Other naturalist approaches to culture closely affiliated with Wilson have similar ambitions to displace the humanities disciplines as interpreters of culture. Most notably, science writer Richard Dawkins and philosopher Daniel Dennett have popularized a theory of "memes"—semiotic units and patterns of information such as a melody, a slogan, a gesture, or a fashion trend. What meme theory suggests is that we understand these phenomena in the same way we do genes, namely in terms of how they succeed, grow, spread and evolve according to the principle of natural selection.[12] Dennett suggests that we view memes as similar to a virus in their transmission patterns. He emphasizes that memes spread through culture in ways best explained by their own fitness at survival—by a "meme's eye view"— and not by their relation to any meaning intended by a speaker or recognized by a listener.[13] To give a personal example of such a phenomenon: recently, I was assigned to teach formal logic at my institution. One thing I have learned while teaching truth tables, with their neat rows of alternating Ts and Fs, is that I cannot rapidly write down the sequence "FFFF-TTTT" without triggering a vivid (and unwelcome) mental recollection of the 1980s hit "Safety Dance" by Men Without

---

[10]   Wilson, *Consilience*, pp. 66–71.

[11]   Ibid., pp. 96–100, 125–130.

[12]   Richard Dawkins, *The Selfish Gene* (Oxford: Oxford University Press, 2006), pp. 189–201.

[13]   Daniel Dennett, *Consciousness Explained* (Boston: Little, Brown & Co., 1992), pp. 199–208.

Hats, which begins with the singer chanting the letters of "safety" four times each. This mental replay does no discernible good to me as an organism, but the meme has apparently infected me to the benefit of *its* own survival, however undeserved it may be. Now most people would tend to write off such phenomena as mental detritus, but for Dennett, memes are the units of all cultural content. He goes so far as to suggest that the human mind is itself a huge complex of memes that process other memes, analogous to the software that allows a computer to run a "virtual machine" such as Word or PowerPoint. While the hardware—brains—are basically the same physiologically, the cultural difference between, say, a Chinese and American mind might be analogous to the difference between Windows and Mac OS.[14] The appeal of this to Dennett, Dawkins and others is that memes seem to offer the prospect of a science of cultural transmission and generally of a scientific approach to culture, eliminating the need to rely on the fuzzy and inexact ways that culture is approached within the humanities.

So, to refocus the issue: the *goal* of sustainability seems best served by treating the *idea* of sustainability broadly, as a bond of identity and responsibility between humanity and nature, and as a common task of human inquiry uniting scientific approaches with ethical principles, spiritual attitudes and cultural pursuits. This is the ideal of the Earth Charter, one I have suggested is worth subscribing to, on both humanist and environmentalist grounds. But when we examine some of the ideologies influential within the sustainability movement, this broad synthesis itself seems difficult to sustain. If human culture were reduced completely to the material components and processes of the natural world, as the proponents of the naturalist approach to culture attempt, it seems there would no longer be any humanity to balance *with* nature.

In a sense, the leading advocates of the naturalist approach to culture turn on its head the modern "doubling" of subjectivity first diagnosed by Foucault, and recounted by Habermas in *The Philosophical Discourse of Modernity*. The modern subject reacted to its double status as transcendental subject and empirical object by attempting to re-conquer objective reality *for* consciousness in such projects as the idealism of Fichte and Hegel, and Freudian analysis that proceeded

---

[14]    Ibid., pp. 210ff.

by the slogan *Wo Es war, soll Ich werden*.[15] By contrast, humanity, in Wilson and Dennett's account, *starts* with the scandal that intuition or first person experience seems to be an ineradicable accompaniment to the observable phenomena of behavior and cognition. They set out to eradicate that alleged scandal, in Wilson's case by putting an empirical consilient science of consciousness in the place of the fuzzy intuition or "folk psychology" of everyday experience, and in Dennett's case by explicitly proposing a "hetero-phenomenology" that directly challenges the presumed irreducibility of intentionality and the first person stance.[16] Both replace the first person stance of experience with a "proper" third person descriptive approach—*Wo Ich war, soll Es werden*. No room for "the human" here.

Further, if cultural naturalism is right to unveil the everyday language of human experience and its scholarly elaborations as crude and inadequate approximations of knowledge now thankfully available in scientific form, one has to ask whether the confluence of scientific, cultural, spiritual and scholarly voices endorsed by the Earth Charter really has any point. If science is the one legitimate mode of describing reality; and if, as Sam Harris recently suggested in *The Moral Landscape*, it suffices for ethics as well,[17] it would seem what would be called for is something closer to the monological approach of the Brundtland report, only this time rewritten by biologists instead of policy wonks. Our question, then, becomes whether in the naturalist intellectual environment inhabited by many people in the sustainability community, the humanities and the sciences can meet in dialogue at *any* level. Further, we must ask whether the ideal of sustainability is *itself* sustainable, once the internal logic of naturalist ideology has effectively purged any humanism from the idea.

I will claim that sustainability—the idea and the movement—is *not* sustainable when thought apart from humanism. Further, I would like to suggest that the notion of *integrity of life*, as developed by David Klemm and William Schweiker in *Religion and the Human Future: An Essay on Theological Humanism*, represents a particularly viable model for conceiving sustainability today, an alternative to the bloodless policy-speak of the Brundtland report or the ultimately self-defeating

---

[15]   Juergen Habermas, *The Philosophical Discourse of Modernity*, trans. Frederick Lawrence (Cambridge, MA: MIT Press, 1987), pp. 261ff.

[16]   Dennett, *Consciousness*, p. 72.

[17]   Sam Harris, *The Moral Landscape: How Science can Determine Human Values* (New York: Free Press, 2010).

scientism of Wilson and his followers. Briefly stated, *integrity* names both a wholeness of life goods, and the *activity* of integrating those goods *into* wholes, guided by an ethical commitment to respect and enhance the integrity of life for oneself and others.[18] The task of selfhood on this account is, *first,* to integrate the goods of life into some livable form,[19] those goods being divided into basic life goods, social goods, reflective goods and goods of locality; *second*, to maintain a responsible commitment to the good of *others*, guided by norms of moral action, understanding that "the integrity of one's own life cannot be directly aimed at or achieved, [but] arises in and through a life dedicated to respecting and enhancing the integrity of life in, with, and through others"[20]; *third,* to orient oneself toward a spiritual ideal in which "What seems to be of unsurpassable importance is the right and responsible unity of power and life as the integrity of life."[21] Integrity names a model of humanity, and a norm for the thinking, interpreting and acting activities which integrate life into individual, intersubjective and spiritual wholes.

*Integrity*, so conceived, offers some immediately apparent benefits to anyone trying to link humanism to sustainability concerns. For one, Klemm and Schweiker posit integrity as an ideal of humanity out of the conviction that the spiritual longing of our age is for an upholding of the forces of life over against forces of disintegration that pervade the economic, ecological, intellectual and psychological realms.[22] Theological Humanism is humanism for an age of crisis, and environmental degradation is among the list of crises calling for integrating response. Further, Theological Humanism insists that the task of integration requires more than just the "lateral transcendence" that calls me to responsibility to other *people*; rather, human integrity refers us to the task of integrating ourselves within life as a whole: "The human struggle for wholeness, for integrity, situates us in the wider complex of life … The challenge is … to fashion a form of thought and a way of life that respects and enhances the integrity of human existence within but not against other forms of life."[23] Finally,

---

[18]    David Klemm and William Schweiker, *Religion and the Human Future: An Essay on Theological Humanism* (Oxford: Blackwell, 2008), p. 83.

[19]    Ibid., p. 75.

[20]    Ibid., p. 85.

[21]    Ibid., p. 92.

[22]    Ibid., p. 90.

[23]    Ibid., pp. 35–36.

Klemm and Schweiker's book itself embodies the interdisciplinary dialogue we identified as important to sustainability, as it incorporates the voices of science, philosophy, the arts and theology.

I would like to push the connection between "integrity of life" and sustainability further now, by looking into one possible *philosophical* grounding for the Theological Humanist ideal of integrity, drawn from David Klemm's reading of Schleiermacher's principle of Individuality. As Klemm has shown us, Individuality is not only central to understanding Schleiermacher's theology and philosophy, but can also be read as the grounding principle for Paul Ricoeur's hermeneutics.[24]

The principle of Individuality appears most directly in Schleiermacher's philosophical lectures on *Dialectic*, a work Klemm has done much to help English language readers access. Schleiermacher's work is grounded in *dialogue*. Starting from the fact of dispute between different speakers, it examines the grounding principles under which that dialogue can be resolved in knowing, that resolution being guided by the criteria of *intersubjective agreement* and *correspondence between thinking and being*. The latter criterion demands that thought presuppose some transcendent ground of the unity of thinking and being. The individual human self is the finite "analogue" of that transcendent ground, accessed in an intuition of "immediate self consciousness" as feeling.[25] The principle of Individuality, then, enters dialectic at two levels. First, as the principle for a modest ontology of objects,

> It states that the universal element of an object of knowledge can never be fully abstracted from the particular element in which it appears, any more than the particular element can be derived from the universal element ... [T]he most essential element of an object is the third individualizing element "mediating" between the universal and the particular.[26]

---

[24] David Klemm, "Individuality: The Principle of Ricoeur's Mediating Philosophy and its Bearing on Theology of Culture," in David Klemm and William Schweiker (eds), *Meanings in Texts and Actions: Questioning Paul Ricoeur* (Charlottesville: University Press of Virginia, 1993), pp. 275–291.

[25] David Klemm, "Schleiermacher on the Self: Immediate Self-Consciousness as Feeling and as Thinking," in David Klemm and Gunther Zoeller (eds), *Figuring the Self: Subject, Absolute and Others in Classical German Philosophy* (Albany: SUNY, 1997), pp. 170–173.

[26] Ibid., p. 171.

Second, as philosophy of human selfhood, it steers between the various dualist and idealist options of modernity:

> Schleiermacher stands between Kant on the one hand and Fichte and Hegel on the other hand. Schleiermacher claims less than the absolute idealist position, for Schleiermacher claims that the intuition of the self is not purely an *intellectual* intuition, self-produced in thought when thought thinks itself, as it is for Fichte and Hegel. But Schleiermacher … claims more than the critical philosophy, for the intuition of the self is not merely an idea of pure reason … Schleiermacher's notion is determined by the principle of *individuality*, the principle of the unity of the intelligible and the sensible.[27]

I believe there is good warrant for reading Schleiermacher's principle of Individuality as a major philosophical source for the idea of integrity of life in the Theological Humanism of Klemm and Schweiker. But rather than demonstrating that, I'll assume it, in order to move on to the question of how reading *integrity* in terms of Individuality may help humanism respond to the aporias and inadequacies of naturalist ideologies of sustainability such as Wilson's.

First, reading integrity in terms of Individuality helps mitigate the *metaphysical* problems that make it difficult to think sustainability as a coexistence of humanity and nature. The philosophical project of modernity called for the principle of humanity, the thinking "I", to reconquer objectivity and nature along with it for thought. This move issued philosophically in idealism and, at least in the Heideggerian account, contributed to the crisis of overhumanization by issuing in the "age of the world picture" and the technological worldview.[28] Conversely, the naturalism of Wilson and Dennett calls on objective study of nature to be the means by which science can explain and ultimately conquer subjectivity, dissolving the conscious thinking "I" as a reference point for inquiry. Ironically, Wilson's naturalism also renders the world as Cartesian grid, and thinks nature technologically as much as modernity did, albeit in terms of biochemical R&D rather than factories and tractors. To redeem the promise of the Earth Charter,

---

27   Klemm, "Individuality," pp. 279–280.
28   Martin Heidegger, *The Question Concerning Technology and Other Essays*, trans. William Lovitt (San Fransisco: Harper, 1982).

which speaks of the sustainability of "one whole earth community," we need to operate with an ontology that allows the thinking being of humanity to coexist with natural being. Individuality provides this, in that it finds the first principle not in a dualism of thinking and being, universal and particular, but in the mediation between them.[29] The *integrity* of Theological Humanism, thought as the integrat-*ing* activity that works out this mediation, can be fruitfully read as the living enactment of Schleiermacher's principle of Individuality. Wilson's consilience has *ambitions* to be the principle that explains individual entities; but consilience never really articulates the unity of individual beings, remaining reductionist and one-sided through and through.

Second, naturalist accounts of sustainability can find themselves caught in an unresolved tension between *feeling* and *reason*. This is so especially for E.O. Wilson, whose works exhibit an unusually high rhetorical pitch for a scientist. He appeals to emotion frequently, seems to understand that the cultivation of "biophilia" needed to promote sustainable action will require inspiration, and generally claims to have a high regard for literature and the arts. Yet Wilson assumes that feelings and artistic expressions have no *meaning* accessible to the thinking subject: "Works of art communicate feeling directly from mind to mind, with no intent to explain why the impact occurs."[30] Wilson is at a loss to account for artistic creativity largely because he thinks feelings have no cognitive content by themselves. For him, the affective realm can only be approached rationally by regarding emotion as the felt impact of a human nature that is explicable only by science: "Artistic inspiration ... rises from the artesian wells of human nature. Works of enduring value are truest to those origins. It follows that even the greatest works of art might be understood fundamentally with knowledge of the biologically evolved epigenetic rules that guided them."[31] Ultimately, then, the life of feeling is a temporary stopping point on the road to adequate scientific explanation of human nature. But in that case it is unclear why a scientist should seek to inspire as much as Wilson does.

The integrity of life read in terms of Schleiermacher's Individuality principle does not run into this difficulty. For Schleiermacher, feelings *do* have cognitive

---

[29]   Klemm, "Schleiermacher on the Self," p. 171.
[30]   Wilson, *Consilience*, p. 218.
[31]   Ibid., p. 213.

content. They are determinate modifications of immediate self-consciousness, the felt manifestation of Individuality; which, as we recall, is the analogue for the transcendent ground of objects as mediated unities of universal and particular.[32] As such, feeling is differentiated into spheres in connection with different objects of knowledge, and the affective realm is continuous with the ideal of objective knowledge: "[In] the nature feeling ... the self becomes aware of its bodily existence as a whole in relation to what is outside itself as a whole, and feels itself as part of the whole of nature. *This feeling of the whole of nature is mediated by means of objective consciousness.*"[33] For integrity of life thought as Individuality, this "nature feeling" is as well grounded as the objective knowledge accompanying it, and sustainability discourse so thought can appeal to both objective knowledge and feeling without contradiction.

Third, as I mentioned already, the ideology of naturalism makes it difficult to carry out dialogue between different disciplinary voices without reductionism. Indeed, Wilson does not regard reductionism as any kind of problem at all, pleading "guilty, guilty, guilty" to the charge.[34] This, of course, belies his claim that the problems of sustainability will have to be addressed in dialogue with a variety of disciplinary voices—what's the point of conversation if the non-scientific disciplines do not talk sense? But a humanism based on the idea of integrity of life places a premium on human linguistic expression and dialogue. Again, Klemm's work on Schleiermacher's Individuality principle helps shed light on this, especially inasmuch as Klemm reads Individuality as a grounding idea for Ricoeur's hermeneutics. Klemm reminds us that Schleiermacher's work is not simply about feeling, but that the Individuality principle is manifest principally in *language*: "It can be argued on the basis of a close reading of Schleiermacher's text, that by *Gedankending* [thought-thing], Schleiermacher means *language*. Language, conceived as a historically determinate system of signs, makes possible the synthesis between thought and percept, because language is both thought and thing."[35] Language itself, on this account, becomes the medium for the *integration* of experience; one that fully articulates the range of discourses covered in the

---

[32]   Klemm, "Schleiermacher on the Self," p. 178.

[33]   Ibid., p. 179, emphasis mine.

[34]   Wilson, *Consilience*, p. 11.

[35]   Klemm, "Individuality," p. 243.

*Dialectic*, from expression of feeling to rationally justified objective knowledge. Consequently, this philosophy of language can provide philosophical grounding for dialogue between different modes of linguistic expression, including those with relatively more investment in rationality and those more directly expressive of feeling. Klemm takes the Individuality principle also as key for Paul Ricoeur's hermeneutics. On his reading, Schleiermacher's cautions about one-sidedness, and his principle that universal and particular can never fully be abstracted from one another, become manifest in Ricoeur's dialectic of explanation and understanding, the pattern whereby he carried out his many dialogues between the humanities and scientific and other explanatory disciplines. The integrity of life, thought hermeneutically, can thus account for the dialogue of voices and approaches in ways that are non-reductive.

Fourth and finally, the Earth Charter casts sustainability—the coexistence of humanity and nature—as a *spiritual* ideal, bringing into play religious dimensions of human experience and valuations of nature as sacred. Wilson, too, seems to see some value in religious approaches to nature, and his own writing sometimes exhibits a spiritual—or as he puts it a "mystical"—tone. But Wilson's approval for "green religion" is really just pragmatic and rhetorical. Ultimately for him, the object of reverence is the process of scientific inquiry itself.[36] Wilson's co-workers in the naturalistic approach to culture are more frankly—and famously—anti-religious, making up the ranks of the so-called "New Atheists." The spiritual dimension of sustainability does not seem to fare well under the naturalist ideology of Wilson & Co. Theological Humanism, by contrast, produces a theology that is friendly to the spiritual dimension of sustainability, as it identifies "God" with the integrity of life across all realms of life: "Insofar as 'God' is the integrity of life—that is, the power of life toward its ever renewed integration of power and life sensed and held as ultimately important and real—then conscience is a sense of the divine, a capacity for what we can call or name God."[37] Indeed, it may be fair to say that in Theological Humanism, it is the identification of integrity of life with God that prevents integrity from being thought as a purely intra-human affair; it opens up humanism beyond "lateral transcendence" to think human life within and not against the wider community of life. Again, identification of integrity of

---

[36]   Wilson, *Consilience*, pp. 6, 265.
[37]   Klemm and Schweiker, *Religion and the Human Future*, p. 93.

life with God seems to find philosophical grounding in David Klemm's work on Schleiermacher, as for instance when he describes the Ideal goal of dialectic as "God—the absolute ground or unity of thinking and being, conceived as source and goal of all mediating activity."[38]

For all these reasons, I would propose that advocates of sustainability jettison the naturalist ideology that often accompanies sustainability discourse, however admirable the practical initiatives of E.O. Wilson and others like him may be. And I would suggest that they take a second look at humanism—especially humanism thought in terms of Klemm and Schweiker's idea of the integrity of life. Integrity of life, I have suggested, names an ideal that would allow us to think sustainability, not as a "bad infinite" indefinitely extending the current pattern of using nature for human need, as the Brundtland report would have it, nor as a conversation between humanity and nature in which the human voices get silenced by reductionism, as happens in Wilson's "consilient inquiry." Rather, to think sustainability as integrity of life would be to see sustainability in the *integrating* of the goods of human life with those of the natural world. For scientists, this would mean a difficult dialogue with the humanities; but in it, an opportunity to reconnect with the language of the lifeworld and make the often silenced voice of scientific expertise heard in the public square. For humanists, it means broadening the focus on human life to include the natural world that humanity is "within and not against," and perhaps taking up the difficult questions of what significance "the animal" or genetic diversity might have for the humanities. But it also empowers us to defend *mimetic* diversity—that's "mimetic" not "memetic"—whenever reductionism threatens to silence one of the configurations of human meaning-making. For all people, it holds out hope—hope that human life can itself be sustained in and through taking responsibility for the sustenance of life as a whole; a responsibility admirably expressed in Theological Humanism's imperative of responsibility: *in all actions and relations respect and enhance the integrity of life before God.*[39]

---

[38]    Klemm, "Individuality," p. 284.
[39]    Klemm and Schweiker, *Religion and the Human Future*, p. 55.

**Selected Bibliography**

Earth Charter Initiative, "The Earth Charter," http://www.earthcharterinaction.org (accessed June 19, 2011).

Klemm, David, "Individuality: The Principle of Ricoeur's Mediating Philosophy and its Bearing on Theology of Culture," in David Klemm and William Schweiker (eds), *Meanings in Texts and Actions: Questioning Paul Ricoeur* (Charlottesville: University Press of Virginia, 1993), pp. 275–291.

Klemm, David, "Schleiermacher on the Self: Immediate Self-Consciousness as Feeling and as Thinking," in David Klemm and Gunther Zoeller (eds), *Figuring the Self: Subject, Absolute and Others in Classical German Philosophy* (Albany: SUNY, 1997), pp. 169–190.

Klemm, David and William Schweiker, *Religion and the Human Future: An Essay on Theological Humanism* (Oxford: Blackwell, 2008).

Wilson, Edward O., *Consilience: The Unity of Knowledge* (New York: Knopf, 1998).

Chapter 5

# The Practice of Memory

W. David Hall

In *Religion and the Human Future*, David Klemm and William Schweiker articulate and defend the position of theological humanism as a way "of being religious in which religious and other authorities are submitted to criticism and tested in light of actions and relations that respect and enhance the integrity of life."[1] The part of their position that will be of principle interest here is the moral imperative that advances out of this position. On my reading, the imperative to respect and enhance the integrity of life before God, though a powerful one, encounters a critical question yet to be adequately dealt with: how is it that we come to know and understand life in its variegated forms as an object of moral respect? Or, more pointedly, if less concisely put, how can one become attuned, however imperfectly, to the integrity of life as a moral duty and to what extent can one conceive this duty as pertaining to the divine, especially in an age of instrumental rationality that functions precisely on the analytical disintegration of complexity in the interest of technical/scientific knowledge? It seems that understanding the imperative itself entails non-reductive forms of cognition that are somewhat inimical to methods of reasoning that drive the modern striving for knowledge.

This chapter explores the Renaissance humanist tradition, particularly the manner in which this tradition gets distilled in the thought of Giambattista Vico, as a resource for theological humanists' attempts to construe the integrity of life before God. I will argue that Vico's threefold account of memory as containing within itself *memory* proper, *imagination*, and *invention* can be conceived as a philosophical practice the cultivation of which militates against reductive thinking. Conceived this way, the cultivation of memory provides the basis for

---

[1] David E. Klemm and William Schweiker, *Religion and the Human Future: An Essay on Theological Humanism* (Malden, MA: Blackwell Publishing, 2008), 3.

a non-reductive form of reasoning that witnesses to the object as an integral part of the whole, understands any particular life form as a participant in the overall integrity of life as such, and perceives the divine as the background against which that integrity is, however partially and imperfectly, re-membered.

The argument will be presented along three intersecting paths. I will begin by articulating Klemm and Schweiker's position and what I take to be its strengths and weaknesses. I will then explore the humanist idea of a topical philosophy and explain why it offers hope for an adequate understanding of the integrity of life as an object of moral concern. I will conclude by examining Vico's threefold account of memory and its possibilities for a non-reductive form of knowledge, one that allows for a conception of the integrity of life before God in its full complexity.

## On the Integrity of Life Before God

Given the constraints of space, my treatment of Klemm and Schweiker's position will be cursory at best and must presuppose some familiarity with the ideas. Broadly speaking, however, Klemm and Schweiker seek to articulate a position that avoids what they take to be the two primary ideological threats to human and non-human life in the global age: *overhumanization*, or the tendency to restrict moral concern strictly to the human realm and to reduce concern for the non-human world to utilitarian means of satisfying human wants and needs, and *hypertheism*, or the reemergence of neotribalism in what we might call a "post-secular" age and the tendency to restrict claims to truth and value to narrative resources of one's own insular community.[2] This position attempts to offer a third way that conceives of the human *and* non-human world as possessing an inherent value that is sanctioned by the divine, and that resists the reduction of life to utilitarian calculation (the *theological* in theological humanism). At the same time this position resists the drift toward neotribalism, arguing instead that religious (and other) traditions offer distinctive, but not uniquely legitimate, articulations of the human and non-human

---

2   By the term "post-secular" I mean to indicate the empirical invalidation of the "secularization thesis" proposed by late nineteenth and early twentieth century sociologists, the idea that religious belief would continue to decline and eventually be overtaken by scientific-technological rationality and a purely secular worldview.

worlds and their value, and seeks to locate means for discussion from within and across traditions (the *humanism* in theological humanism).

As I cannot hope to deal with the complexities of Klemm and Schweiker's ideas *in toto*, I will focus on the moral imperative that grounds their position: "The imperative of responsibility at the heart of theological humanism is this: *in all actions and relations respect and enhance the integrity of life before God.*"[3] In what follows, I will briefly discuss the contours and appeal of this imperative and its fundamental problem as Klemm and Schweiker present it: given that the "integrity of life" is the object of moral concern, how can this reality become an object for consciousness? Here, I think Vico's ideas offer promising possibilities.

Klemm and Schweiker's formulation of the imperative is particularly appealing for two reasons. First, it affirms human capability and freedom within limits. In all actions and relations we are to *respect* and enhance the integrity of life. The imperative directs us to use freedom to enhance wherever possible and whenever appropriate, but always under the primary criterion of respect; if enhancement of any form of life (ours or others) works contrary to our respect for life in its integrity, we should not so act. Second, the imperative offers a complex and dynamic view of the realm of moral concern; it is not life qua life that is to be respected and enhanced, but the *integrity* of life, i.e., the complex and dynamic interrelation of life forms. This complex understanding of the integrity of life protects against an overly simplistic notion that we ought in all cases respect and enhance whatever life forms we encounter. Besides its naïveté, the fulfilling of such an imperative would be simply impossible: to eat is to destroy life (whether animal or vegetable) in the service of preserving and enhancing life; to practice medicine is to destroy life (viral, bacterial, or parasitical) in the service of preserving and enhancing life; to build a house is to kill and/or displace life in the service of preserving and enhancing life. Klemm and Schweiker argue that it is not life, but the complex interrelation of life forms and their continued possibilities for greater integrity that is to be respected and enhanced. "There are situations," they argue, "in which life can and may and must tragically be sacrificed precisely to respect and enhance its integrity ... Against those who deny the sanctity of life this ethics insists that life has great dignity and intrinsic worth. Against those who insist on the sacredness of life, this ethics argues the integrity of life, and not life itself, bears intrinsic

---

[3]    Klemm and Schweiker, *Religion and the Human Future*, 82.

value."[4] In all our actions, then, we ought to aim to secure certain intrinsic goods (physical, social, reflexive, natural, and spiritual) that promise to promote the continued integrity of life.

But, the complexity with which Klemm and Schweiker map the moral realm and the capacity and limits of human freedom, which is its strength as a moral position, encounters problems in another sense, at least as they have discussed it: how can we know the integrity of life? How can we determine which actions will enhance while still respecting? How do we know which forms of life can and must legitimately be sacrificed in the interest of preserving integrity? Given that the moral realm is complex, interactive, dynamic, and, as such, continually changing, it is not clear how we can know it, and, without knowledge, it is not clear how we ought to act toward it in specific circumstances. This aspect of the integrity of life is further complicated by the fact that Klemm and Schweiker claim that our efforts to respect and enhance it continually take place "before God." On this reading the claim of the integrity of life is, at the same time, the claim of the sacred upon us. "[Sacred power] is," Klemm and Schweiker explain,

> the appearance – the incarnation – of the integrity of life in stories of courageous or creative individuals or communities, in the sight of an integral ecosystem, in the experience of truthfulness in a loved one's death, or in the wholeness of a perfect symphony or novel … In principle, anything whatsoever can strike us with the claim of the integrity of life as a concrete and local event, even when we see the opposite in injustice or falsehood that affronts us and demands that life *should not* be this way. This religious arousal of a sense of ultimate significance in this time and place also carries with it an absolute claim to the integrity of life universally speaking.[5]

Their presentation of the nature and scope of the sacred seeks to avoid what they take to be the dual pitfalls of a tacit reliance on an exclusivist, traditional theism (a part of what they designate "hypertheism"), or a narrowly atheistic dismissal of the divine (a dimension of what they call "overhumanization"). Thus, the problem of moral knowledge is also one of religious knowledge: how do we conceive

---

4   Klemm and Schweiker, *Religion and the Human Future*, 84.

5   Klemm and Schweiker, *Religion and the Human Future*, 54–55.

and make intelligible the confrontation with phenomena as at the same time a confrontation with the sacred?

Klemm and Schweiker suggest that claims of the integrity of life are recognized in *conscience*, conceived as a "primary mode of being human as an agent in the world."[6] In this sense, conscience is the manner in which, or the faculty through which, an agent recognizes the claims of particular life forms to the intrinsic goods that ground integrity and at the same time perceives this claim as an indication of the divine. But, it is not clear that conscience can itself articulate the *integrity* of life, make it intelligible as an object of respect, and explain *how* we ought to strive to meet claims to intrinsic goods where appropriate, or when we ought to *sacrifice* life in the service of life. Conscience is the faculty that focuses attention on the moral and theological claims of a situation. But how does that experience rise to the level of meaning? How do we finally make sense of experiences of the claim of integrity and, more importantly, how do we move from experience to judgment, from "is to ought"? Purely logical, analytic, or critical epistemologies are not helpful here for at least two reasons: first, they tend to be suspicious of experience and move away from it in favor of logical principles. Second they tend to reduce complexity in the interest of clarity. What we need is a position that does not shy away from the experience of complexity as a *source* of knowledge. It is my contention that the Renaissance account of imagination and invention, and Vico's presentation of the role of imagination in memory in particular, provides the outlines for such a position.

## Topical Philosophy: Vico's Critique of Descartes

Ernesto Grassi has argued that what most starkly contrasts the Renaissance humanists' approach to philosophical knowledge and the modern philosophical tradition initiated by Descartes is the emphasis they placed on the idea of *ingenium* in human knowledge. This term is difficult to translate, but might best be thought in terms of ingenuity, invention, or creativity. *Ingenium* is the means through which the human encounter with reality becomes manifest in linguistic meaning. Grassi traces the emergence of this term in the Latin tradition from the poets to the

---

[6]  Klemm and Schweiker, *Religion and the Human Future*, 85.

classical rhetoricians. It is with Cicero that the primary influence of the classical Latin world upon humanism is most pronounced:

> In the Latin tradition, "ingenium" is used concerning the behavior of animals in general and human activity … Cicero describes the ingenium as an "archaic," that is, a primal, non-reducible, and dominant power: as such, ingenium lifts man above the habitual forms of thinking and feeling: "Magni autem est ingenii sevocare mentem a sensibus et cognitationem ab consuetudine abducere." It unites man with the Divine and, therefore, enables him to recognize the laws of the universe which are an expression of the godhead.[7]

*Ingenium* operates on two levels. As a principle of life in general, it represents the animal drive to perpetuate existence in the face of the exigencies of reality. The animal response to the realities of the here and now is, therefore, ingenious, inventive; the drive to maintain existence is creative. In the human, however, *ingenium* reaches a higher pitch. In the human, *ingenium* represents the ability to rise above mere drives and habitual modes of behavior in order to contemplate the very structure of reality. In both cases, the spur that mobilizes ingenious activity is *necessitates*.

For the humanists, necessity is, in a very immediate sense, the mother of invention. For brute animal life, *ingenium* takes the form of instinctual and habitual forms of behavior necessitated by the struggle to perpetuate existence. In human life, however, *ingenium* takes on more complex forms. All forms of human life are the effect of human ingenuity in response to the necessities of nature, including philosophy. Indeed, philosophy, that form of life in which humanity lifts itself to contemplation of the laws governing reality, is ingenious activity *par excellence*.

One place where the differences between a purely logical, scientific philosophy and a humanist "topical" philosophy become pronounced is Vico's criticism of the Cartesian method. As is well known, Descartes asserted that if the philosopher as scientist were able to locate a single indubitable first principle, he should be able to methodically reconstruct an entire system of clear and distinct ideas about reality. The Cartesian philosophical enterprise is, therefore, the attempt to locate such

---

[7]    Ernesto Grassi, *Renaissance Humanism: Studies in Philosophy and Poetics* (Tempe: Medieval and Renaissance Texts and Studies, 1988), 68.

a first principle, the "cogito," and a rational method by which to move from the first principle to an understanding of the world. Descartes described the method as such:

> I believed the following four rules would be sufficient, provided I made a firm and constant resolution not even once to fail to observe them: The first was never to accept anything as true that I did not know evidently to be so; that is, carefully to avoid precipitous judgment and prejudice; and to include nothing more in my judgments than what presented itself to my mind with such clarity and distinctness that I would have no occasion to put it to doubt. The second, to divide each of the difficulties I was examining into as many parts as possible and as is required to solve them best. The third, to conduct my thoughts in an orderly fashion commencing with the simplest and easiest to know objects, to rise gradually, as by degrees, to the knowledge of the most composite things, and even supposing an order among those things that do not naturally precede one another. And last, everywhere to make enumerations so complete and reviews so general that I would be sure of having omitted nothing.[8]

Vico was a product of the humanist rhetorical tradition and held the chair in rhetoric at the University of Naples at a time when Cartesian critical philosophy was beginning to exert dominance. Descartes' dismissal of rhetoric is well known, as is his suspicion of imaginative, undisciplined, and unmethodical forms of thinking and observation.[9] The method, which made Descartes so attractive to many of his contemporaries, presented both philosophical and pedagogical problems for Vico. Against those arguing for pedagogical reform at the university, Vico asserted that students' education ought to begin with the *ars topica*, the classical rhetorical topics, because a facility with topics feeds the imagination and makes the mind acute and inventive (*ingegno*). He was discouraged by what he

---

[8] Rene Descartes, *Discourse on Method and Meditations on First Philosophy* (Indianapolis: Hackett, 1993), 11.

[9] "I held eloquence in high regard and I loved poetry, but I believed that they were both gifts of the mind – not fruits of study. Those who possess the most forceful power of reasoning and who best order their thoughts so as to render them clear and intelligible can always best persuade one of what they are proposing, even if they speak only the dialect of Lower Brittany and have never learned rhetoric" (Descartes, *Discourse on Method*, 4).

saw as the growing dominance of Cartesian "critical philosophy." "In our days …
philosophical criticism alone is honored. The art of 'topics,' far from being given
first place in the curriculum is utterly disregarded … We hear people affirming
that if individuals are critically endowed, it is sufficient to teach them a certain
subject, and they will have the capacity to discover whether there is any truth in
that subject."[10] Vico argued instead for the primacy of rhetoric in the university's
curriculum, and especially the teaching of rhetorical topics:

> I think young men should be taught the totality of science and arts, and their
> intellectual powers should be developed to the full; thus they will become
> familiar with the art of argument, drawn from the *ars topica*. At the very outset,
> their common sense should be strengthened so that they can grow in prudence
> and eloquence. Let their imagination and memory be fortified so that they
> may be effective in those arts in which fantasy and the mnemonic faculty are
> predominant. At a later stage let them learn criticism, so that they can apply
> the fullness of personal judgment to what they have been taught … Were this
> done, young students, I think, would become exact in science, clever in practical
> matters, fluent in eloquence, imaginative in understanding poetry or painting,
> and strong in memorizing what they have learned in their legal studies. Let their
> imagination and memory be fortified so that they may be effective in those arts
> in which fantasy and the mnemonic faculty are predominant. At a later stage let
> them learn [methodological] criticism, so that they can apply the fullness of their
> personal judgement to what they have been taught.[11]

But Vico offered philosophical criticisms of the Cartesian dismissal of rhetoric as
well. Topics (*topoi* in Greek, *loci* in Latin) are standard lines of argumentation that
serve to ground arguments. Aristotle distinguished 28 such *topoi* in the *Rhetoric*
(bk. II, ch. 23), ranging from seemingly empirical principles—relations of cause
and effect, temporal succession, etc.—to purely impressionistic inferences—e.g.,
similitude, possible motive for action. The catalogue of topics changed throughout
the classical, Medieval, and Renaissance traditions, but the basic understanding

---

[10]    Giambattista Vico, *On the Study Methods of Our Time*, trans. Elio Gianturco
(Ithaca, NY: Cornell University Press, 1990), 14.

[11]    Vico, *On the Study Methods of Our Time*, 19.

of what they are and how they function remained largely the same: topics maps the "places" (topography or location) where the initial means of mounting an argument, whether dialectical or rhetorical, are found. The mind schooled in the topics is able to "find" the proper argument. Thus, Vico, against Descartes, re-established the connection between rhetoric and critical philosophy, but on grounds much different than traditionally understood, for instance, in Aristotle.

Aristotle viewed rhetoric as a companion to dialectic, i.e., philosophy proper. While dialectic is concerned with logical proofs, rhetoric is concerned with probabilities and means of persuasion. Both partake of topics, but for different purposes: dialectic adopts topics as first principles from which to derive rational proofs, rhetoric to discover persuasive arguments. Both use syllogistic reasoning: dialectic employs true syllogisms to articulate necessary truths; rhetoric employs enthymemes, practical syllogisms, to articulate probable truths. So conceived, rhetoric is a secondary discipline concerned either to elicit non-philosophical appeal among the uneducated for purely rational knowledge, or to articulate probabilities where necessity cannot be determined.

In important ways, Vico reversed the order of priority between dialectic and rhetoric, between critical philosophy and topics. His treatment of the problem is much more in line with the Latin rhetorical tradition embodied most clearly in Cicero. In *Topics*, Cicero argued that there are two interrelated aspects of argumentation: invention and judgment. "Aristotle was the founder of both in my opinion. The Stoics have worked in only one of the two fields. That is to say, they have followed diligently the ways of judgment by means of the science which they call *dilektikh* (dialectic), but they have totally neglected the art which is called *topikh* (topics), an art which is more useful and certainly prior in the order of nature."[12] Both dialectic and topics contribute to wisdom, and while wisdom lacks virtue without judgment, it lacks voice and appeal without invention.

Part of the reason for the shift of emphasis in the Latin rhetorical tradition is that argumentation was more firmly grounded in oratory than in the Greek tradition. In a context where argumentation is primarily performative, a firm command of topics is paramount in order to be able to construct arguments extempore. Thus, invention precedes proof, and topics takes precedence over dialectic. John D.

---

[12]  Marcus Tullius Cicero, *Topica*, Loeb Classic Library (Cambridge, MA: Harvard University, 1949), 2.6–7.

Schaeffer has argued that Vico's Naples had more in common with classical Rome than with modernity in this sense; it was a society governed in important ways by oral practices:

> The University of Naples and the law courts were the two focuses of that practice, and these two institutions formed the immediate context of Vico's rhetorical theory ... The university and the law courts continued to feature oral performance and adversarial thinking in ways that decisively shaped their practices – and their supporting theories. Because they were arenas of social conflict, the university and the courts were also the focal points of reform, and reformers competed for their control.[13]

The exigencies of oral performance shaped Vico's understanding of rhetorical theory and university education. He emphasized the importance of *memorization* of the topics in order to make the mind inventive in argumentation, but he suggested further that education in topics shapes the mind in its capacities to engage the world. It instilled both an imaginative wonder about things in general and an ingenuity in making sense of them.

The Cartesian turn to the idea too quickly reduces out aspects of the object in question. Vico explains:

> But if someone is confident of having looked all through a thing in a clear and distinct mental idea [of it], he can easily be mistaken and may often think that he knows the thing distinctly when he has still only a confused knowledge of it, because he does not know all [the elements] that are in the thing and which distinguish it from others. But if he will scrutinize all the "places" distinguished in the *Topics* with a critical eye, then he will be certain that he knows the thing clearly and distinctly because he has turned the matter over in his mind and answered all the questions that can be asked with respect to the subject under

---

[13]    John D. Schaeffer, *Sensus Communis: Vico, Rhetoric, and the Limits of Relativism* (Durham, NC: Duke University Press, 1990), 35.

discussion. *And by completing this process of questioning, topics itself will become criticism.*[14]

Far from leading to unclarity and self-deception, as Descartes asserted, Vico argues that rhetoric grounds the questioning that leads to clear and distinct ideas, precisely in its topical focus on memory, imagination, and invention. Grassi has characterized Vico's thought as a *topical philosophy*, as opposed to a critical philosophy in the Cartesian vein. For Vico, only a topical philosophy can deal with the reality and complexity of the things themselves.[15]

Commenting on Vico's criticism of the Cartesian method, Grassi states:

> Vico's rejection of the critical method, and of the rationalism connected with it, is based on the recognition that the original premises as such are nondeducible and that the *rational process* hence cannot "find" them; that, moreover, rational knowledge cannot be a determining factor for rhetorical or poetic speech because it cannot comprehend the particular, the individual, i.e., the concrete situation; and since the critical method always starts with a premise, its final conclusions are necessarily valid only generally … Vico repeatedly defends topics against the prevalence of rational activity on the grounds that the premises from which conclusions are drawn have to be "perceived" to begin with. This perception is the function of topics because, and here the new important term appears, they come from the *ingenium* and not from the *ratio* … *Ingenium* is the source of the creative activity of the topics.[16]

In articulating the idea of a topical philosophy, Grassi intends to indicate the importance Vico placed on the creative, inventive faculty of mind that gives rise to, that "finds," the first premises upon which the deductive process can then proceed. This finding is an activity of *ingenium* not *ratio*, of invention and ingenuity, not logic and deduction.

---

[14]   Giambattista Vico, *On the Most Ancient of the Italians, Unearthed from the Origins of the Latin Language*, trans. and intro. by L.M. Palmer (Ithaca, NY: Cornell University Press, 1988), 101.

[15]   Ernesto Grassi, *Rhetoric as Philosophy: The Humanist Tradition*, trans. John Michael Kois and Azizeh Azodi (Carbondale, IL: Southern Illinois University Press, 2001).

[16]   Grassi, *Rhetoric as Philosophy*, 44–45.

In the end, philosophy, like all human activities and institutions, is the labor of ingenuity; it is work: human labor with the goal of wresting meaning from nature. Work is the process through which humans "humanize" nature, i.e., adjust nature to human need. But, as Grassi indicates, for Vico and the humanists, human work, especially philosophical work, is not just mechanical manipulation of the natural world. Human work is profoundly symbolic: "Work … is to be understood as a function both of conferring a meaning and making use of a meaning, never as a purely mechanical activity or a purely technical alteration of nature detached from the general context of human functions. Otherwise it would consist merely of an inexplicable act of violence to devastate nature."[17] And this labor, the ingenious human response to necessity, is not a rational act, not founded in *ratio*, but in something more original, an act of imagination:

> But how does this "humanization of nature" take place if not through *ratio*? We already said that nature possesses a meaning only in regard to human needs. This presupposes that we discover a relationship, a *similitudo*, between what the senses reveal to us and our needs … Insight into the relationships basically is not possible through a process of inference, but rather only through an original *in*-sight as invention and discovery [*inventio*] … Since such a capacity is characteristic of fantasy, it is this, therefore which lets the human world appear. For this reason it is expressed originally in metaphors, i.e., in the figurative lending of meanings.[18]

The first acts, the first human works, through which the human world comes into existence are metaphorical interpretations, the yoking together of sensual experience and need. The faculty through which these metaphors come to light is not reason, but *fantasia*, imagination. Imagination is our most basic commerce with the world; it provides the basic materials upon which human ingenuity builds. Philosophy, like all human works, is grounded, according to Vico, not in rational deduction, but in facility with metaphors, in imagination and invention.

---

[17]  Ernesto Grassi, "The Priority of Common Sense and Imagination: Vico's Philosophical Relevance Today," in *Vico and Contemporary Thought*, ed. Giorgio Tagliacozzo, Michael Mooney, and Donald Phillip Verene (Atlantic Highlands, NJ: Humanities Press, 1976), 174–175.

[18]  Grassi, *Rhetoric as Philosophy*, 6–7.

**Practicing Memory**

In *The New Science*, Vico speaks of memory as such: "Memory thus has three different aspects: memory when it remembers things, imagination when it alters or imitates them, and invention when it gives them a new turn or puts them into proper arrangement and relationship."[19] On this understanding, memory is at once a pulling of the object out of the flux of sensation such that it becomes present, even in its physical absence, to the mind (*memoria*), an imaginative construal of intelligibility (*fantasia*), and an inventive "placing" of the object in a context (*ingegno*) such that it becomes meaningful. The simplest way to explain how this happens is to adopt Vico's own privileged account of the act of memory, the initial act by which humanity lifted itself out of brute animal existence.

On Vico's account, the first act by which humanity elevated itself out of the flux of sensation that characterizes bestial nature was an imaginative one. The first humans were thrown into reflective consciousness through fear of the thunderclap; they came to conceive thunder as a sign of Jove. But it is important to be clear what he means here. Vico asserts that Jove is not conceived in this primordial scene as the source of thunder, rather Jove *is* thunder. Or, more accurately, thunder, as it rumbles in the sky, *is* the voice of Jove. Further, the sky, from which thunder rumbles, is not the abode of Jove, the sky *is* Jove. Jove becomes for the first humans the first *universale fantastico*, the first imaginative universal by which humanity *makes* the world intelligible. Imaginative universals function for the first humans, according to Vico, the same way that abstract categories function in rational metaphysics: they serve as exemplars that establish genera by which the world is organized. Unlike rational genera, they are not abstracted from particulars, rather the reverse: particulars are aggregated under the imaginative universal and become meaningful through it. But how is this an act of memory? For Vico, the capacity for memory is one of the principle things that distinguishes human from non-human. Non-human life exists in pure flux; sensation follows sensation without any becoming fixed and determinative. Fear of Jove, then, is the first act of memory, the first fixing of a sensation, the thunderclap, as a determining event. Based on the recollection of the now absent sensation, humans employ imagination, the second aspect of

---

[19]    Giambattista Vico, *The New Science*, trans. Thomas Goddard Bergin and Max Harold Fisch (Ithaca, NY: Cornell University Press, 1984), 313–314.

memory to form an intelligible image, the imaginative universal. Finally, through inventiveness and ingenuity, the third aspect of memory, they construct a world around this first image; the world becomes populated by gods—the progeny, consorts, and/or rivals of Jove.

Vico's account is particularly apt in addressing Klemm and Schweiker's position for three reasons: first, Vico's system of thought stands as a polemic against the Cartesian method that is at least partially responsible for contemporary reductive forms of thinking. Vico's account of memory allows for a confrontation with the world not grounded in general principles but in an original, imaginative insight into particular situations freighted with moral meanings. Indeed, Vico might be viewed as a precursor to and foundation for the very sort of hermeneutical understanding that Klemm and Schweiker assign to conscience.

The second aspect that Vico's account lends to theological humanism is the theological character of his own understanding of memory. Vico conceived the first act of memory, by which humanity comes into existence, as a memory of Jove. The thunderclap that signifies Jove's existence is the first object that arises out of the flux of sensation and becomes fixed before the mind, imagined in intelligible form, and established within a world of meaning. The foundation of the human world is itself a theological event; the "theological poets" were, for Vico, the first philosophers, Homer above all others. It would be foolhardy to adopt Vico's presentation of these events uncritically; his narration of the primordial event is hardly an argument. Donald Verene likens Vico's account to the fables that were so much a part of Vico's concern. On Vico's understanding, imaginative universals are themselves relayed poetically through narration, through myths or fables (*vera narrativa*). Fables, then, narrate the coming to be of human understanding of the world. Donald Phillip Verene describes the relationship between imaginative universal and fable as such:

> Vico defines fables as "imaginative class concepts" (*generi fantastici*). For Vico, fables are not embellishments of actual events or historical figures … Events themselves are given form through fables … The *universale fantastico* is a way of making intelligibility. It is a conception of how intelligibility takes place at the origin of human mentality, at the beginning of the human world. The fable,

which depends upon the mind's power of *fantasia*, is the means by which the world first takes on a shape for the human.[20]

Thus, for Vico, the first human acts, i.e., works which eventually lead to the formation of the institutions that compose the human world, were imaginative, metaphorical acts eventually narrated in the form of myths; his account is, as such, "fabulous." More problematic still is his attempt to mark different trajectories for the pagan and Judeo-Christian worlds. Nonetheless, his thought gives us important food for thought in making sense of the "theological" part of theological humanism. For Vico, the gods remain a fundamental aspect of the human condition, even if not explicitly so. To make sense of the world is, on some level, to *be* theological.

This theological aspect of his thought leads to a third offering to theological humanism. Vico's ultimate concern was the location of a *sensus communis*, a common sensibility *and* sense-making, that grounds the moral life of humanity. In the *New Science*, Vico characterizes *sensus communis* as the unifying ground that directs human experience and choice toward human needs and utilities. He calls it "judgement without reflection, shared by an entire class, an entire people, an entire nation, or the entire human race,"[21] and he suggests that it is the effect of divine providence. Speaking of the relationship between imaginative universals and *sensus communis*, Jon D. Schaeffer explains:

> This *sensus communis* is a "common sense" in a very literal and strict sense: the community learns to arrest its sensations, perceive them, and respond to them as a community. From the original imaginative universal, Jove, come others that advance the community's self-understanding and certify its social institutions by providing a "sensory topics" that organize[s] and interpret[s] other, more complex sense perceptions ... Such images become, like Jove, true fables that fuse sensation, affection, and action to certify as true the reality they reflect and create.[22]

---

[20]   Donald Phillip Verene, *Vico's Science of the Imagination* (Ithaca, NY: Cornell University Press, 1981), 71.

[21]   Vico, *The New Science*, 63.

[22]   Schaeffer, *Sensus Communis*, 91.

Thus, *sensus communis* directs imagination and invention toward the accomplishment of action that serves common needs and desires; what was brought to experience in memory, made intelligible in imagination, and made meaningful in invention, becomes directed by judgments about the proper actions to secure the common good.

## Re-membering the Integrity of Life Before God

I have suggested that Vico's account of memory is particularly helpful in addressing a fundamental weakness in Klemm and Schweiker's position; that weakness concerns a general lack of articulation of how we could come to know and understand the integrity of life before God. Given the dynamic and interrelational character of the integrity of life, we need an equally dynamic epistemology to rise to its challenge; contemporary rationalistic, analytic ones will not do the job.

Vico's account of memory, with its focus on imagination and creativity, is particularly promising. As conscience directs attention toward experiences qualified by moral values, imagination strives to make those experiences intelligible and creative ingenuity strives to place them within an overall system of meaning. Such strivings, partial and imperfect as they will always be, are directed by the *sensus communis*, the unreflective judgments that bind action to the common good. Vico offers the possibility that we might re-member the integrity of life before God as it is incarnated in specific instances of moral demand.

## Selected Bibliography

Grassi, E. 2001. *Rhetoric as Philosophy: The Humanist Tradition*. Trans. John Michael Kois and Azizeh Azodi. Carbondale, IL: Southern Illinois University Press.

Klemm, D.E. and W. Schweiker. 2008. *Religion and the Human Future: An Essay on Theological Humanism*. Malden, MA: Blackwell Publishing.

Vico, G. 1984. *The New Science*. Trans. T.G. Bergin and M.H. Fisch. Ithaca, NY: Cornell University Press.

Vico, G. 1988. *On the Most Ancient of the Italians, Unearthed from the Origins of the Latin Language*. Trans and intro. by L.M. Palmer. Ithaca, NY: Cornell University Press.

Vico, G. 1990. *On the Study Methods of Our Time*. Trans. Elio Gianturco. Ithaca, NY: Cornell University Press.

# Chapter 6

# Dwelling Theologically

Daniel Boscaljon

The past decade reminds us that we have not yet learned how to dwell appropriately on the earth. The financial crisis of 2008 presents recent symptoms of our failure, as families were thrown from empty homes, while large buildings were left rusting. The deeper problems lie not with the manifestation of failure, however, but in the tragedy of the wrong kind of success. The structures that continue to be constructed and sold in the United States testify to a preference for McMansions and strip malls: each manifests a corporate universality that successfully secularizes space into empty repetitions of the same. Hills are flattened, valleys are filled, wetlands are dried, rivers are straightened. Fields and grassland provide fresh crops of single-family homes in neighborhoods that testify to the efficiency of mass production. In a mobile society where humans move across the country for education and employment, such structures undoubtedly are meant to evoke a feeling of comfort, as though one can find one's home wherever one looks. Everything looks the same.

The middle-class hunger for empty repetitions reveals a profound change in the way that humans approach houses: with frequency, we have only a superficial relationship with the environments that we build around ourselves. Yi-Fu Tuan acknowledges, "In the modern world people do not ... build their own houses," so that now "Rites and ceremonies that focus on the building activity, which used to be thought of as the creation of a world, have greatly declined."[1] Building materials were largely procured from nearby natural sources, allowing the home to be a redistribution of the abundant goods that surrounded the area. Once built, the land was handed down within the family and the house was a part of the land: the

---

[1] Yi-Fu Tuan, *Space and Place: The Perspective of Experience* (Minneapolis, 1977), p. 116.

life of the building, the land, and the people were intertwined. By contrast, houses today are legal documents that abstractly narrate the dimensions and value of the lot, the age of the appliances, significant damages and repairs, levels of radon. Lumber and stone for construction are processed and shipped in from around the country to be constructed against the land. Before, humans invested in their homes: Americans today consider houses as investments.

My interest here is not in describing the financial cost of housing decisions: instead, I argue that the existential cost of how we live threatens our ability to reflect theologically or discern which ideals are good pursuits. To do this, I will advocate for a stronger sense of the relationship that connects theology and dwelling. In particular, I will argue that theology and dwelling have a reciprocal effect on each other: theology is framed by our dwelling places, and true dwelling requires theology. Most of the argument will proceed within the space cleared and defined by Heidegger's later essays, although my work is less to clarify Heidegger than to build upon the foundation that he constructed. I begin with a brief definition of dwelling extracted from Heidegger, and then discuss Arthur Miller's *Death of a Salesman* as an example of the existential crisis spawned by the way we live. Third, I return to Heidegger for his explanation of what it means to dwell poetically, and then explore other modes of human relations in space that Heidegger does not attend to—namely occupying and living—with reference to Robert Scharlemann's work concerning levels of experience. I follow this with a brief meditation on what it means to build reflectively and will conclude with an explanation of how to dwell theologically. In total, this will disclose the deeper truth underlying the cliché that "home is where the heart is": because our places for dwelling enable or hinder our pursuit of ideals, they also frame our theological reflections.

## Dwelling

Between his writing of *The Origin of the Work of Art* and his thinking in the later essays, Heidegger makes two important shifts. First, his key examples shift from privileging art as sites unique in their revelatory potential to focusing instead on ordinary things. This change is marked through Heidegger's term *dwelling*, a word he unfolds most productively in his essay "Building, Dwelling,

Thinking." This essay, along with "The Thing" and "The Question Concerning Technology," features a development from Heidegger's initial understanding of what contributes to a human environment. In *Origin*, Heidegger argued that the work of art came with putting "world" in conflict with "earth," and excluded merely equipmental things as capable of displacing humans from their ordinary ways of being. The later Heidegger is more concerned with our habitual way of being and our way of inhabiting the world, and thus attends to ordinary objects such as a jug, a bridge and a chalice. A second major change in Heidegger's thinking comes in his understanding of world: the nuanced replacement is *Das Geviert*, or the Fourfold of earth and sky, mortals and divinities. Equipmental objects in the later essays serve as locations that gather and bring to rest these four forces in a unique fashion—each in its own way. This shift allows Heidegger to emphasize integration instead of the points of rupture and disconnect seen in *Origin*'s emphasis on conflict and displacement.[2]

We dwell as a part of our everyday lives—Heidegger argues that being on the earth involves building as dwelling, and anchors this in the everyday human experience, an experience which, he explains, "is from the outset 'habitual'—we inhabit it."[3] Externally, we witness dwelling when we engage in construction and cultivation with the intention of cherishing, sparing and preserving—terms anchored in the German term *bauen*. Heidegger's decision to anchor dwelling's fundamental character in sparing and preserving reinforces dwelling as the human cognate of the gathering accomplished in our artifacts.[4] Additionally, it is this character that allows us to characterize places of true dwelling: these are places constructed as spaces of preservation, mindful of allowing what it gathers to stay as it is. Places that do not allow for this type of freedom fail to meet the standard of dwelling.

---

[2]  Heidegger's essays that I reference are collected in *Poetry, Language, Thought*, edited by Albert Hofstadter (New York, 1975), with the exception of "The Question Concerning Technology," which appears in *The Question Concerning Technology*, translated and edited by William Lovitt (New York, 1977) and "Memorial Address," which appears in *Discourse on Thinking*, translated by John M. Anderson and E. Hans Freund (New York, 1969). Due to the continuity of thinking, I will refer to general themes gathered in these selections and will make specific notes only when I engage in direct quotations.

[3]  Heidegger, *Poetry, Language, Thought*, p. 147.

[4]  Ibid., p. 149.

The point of continuity throughout these essays rests on the pivotal role language plays in allowing us to dwell in spaces. In *Origin*, the role of language was framed as a projective sketch that allowed for the human conception of time, history and culture. The later essays also attend to the important role that language plays as a manifestation of human potential: as Heidegger understands through the poetry of Hölderlin, humans dwell poetically, brought into an awareness of our world through the mediation of language. But the gift of language in allowing for humans to participate in the process of revealing and concealing, *poiesis*, is problematic in that it can close us off from "the piety of questioning."[5] This is the final warning of Heidegger's *Question Concerning Technology*—the blindness spawned by being *enframed* by a desire for quantification, calculation and regulation is mirrored in poetry's own self-enclosed world. Heidegger's inability to resolve the issue stems, ultimately, from his refusal to understand the power of the God-word, theology. As I will argue in the conclusion, it is solely through theology that we can dwell in a manner that reflexively allows us to pursue ideals in a way that remains mindful of the space for freedom.

## Dwelling in *Death of a Salesman*

Revived on Broadway to rave reviews in early 2012, *Death of a Salesman* exemplifies the dangers of calculative thinking by displaying the damage done when one does not undertake dwelling. Arthur Miller depicts a man annihilated by a calculated pursuit of abstraction, a lifestyle tragically familiar to us now. Miller's characterization of Loman's house as the place that could have integrated Willy with his family, with nature, and with a more authentic self-knowledge reinforces both the importance of dwelling—and suggests the likelihood that fewer people know what it means to dwell. In many ways, *Death of a Salesman* exemplifies what Heidegger refers to as "unpoetic dwelling," a state that derives "from a curious excess of frantic measuring and calculating."[6] As Heidegger makes clear, unpoetic dwelling is a possibility only because humans are capable of dwelling poetically: we recognize this truth in understanding Willy Loman as a tragic figure.

---

[5]   Heidegger, *Question Concerning Technology*, p. 35.
[6]   Heidegger, *Poetry, Language, Thought*, p. 228.

The type of thinking, which he argues is caused by *"Ge-stell"* or "enframing,"[7] he describes as being a greater danger than nuclear annihilation. Heidegger warns,

> that the approaching tide of technological revolution in the atomic age could so captivate, bewitch, dazzle and beguile man that calculative thinking may someday come to be accepted and practiced *as the only* way of thinking. What great danger then might move upon us? Then there might go hand in hand with the greatest ingenuity in calculative planning and inventing indifference toward meditative thinking, total thoughtlessness. And then? Then man would have denied and thrown away his own special nature—that he is a meditative being. Therefore, the issue is the saving of man's essential nature. Therefore, the issue is keeping meditative thinking alive.[8]

Although the speech was delivered over 50 years ago, the point remains as timely as Miller's play. Although the capacity for meditative and reflective thinking obviously exists, the increasing domination of calculative thinking infects all domains of human existence.

Critics often discuss Arthur Miller's *Death of a Salesman* in terms of its critique of the American dream, and, if it is mentioned at all, the function of Willy Loman's house is used as a means to the end of that argument. Focusing on the house, however, reveals Miller's insight into the nature of American dwelling. The house not only frames the stage but also the script; understood as a comment on how we dwell, Miller's play also condemns the American tendency to dwell abstractly. In a modern world, abstract dwelling has many advantages: increased mobility in the pursuit of a better 401k portfolio requires that we remain separated from the spaces that we call home. The play foretells our situation in the twenty-first century, as we find places that allow us to ignore our mortality, godless spaces made of unnatural materials that prevent us from witnessing the sky. Our inability to integrate, our failure to dwell, has produced a nation of people who, like Miller's protagonist, feel "temporary" about themselves.[9]

---

[7] Heidegger, *Question Concerning Technology*, pp. 26–30.

[8] Heidegger, *Discourse*, p. 56.

[9] Arthur Miller, *Death of a Salesman* (New York, 1976), p. 51.

Miller's play speaks prophetically as he looks at the nuances of the term "building" that emerge in the business culture of the 1950s. Willy, speaking with his brother Ben, describes how he is "building something at the firm." His brother Ben responds by saying "What are you building? Lay your hand on it. Where is it?" Willy then discusses the advantages of capitalistic abstraction, saying "You can't feel it with your hand, but it's there." He later praises the benefits of abstraction, stating "[t]he whole wealth of Alaska passes over the lunch table at the Commodore Hotel" in an abrupt about-face from his earlier appreciation of timberland and the outdoors.[10]

The play ends as the temporary nature of Willy Loman's dwelling, caused by his pursuit of abstraction at the expense of concrete goods, becomes a source of very real despair. Realizing that he has nothing planted, that he doesn't "have a thing in the ground",[11] Willy is unable to apply this belated realization of the value of concrete goods to his own life, as he feels that he is "worth more dead than alive."[12] This conclusion is the result of a mistaken belief that he has a life insurance policy, but, more importantly, is due to a lifetime investing in calculated values of abstraction. In the final scene, the older son reflects, "there's more of [Willy] in the front stoop than in all the sales he ever made."[13] This locates the tragedy in Willy's inability to reflect on how to integrate himself with his home, his dwelling space. Willy's wife speaks the final words: "I made the last payment on the house today. Today, dear. And there'll be nobody home. We're free and clear. We're free ... we're free ..."[14] Linda's last lines linger in the audience's ear as an ironic note: the freedom they attained is of the wrong kind.

**Dwelling Poetically**

Having detoured through Miller's criticism of calculation and abstraction, I will briefly return to Heidegger to describe the threefold nature of poetic dwelling. Originally and most essentially, poetic dwelling arises in a response to the language

---

[10]   Ibid., pp. 85–86.
[11]   Ibid., p. 122.
[12]   Ibid., p. 98.
[13]   Ibid., p. 138.
[14]   Ibid., p. 139.

that precedes our awareness of it, and thus incorporates our efforts to receive and respond mindfully to the mystery surrounding us. Additionally, poetic dwelling comes through the recognition of actual narratives that inform a society's culture and traditions. Finally, poetic dwelling emerges through the appropriation and incorporation of artifacts into dwellings that spring forth as human realizations of the truths disclosed by the dominant narrative.

In his essay " ... Poetically Man Dwells," Heidegger argues that the primary work of dwelling is based in language—more specifically, the human *response* to language. He writes that "Poetry first of all admits man's dwelling into its very nature, its presencing being. Poetry is the original admission of dwelling": the human ability to hear and respond to language that summons us allows us the freedom to dwell, gathered by language, which is "the highest and everywhere the first."[15] To achieve freedom in this situation, to dwell poetically, Heidegger writes that humans must remain mindfully open in responding to the beckoning of language.

Heidegger offers a second conception of what it means to dwell poetically in this essay, one that looks to the human activity of building. The origin of this building comes in speech, a saying that is not "building in the sense of raising and fitting buildings." Dwelling in this sense provides the narrative structure for the growth and development of society, framing the nation or culture of people through what Heidegger elsewhere calls a "projective sketch."[16] Absent this poetic structure, Heidegger argues that no sense of history or dwelling would be possible because the narrative informs and infuses the creation of the art and artifacts—*techne*—of that society. Dwelling cannot exist without the projective sketch that frames houses, stories and things as a referential anchor. Yet, the capacity for dwelling that allows for the integration of people with houses also shatters individuals who dwell unpoetically, putting their stories at odds with their concrete reality.

The emphasis shifts yet again in his essay "Building, Dwelling, Thinking" as Heidegger focuses on the work of construction and cultivation as objectively important activities in human dwelling. It is in physically restructuring our environments that we are able to appropriate the earth around us, to alter and change it in a way that fulfills our needs, to allow it to reflect the truth of the

---

[15]  Heidegger, *Poetry, Language, Thought*, p. 227.

[16]  Heidegger, *Poetry, Language, Thought*, pp. 74–77.

projective sketch that guides how we remember our pasts and anticipate our futures. As mentioned above, things, in Heidegger's essay, are important not as possessions but as loci of meaning that contain a truth about both the self and the world, integrating and preserving *Das Geviert* and its dimensions of the mortal, the divine, the earth and the sky. The abstractions admired and desired by Willy Loman do not permit the elements of the Fourfold to be gathered together. Earth, sky and divinities cannot be calculated: reducing the world to numbers maximizes efficiency but impoverishes the world to a corresponding degree. Although this increases calculability, it impoverishes the world to a corresponding degree.

Understanding how poetic dwelling merges manifestations of revelation, creation and appropriation to form spaces intended to spare things as they are, I will now depart from Heidegger in order to explore the actual spaces through which we live and move. This will indicate ways that buildings and structures determine our thinking and habits, following Tuan's insight that "the building or architectural complex stands as an environment capable of affecting the people who live in it."[17] To pursue the nature of this affect, I will outline how concrete buildings encourage specific modes of experience, as distinguished by the work of Robert Scharlemann.[18]

## Occupying and Living

The most basic experience of dwelling is occupying, which occurs with a first order awareness of one's surroundings: because this excludes the self, this experience occurs as one occupies the borders of a space without adding to it. We occupy many spaces during the course of a day, simply passing through without giving *where* we are any attention. The experience of occupation occurs as we interpret the space as transitory—one that we will move through (either spatially or temporally) en route to another destination. Occupancy is necessary to dwelling, but is not sufficient: the experience of occupation conceals the truth of the space where one is by revealing its potential as a means to a different end.

---

[17]   Tuan, *Space and Place*, p. 102.

[18]   Robert Scharlemann, *The Being of God: Theology and the Experience of Truth* (New York, 1981).

Much of the United States consists of spaces whose sole function is to contain a body for a short period of time: waiting rooms, lobbies and classrooms reveal their transitory quality in the absence of any anchor that allows spaces to feel homelike. Uncomfortable chairs discourage even weary travelers from fulfilling a desire to linger. Grey walls, nondescript tile or carpet, and the anonymity of others nearby render these spaces unremarkable. Often interchangeable, such anonymous spaces succeed when they promote human inattention: forgetfulness allows humans to see their bodies as objects to be regulated and controlled. When we find the abject markers and reminders of another's presence—stains or refuse—we react with disgust.

The experience of occupying not only contextualizes Heidegger's notion of dwelling, but also attends to how the spaces we inhabit encourage certain attitudes toward our environments. The spaces that gather what is anonymous in order to promote uniformity are appropriate in their context, and fulfill their purpose when they exhaust themselves in the event of duration. Such spaces are problematic only when they leave a remainder, when our experience of chain restaurants, bus stops or hotel rooms feels familiar to us. Accustomed to moving through anonymous environments, we are both less likely to notice other environments better suited for dwelling, and are more likely to feel at home in empty spaces that resist our integration with it. Once these spaces feel like home and we desire their abstraction and blankness, we follow the example of Willy Loman. Feeling temporary about ourselves, we forget how to dwell. The abstract nature of occupying a space precludes our ability to spare or preserve.

Second, the term "living" designates the experience of dwelling at the level of self-awareness, when one is aware of both self and space through knowing that one is engaged in occupation. *Living* in a space permits me to attest "I am here," as both the "I" and the "here" emerge as distinct entities. Yet while the individual who lives in a space affirms and is affirmed by the things that emerge and present themselves, the space is still one marked more by opposition than familiarity. Living (especially when understanding it as other than a synonym for dwelling) occurs in a state of tension, as the "I" and the "here" become juxtaposed temporally without being bridged or integrated. Saying "This is where I live" therefore has an unspoken implication of "for now." Often uttered with resignation, "living at the office" has a negative connotation. Even expressions framed in a more positive sense, such as when one is "living it up" or exclaims "this is really living!" are uttered with a nod to the temporary nature of the situation. One *lives* when one is on vacation or visiting a location for only a short while. Such spaces encourage an awareness of the self in relation to the space without permitting the self to engage in the co-presencing or co-responding that occurs where one dwells.

Like occupation, living occurs in a variety of environments: tourist sites, places of employment, the houses of one's friends or relatives. Without the nourishment that time provides, living does little more than remind us of possibilities that we do not actualize. Sensing an imminent departure, we hesitate and do not allow the space to gather us. Although it is necessary to experience the self's relation to the space one is in for dwelling to occur, it also is not sufficient. As with occupying, the space itself guides our experience of living: knowing it to be already marked with a temporal ending in the near future, we do not allow ourselves to integrate with it.

**Building Reflectively**

Although we occupy and live at a shallow level, the actual design and construction of spaces necessarily occurs at what Scharlemann would call the reflective level of consciousness. Heidegger accounts for this in *The Question Concerning Technology* when discussing the interconnected nature of *poiesis* and *techne*: both are modes of revealing, and the works of art and engineering are rooted in *physis*, or ways of letting things emerge.[19] The things we make—including constructing and cultivating as modes of building—are crafted from a paradigm incorporating judgments about what values frame the production of the thing at hand. After its construction, a thing continues to participate in the paradigm—although not exclusively. On the one hand, things depend on our watchfulness in order to disclose the Fourfold, even if they were created with the intention of preserving it. On the other hand, the things surrounding us orient us into a type of thinking that becomes habitual. World emerges through human co-responding.

Human construction is determined by which one of two primary orientations to space is dominant. Belden Lane describes these orientations with the Greek terms *topos* and *chora*. Aristotle's sense of *topos* conceives of space as an empty,

---

[19]   Heidegger, *Question Concerning Technology*, p. 13.

anonymous grid in which all space between regulated points is identical, "an inert container exerting no particular influence on the creatures or objects within it."[20] Modern cities are largely built on technological grid systems that allow for the efficient use of empty spaces: the logic of these cities, which spread in subdevelopments and strip malls, maximize the ability to calculate, organize, secure and control the flow of human traffic and the natural world around it. Buildings—apartments and stores—are constructed abstractly to maximize the number of those willing to rent the space. Even classrooms are designed with a desire for the temporary. Cities urge our perpetual displacement into a series of houses that we are increasingly unable to commit to experiencing as a home. The danger to humans arises as our unthinking acceptance of a shallow environment seems more comfortable and familiar to us than a nourished place of dwelling, which offers a complex topography capable of expanding our thoughts and capacities. The brutal efficiency of temporary spaces, even when technological systems of production are successful and seem to meet our basic needs, does not foster poetic dwelling. These places push us away from integrating ourselves with our surroundings. Occupying and living, we are diminished.

Lane argues that the alternative to *topos* and technological spaces is Plato's sense of *chora* space, which emphasizes the "capacity of a place to resonate to the immediacies of human experience. Place as *chora* carries its own energy and power, summoning its participants to a common dance, to the 'choreography' most appropriate to their life together."[21] Because our spaces shape our thinking, the motivation for Heidegger's insistence that poetic dwelling also includes an element of building becomes clear. While it is not impossible to preserve the Fourfold at Applebee's, it is far easier to preserve it when one constructs a house with one's family, situating it in the hillside near the water. The land gathers the house, which the family constructs to protect the location that gathers it. *Chora* space is one way of expressing the call of language to humans, the call that frames humans as beings who respond instead of assert. This understanding of space, where humans are grasped by and conform to the surrounding world, seems

---

[20]   Belden C. Lane, *Landscapes of the Sacred: Geography and Narrative in American Spirituality* (Baltimore, 2001), p. 39.

[21]   Ibid.

most prone to allowing for poetic building capable of staying and preserving the interrelation of the Fourfold.[22]

Poetic dwelling occurs when humans experience space and time at the reflective level, rendering a judgment that integrates self and environment as an object of thinking. Dwelling adds this integration to the experiences of occupying and living, binding us to the place that gathers what one evaluates as good. These goods, identified by David Klemm and William Schweiker, include natural, social and reflective goods.[23] The house constitutes a basic good of shelter, and often integrates natural goods of wood, stone and water. Homes provide a social space where we gather with family and friends. Also, homes preserve space for reflective goods—creative works that we both make and enjoy. The house, integrated, provides a closed world of meaning, one reflected and contained in the totality of things gathered in the house. We dwell here poetically, incorporating what Heidegger would call "the divinities," but a gap persists between these and what Klemm and Schweiker recognize as "before God."[24] Absent the God-word, theology, and enframed by our time in shallow spaces, even our homes may fail to become a place characterized by sparing or preserving.

## Dwelling Theologically

While it is clear that calculative thinking and the technological living that it promotes are problematic, to dwell poetically is not necessarily an adequately robust alternative. An unquestioning anti-technological fundamentalism is no better than a technologically enframed posthumanism. These, in fact, are variations on what Klemm and Schweiker identify as the twin perils of *overhumanism* and *hypertheism*. The solution, following their guidance, arrives neither in shunning technology nor in despising poetry. A third way, one that bursts forth the potential for openness, is necessary for humans to maintain questions and the piety of thought.

---

[22]   Heidegger, *Poetry, Language, Thought*, pp. 157–159.

[23]   David E. Klemm and William Schweiker, *Religion and the Human Future: An Essay on Theological Humanism* (Hoboken, 2008), pp. 75–82.

[24]   Ibid., p. 82.

Heidegger desires that the poetic incorporation of the divinities into the Fourfold produce a space that preserves what is unknowable, arguing that the poet "calls in the sights of the sky, that which in its very self-disclosure causes the appearance of that which conceals itself, and indeed *as* that which conceals itself." Continuing, he adds, "In the familiar appearances, the poet calls the alien as that to which the invisible imparts itself in order to remain what it is—unknown."[25] A problem emerges, however, in that integrating the unknowable, bringing near the mysterious, is at most necessary—but not sufficient—for the production of questions. Especially given Heidegger's recognition that the poetic also produces a single-mindedness, something more is needed. At most, it would seem that the poetic and the technological as modes of dwelling manifest what Scharlemann might recognize as a conflict between religious and reflective paradigms of thinking.[26] Calculative thinking and meditative thinking cling to different values that the rival paradigm does not recognize. In our time, we face two modes of reflective thinking that promote rival visions of humanity, neither of which seem to find an outside from which to challenge their own perspective.

Theology seems like an unlikely place to turn for answers, and yet the word "God" itself perhaps has not yet lost its power to disrupt and unsettle enclosed human environments. David Klemm points this out in his introduction to Ebeling's essay "God and Word," arguing that a godless linguistic situation—one still present in our time—demands reflecting on the nature of the word God. Klemm finds through Ebeling that "the language we receive obliges us to speak about God, yet that language does not permit us to do so." Stepping past the shallow dichotomy of what language permits, Klemm argues that the purpose of words is to summon or enable a reality they describe: the word God is a "word of words" as it "manifests the basic human situation as a linguistic situation" in which we are "given a language, called upon to speak, and made answerable to the situation in which we find ourselves." Finally, Klemm reminds us that only God can authorize the use of the word God. Because *"God is God as the word that brings our own*

---

25    Heidegger, *Poetry, Language, Thought*, p. 225.
26    Scharlemann, *Being of God*, p. 28.

*situation to light*,"[27] it is necessary to exercise a healthy restraint before speaking the word.

The God-word, theology, exposes the relative limitations of human-based linguistic worlds, questioning both human calculation and the poetic projection of worlds by forcing us to reflect on the fact that we (and our worlds) are merely finite. The status of "God" as the word of words means it is also an un-word, one whose power comes in denying our assumptions of referentiality by exposing the existence of an actual absolute, that which is not anchored or summoned by language. Our reflexive awareness of our finitude allows for meditative thinking and an openness to testing what seems certain. Poetic and calculative forms of dwelling affirm only their own truths, but theology provides a self-critical stance of openness that declares all linguistically revealed truths are contingent and relative. By integrating the God-word into theological dwelling, we engage in reflexive thinking that questions whether one's engagement with the world spares God as God. As Klemm and Klink write,

> To pass this test, the depth construed as symbol must itself affirm both a critical No and an affirmative Yes as to whether the symbol makes manifest God as the ultimate depth. No, the symbol of the depth is not a literal representation of God in some element or relations among elements within the structure. Yes, the symbol nonetheless manifests the depth dimension in and through the structure. The point is that the theological depth of a structure is both immanent in and transcendent to that structure.[28]

The integration of the God-word through theological dwelling permits us the freedom to see the boundaries and limits of our own worlds and dwellings. Dwelling is and is not ultimate: it allows a truth to manifest without incorporating it completely. Heidegger reminds us that boundaries, rather than being where something stops, is rather where something begins its presencing.[29] The beginning of theology is also the beginning of reflexive dwelling, a dwelling that is able

---

[27]    David E. Klemm, *Hermeneutical Inquiry, Vol. I ,Interpretation of Texts* (Atlanta, 1986), pp. 193–194.

[28]    David Klemm and William Klink, "Constructing and Testing Theological Models," *Zygon: A Journal for Religion and Science*, 38/3 (2003), p. 519.

[29]    Heidegger, *Poetry, Language, Thought*, p. 154.

to appropriate its own linguistic situation as one integrating the absence of God, which Heidegger allows poetically, but also the presence of God, which only appears theologically. We dwell theologically as we project boundaries into the world that allow for the possibility of God's coming to presence within them. This possibility is spared and preserved.

The truth found by dwelling theologically exposes God even in those places more conducive to mere occupation. Although hotel rooms or airport lounges seem alien to God as they operate with a reductive understanding of the human condition, dwelling theologically reveals the truth of God, who appears here as that which is alien and anonymous—but still present, nonetheless.[30] The God-word interrupts the calculative reduction by exposing that God persists even in these places. Especially as few of us are equipped to build our own homes or choose lakeside locations, we must learn to dwell theologically even in the barren and empty spaces that hinder poetic dwelling.

Theology, incorporating the God-word into our vocabulary as we dwell as mortals on the earth, is a necessary corrective to the technological and poetical organizations that structure twenty-first century human existence. Avoiding both the grasping projection of *topos* space and the responsive organization of *chora* space, dwelling theologically reminds us that freedom comes in holding these reflective modes of dwelling in tension. Learning to dwell theologically allows us to constantly carry with us the "before God" that informs how we respect and enhance the integrity of life in our actions and relations.[31] It is in this sense that theology provides the truth of the experience of dwelling—by reminding us that our experiences of dwelling liberate us only by preserving boundaries that blind us to its limitations. We dwell on the earth comfortably, and perhaps with moments of authenticity—but not always in the unearthly abyss cleared by the name of God. Today is still the right time to speak of God, because only this word "is capable of saying what the situation in reality is."[32]

Ultimately, it is because dwelling exists before and as our moments of deepest living that it ought to be understood as the concretization of theology. A theology

---

[30]   Thomas J.J. Altizer, *Total Presence: The Language of Jesus and the Language of Today* (New York, 1980), pp. 19–20, 35.

[31]   Klemm and Schweiker, *Religion*, p. 82.

[32]   Scharlemann, *Being of God*, p. 117.

abstracted from its time and place risks building and dwelling in a castle in the air. Unmoored theological speculation partakes in the fate of Willy Loman, desperate to find a space for integration but habituated to a blindness that conceals its ownmost possibility. Theologians need to remember the importance of dwelling—including calculative frames, poetic projections and concrete structures—and learn to show the appropriateness of God to these specific contexts in a way that expands the human capacity for theological dwelling.

How one gathers, what one integrates, the ideals that one strives for—these are all reflected and preserved in the space within which one is found to dwell. The products of our hands, our minds and our hearts—our theologies—are integrated with and as our space of dwelling. Beyond poetry—which can gather, at most, the traces of absent divinities of closed poetic worlds—the God named by philosophical theology integrates within our dwelling the terrifying openness that the word God provokes.

## Selected Bibliography

Altizer, Thomas J.J. *Total Presence: The Language of Jesus and the Language of Today*. New York: The Seabury Press, 1980.

Heidegger, Martin. *Discourse on Thinking*, trans. John Anderson and E. Hans Freund. New York: Harper & Row, 1969.

Heidegger, Martin. *Poetry, Language, Thought*, trans. and ed. Albert Hofstader. New York: Harper & Row, 1975.

Heidegger, Martin. *The Question Concerning Technology*, trans. and ed. William Lovitt. New York: Harper & Row, 1977.

Klemm, David. *Hermeneutical Inquiry, Volume I: Interpretation of Texts*. Atlanta: Scholars Press, 1986.

Klemm, David and Klink, William. "Constructing and Testing Theological Models." *Zygon: A Journal for Religion and Science*, 38/3 (2003), pp. 495–528.

Klemm, David and Schweiker, William. *Religion and the Human Future: An Essay on Theological Humanism*. Hoboken: Blackwell Publishing, 2008.

Lane, Belden C., *Landscapes of the Sacred: Geography and Narrative in American Spirituality*. Baltimore: Johns Hopkins University Press, 2001.

Miller, Arthur, *Death of a Salesman*. New York: Penguin, 1976.

Scharlemann, Robert. *The Being of God: Theology and the Experience of Truth*. New York: The Seabury Press, 1981.

Tuan, Yi-Fu. *Space and Place: The Perspective of Experience*. Minneapolis: University of Minneapolis Press, 1977.

Chapter 7

# Imagination and Fallibility

Forrest Clingerman

## Introduction

We live at the intersection of tipping points: we find ourselves in a world that speeds toward something, knowing that our direction is irreversible and yet our destination is not fully known. We live in the shadow of controversies over human structures—from the definition of the family to the nature of the global community itself. We are inundated by challenges to political authorities and economic systems, disputes over increasingly scarce goods, breakdowns in diplomacy, and increases in partisanship. And most devastatingly, we live on a biological razor's edge, characterized by such things as overpopulation, loss of biodiversity, pollution on an incomprehensible scale, and tragedies like oil spills and the nuclear meltdowns. Manifestations of an "environmental crisis" are no longer in the distant horizon, but very real aspects of the integrity of life on this planet. Our communal and individual lives exist at the confluence of tipping points—and *this* is the situation of theological reflection.

The present chapter seeks to address something that emblematically defines our current precariousness: climate change. Nigel Clark writes, "What if the event of our time turns out to be not so much the knowledge that human action is altering global climate, as the realization that climate is responsive to our nudges only because it is far more precarious than we ever dared imagine?"[1] Similarly James Hansen begins his book *Storms of My Grandchildren* in these stark terms:

> Planet Earth, creation, the world in which civilization developed, the world with climate patterns that we know and stable shorelines, is in imminent peril. The urgency of the situation crystallized only in the past few years ... The startling

---

[1]    Nigel Clark, "Volatile Worlds, Vulnerable Bodies: Confronting Abrupt Climate Change," *Theology, Culture, and Society*, 27 (2010): p. 32.

conclusion is that continued exploitation of all fossil fuels on Earth threatens not only the other millions of species on the planet but also the survival of humanity itself—and the timetable is shorter than we thought.[2]

Climate change can be characterized as a series of free choices that cumulatively tip us toward cascading, self-reinforcing impacts on human and non-human wellbeing. In other words, anthropogenic climate change simultaneously contextualizes and threatens the meaning of human being in the world.

Insofar as one of the core tasks of theology is the systematic reflection on the depth of human being and the interpretation of meaning's presence in the world, there is a dire need to address climate change *theologically*. How might theology address something that occurs at such a global, abstract, yet simultaneously material level? My discussion explores this question in two stages, suggesting a theological pathway for exploration rather than a complete answer. First, I suggest a critique of how religious responses to climate change often focus on personal virtue or systemic transformation, and suggest an alternative. That is, religious responses often separate—or at least inadequately weave together—the individual and the social dimensions. What appears missing is a reflexive thinking that breaks through this bifurcation. We are led to ask: how might we re-imagine a theological response to climate change, so that the focus becomes the space between the inevitable failure to reform our lifestyle and the hope that cataclysm can be (at least somewhat) averted? In other words, what is required is a "third-way thinking," which contributes the possibility of a reflexive and poetic thinking of *climate change as a manifestation of the ground and abyss of human being at the razor's edge.* In the second section of this chapter I offer an example of such "third-way environmental thinking" through a reading of Ian McEwan's novel *Solar. Solar* is the story of where hope and failure meet in the midst of crisis, ideals and all-too-human existence. This novel is not about the truth of climate change—it is about how we envision the truth about ourselves, and make do with the messiness of human existence. In this discussion, what emerges is how fallibility and imagination serve as a frame for theological reflection on climate change.

---

[2]   James Hansen, *Storms of My Grandchildren: The Truth About the Coming Climate Catastrophe and Our Last Chance to Save Humanity* (New York, 2009), p. ix.

## Framing Climate Change for Religious Reflection

How can we model climate change for *theology*?[3] Certainly climatologists offer one way to frame climate change, ornithologists another, economists still another, and so on.[4] But how can *theologians* uniquely frame the question of climate change?

What we are seeking is an appropriate domain for an informal theological model of the complexity of our perception of climate change.[5] For starters, theology is unable to model a simple, uniform thing called "climate change," because climate change is in fact an abstract, contentious, multivalent ideological concept. It carries different meanings in various disciplines of natural and social sciences.[6] In other words, despite the fact that climate change looms over our political, economic, and cultural lives, it is an exceedingly vague and contested term. The discipline of theology is ill-equipped to adjudicate over the scientific controversies or policy dilemmas on their own terms, nor should it attempt to do so.

Even so, many religious communities approach climate change as a "problem" that can be univocally defined by science, economics, or public policy. From such a limited vantage point, the task of environmental theology would appear to be to summarize a presumed consensus of science—that is to say, to summarize what climate change "is"—before resolving the "problem" through vague theological sentiments, moral calculations, and "religious language." In many cases, therefore,

---

[3]   For a detailed discussion of how we frame different aspects of climate change, see Matthew C. Nisbet, "Communicating Climate Change: Why Frames Matter for Public Engagement," *Environment: Science and Policy for Sustainable Development* (http://www.environmentmagazine.org, accessed 11/3/2010).

[4]   The present chapter presupposes but will not focus on issues directly related to climate science. For a basic description of scientific and policy issues, see David L. Downie, Kate Brash, and Catherin Vaughn, *Climate Change: A Reference Handbook* (Denver, 2009).

[5]   For more information regarding theological modeling, see David E. Klemm and William Klink, "Constructing and Testing Theological Models," *Zygon*, 38 (2003): pp. 495–528; Robert Scharlemann, "Constructing Theological Models," in *Inscriptions and Reflections: Essays in Philosophical Theology* (Charlottesville, 1989), pp. 125–140.

[6]   I am not suggesting scientific disagreement regarding the overall acceptance of anthropogenic climate change. There are nonetheless different models and uncertainties that are part of the scientific process. Misinformation about climate change is not simply lack of scientific knowledge, but also problems with the ways climate change is shown in the mainstream media. Cf. M.T. Boykoff and J. Boykoff, "Balance as Bias: Global Warming and the US Prestige Press," *Global Climate Change*, 14 (2004): pp. 125–136.

environmental theology unwittingly consigns religious reflection to the role of rhetorical ornamentation for ethical mandates aimed at the pious. But such an approach does not recognize the underlying reasons for conflict in dialogues about global warming, and thus theological thinking is unable to identify a meaningful role in the debate.

To combat this simplistic view, religious communities must acknowledge that not only is "climate change" mistakenly understood as one thing, so too is religion. This dynamic is chronicled in Mike Hulme's *Why We Disagree About Climate Change*. Hulme writes:

> Our beliefs about the divine, about the spiritual and the transcendent, and about our role in the world as moral agents, shape our sense of duty and responsibility to care for others and for Nature. They affect the way we relate to climate and how we interpret our role in the changes of climate which are occurring ... But we do not all see the world and our relationship with it in the same way."[7] Hulme also notes that "a convergence of lofty moral principles can easily fragment when challenged by the depth and complexity of the issues raised by climate change."[8]

For Hulme, the inadequacies found in many religious responses to global warming are caused by the lack of universally accepted ways to assign blame. When we reduce climate change to mere "problem," there are nonetheless still individual, social, and global factors at work simultaneously. Hulme shows how many religious statements, built on univocal definitions of both climate change and religion, result in a fracturing or bifurcation of responsibility:

> Most established religions in their teachings overtly hold in tension the individual (or personal) and systemic (or structural) causes of moral failure. This failure may be couched using the language of sin, injustice, disharmony or evil, but all share the diagnosis that the world we experience, including our experience of ourselves, does not conform to what intuitively we would like it to be.[9]

---

[7]   Mike Hulme, *Why We Disagree About Climate Change* (Cambridge, 2009), p. 161.

[8]   Ibid., p. 155.

[9]   Ibid., p. 157.

There is an unexamined lack of agreement regarding "religion" and climate change, which leads to a conflict of interpretations and even a failure of understanding.

Theology is well-equipped to concentrate on such conflicts regarding our perception of climate change but instead the often unexamined divergence of interpretations merely results in a bifurcated response.[10] On the one hand, confessional bodies and theologians concentrate on actions that contribute to greenhouse gases, which can be remedied only through individual choices. Such approaches can be taken to the extreme: "Individuals are held accountable for their actions and the services of carbon offsetting companies are held up to be, in a metaphorical sense, equivalent to the selling of indulgences for the remission of punishment of one's sins."[11] On the other hand, religious groups focus on systemic issues, blaming climate change on economic, political, and social structures. When oriented toward structural responsibility, religious statements demand environmental justice, because "it is claimed, all individuals should not be held equally morally culpable for the emissions for which they are responsible."[12] Yet when taken to its extreme, environmental theology becomes satisfied only with a condemnation of neo-liberalism that requires a contradictory dismantling of present social structures from within.[13]

---

[10]    Interestingly, this is not simply a problem in theology, but also in environmental ethics. An excellent example of this is the recent debate surrounding individual choices versus the framing climate change as a "tragedy of the commons." See Mario Hourdequin, "Climate, Collective Action and Individual Ethical Obligations," *Environmental Values*, 19 (2010): pp. 443–464; B. Johnson, "Ethical Obligations in a Tragedy of the Commons," *Environmental Values*, 12 (2003): pp. 271–287.

[11]    Hulme, *Why We Disagree About Climate Change*, p. 158.

[12]    Ibid., p. 159.

[13]    There are a few book-length theological treatments of climate change, and the present discussion could be applied to varying degrees to each. Backing up Hulme's analysis, the tension between the individual and the social is present in many theological works concerning climate change. For example, Carol Robb's *Wind, Sun, Soil, Spirit: Biblical Ethics and Climate Change* (Minneapolis, 2010) places New Testament ethics in conversation with the Kyoto Protocol. In the chapters devoted to New Testament sources, Robb suggests that Jesus and Paul provide an alternative to the concept of Empire and the purity codes of the time; in technical chapters she suggests different scenarios based on structural responses to climate change. In response, Robb suggests a healthy, spiritual community is the appropriate response to the "Kingdom of Oil." But if a healthy community is more of an abstract ideal, she also presents concrete ethical responses that the individual undertakes to engender this community. Thus, she paints responsibility within the tension Hulme shows: theology offers concrete, individually-oriented choices that reflect

The split between the individual and the systemic is clearly troubling because when taken alone, each side is neither the *root* of the theological issue nor the ground for an *adequate* theological response. Instead, this bifurcation shows the limits of our technical and scientific perceptions of climate change. This bifurcation also exposes a limitation in our theological discourse, because "the reasons for the persistent differences lies in the complex ways we see and use climate change as a totem for other, deep-seeded ways in which we view the world."[14]

Does this bifurcation mask a more appropriate way to approach climate change theologically? I would like to suggest that we have reached *the religious crisis of climate change*: theological discussions of climate change tend to lack a reflexive thinking that is necessary for the complexity of our interpretations of "climate change," and also of "religion" itself. The religious crisis of climate change first emerges when we are forced into an unsatisfying bifurcation of individual and social responsibility toward climate change. But what also emerges in the foregoing analysis is that a theological discussion of climate change becomes fatally flawed when it sees "religion" itself is a *simple, uncomplicated perspective* through which to understand global warming. Religion is something else entirely: religion is influenced and changed by personal actions and overarching structures. It develops across the complexity of space and time. It is a contradictory, evolving,

---

"environmental virtue"—support local farmers, for example, or work on removing fossil fuel subsidies. Alternately, theology defines responsibility in terms of abstract, systemic changes: theology promotes the "Kingdom of God" as an alternative to the "Kingdom of Oil." Sallie McFague's *A New Climate For Theology* (Minneapolis, 2008) provides a second example, although it is not as extreme as Robb's work. McFague's theological reflection on climate change centers on the necessity of changing the theological and economic models operative in society. In the first portion of her book, McFague focuses on structural changes in society and religion. But the second half of her book moves toward what might be understood as particular, individualized responses: worship, urban life, hope and despair. For McFague a Christian theological response to climate change must deal with the individual and the structural. In addition to the two examples given, Ernst Conradie's *The Church and Climate Change* (Pietermaritzburg, 2008) suggests an important analogy between climate change and apartheid. But this is within the context of individual responsibility and systemic injustice. Likewise, Michael Northcott's *A Moral Climate* (Maryknoll, 2007) gives a passionate critique of Empire, before analyzing individual actions and social structures related to food, travel, and energy. In these works and others, the focus is on the individual and the social as independent spheres of action, rather than on how these two poles are held together hermeneutically.

[14] Donald Nordberg, "Review Essay: Disagreeing About the Climate," *Business Society*, 49 (2010): p. 550.

and partial manifestation of meaning of human being and action. Theological thinking is a thinking of when religion *becomes* religion—and this occurs at a place marked by the tensional mixture of the individual and the social, not at the bifurcation of the two. Religion and climate change then form an unstable intersection, which is an ideal object for theological reflection.

So what happens when we acknowledge that religion is not an impartial, paradoxically unsituated vantage point? When we see that the bifurcation of religious responses to climate change is not the response to science or policy, but an exposure of the limitations that theological reflection must overcome? Insofar as we ignore these questions, we are unable to fully explore the crisis of climate change—and we also are unable to grapple with the *integrity of life on the ecological balance*. This tipping point is neither a problem of individual actions nor the corruption of the structures of society itself. Instead, theological thinking must savor the desire to entertain the complexity of interpretation, focusing on the tipping point that emerges at the irreducibly varied *interplay* of our religious experience at the brink of individual and social responsibility.

I therefore propose that theological thinking reflects on the crisis of climate science *in and through* a reflection on the theological tipping points of this crisis. That is to say, I wish to advocate a third-way, hermeneutical thinking[15] that seeks to acknowledge, but then to transform, the bifurcation explained above in the context of our age of "heightened reflexivity."[16] As third-way thinking, the task of theological reflection is to think through the ways in which religion and climate change dialectically transform each other.

To introduce how this third-way thinking on religion and climate change is possible, we can take heed of a comment by the theologian Sigurd Bergmann: "climate change challenges and changes images of God and the sacred and their corresponding sociocultural practices. Theologians and scholars of religion are called to reflect this change as well as on how religion might bring about change."[17]

---

[15] For this discussion of theology as "third-way thinking," I am drawing on David E. Klemm and William Schweiker, *Religion and the Human Future* (Malden, 2008), esp. pp. 52ff.

[16] David E. Klemm, "Introduction: Theology of Culture as Theological Humanism," *Literature and Theology*, 18 (2004): p. 244.

[17] Sigurd Bergmann, "Climate Change Changes Religion," *Studia Theologica*, 83 (2009): p. 98.

Bergmann rightly suggests that climate change and religion are engaged in a transformational dialogue. Theologically, "climate change" is not a *thing* to which we apply doctrine, but a *definition* of our human context, which frames issues of value and meaning. Climate change is a name for the material landscape through which our spirit and values are manifested.[18] At the same time, "religion" serves as a key part of the framework through which we develop the concept of climate change, especially in terms of its ideological implications. Religion is the realm of wholeness and hope, which changes in response to different contexts and climates.

Furthering Bergmann's point, we might re-frame our topic through two statements that define the unstable intersection between religion and climate change: first, rather than say "religion *is*," we should say that *religion becomes religion while we think in the midst of a changing climate*. In a complementary fashion, climate change also is unstable: *the climate's alteration is changed when we think about it religiously*. In its attempt at understanding our desire to be at home in the world—to dwell—theological reflection now has the task of thinking reflexively about how religion is situated in a changing climate, and simultaneously how the concept of climate change contextualizes our hermeneutics of religion.

To think about climate change as religion's other, or to think of religion as a changing climate, occurs through "third-way thinking": thinking that moves past unavoidable tensions toward a satisfying mediation. On one hand, theological thinking can reflexively suggest that the idea of *climate change* is not confined to science, economics, or policy—that is, by thinking about our thinking of climate change, we see that it is *more than* a problem, but rather it is an ideology or concept that issues forth from our understanding of the sacred in the world.[19]

---

[18]    In fact, Gallup has found that the majority of the world's adult population is aware of climate change (61 percent overall, 82 percent in the Americas, and 88 percent in Europe). Anita Pugliese and Julie Ray, "A Heated Debate: Global Attitudes toward Climate Change," *Harvard International Review*, 31 (2009): pp. 64–68. Thus Pugliese and Ray write, "In the last several years it has become increasingly clear the extent to which human action is a cause, why climate change is a threat to human and non-human communities, and the uncertainties that still exist in our scientific understanding. Even so, only with the awarding of the 2007 Nobel Peace Prize to Al Gore and the Intergovernmental Panel on Climate Change was global warming cemented in the popular imagination. And in the months before Copenhagen UN meeting in 2009, there was '…a greater sense of urgency than in the past among many global climate scientists and experts, who say climate change is taking place faster than they anticipated.'" (p. 64).

[19]    Hulme, *Why We Disagree About Climate Change*, esp. chapters 1 and 10.

Without this reflexivity, the focus on science and policy calls for change, but only from within the limitations of the system itself. On the other hand, theological thinking can reflexively suggest that the embodied place of religious experience is within a complex, changing climate. Without this reflexivity, a static and disembodied religious voice calls for individual environmental virtue, but without a recognition of the limitations imposed by finitude and embodiment. In short, a reflexive theology offers inroads to a deeper understanding that is hitherto lacking in the scientific, technical, and moralistic proposals for mitigation and avoidance of global warming. At the same time, "Environmental change changes religion, its practices, ideologies and images of God and the sacred."[20]

One of the hallmarks of this third-way thinking is that it is grounded in a mediation between the particular and the universal. We "should insist on a critical principle of mediation between universality and particularity, recognizing that universality without particularity destroys community and personality; but particularity without universality is tyrannical ... [U]niversality seeks concrete instantiation in order to actualize love, gratitude, and respect both for God and for others; and particularity submits itself to tests of universalisability in order to actualize justice."[21] Indeed, this mediation between particularity and universality is at the heart of environmental theology. Environmental theologies—whether focused on climate change, ecojustice, or wilderness debates—manifest this mediating, third-way when reflecting on how particular situations and environments point toward a more general understanding of the ways in which we encounter and interact with what is understood to be the natural world—that is to say, to see how we (as individuals and communities) simultaneously are part of and separate from "nature." What is required, then, is to explore a concrete, particular manifestation of the unstable intersection of religion and climate change, which opens us to the structure that such tensions inhabit.

---

[20]  Bergmann, "Climate Change Changes Religion," p. 103.

[21]  David E. Klemm, "Humanism and Frayn's Play *Copenhagen*," *Literature and Theology*, 18 (2004): p. 306.

### Third-Way Theological Reflection and Ian McEwan's *Solar*

Third-way theological thinking situates—through indirect, particular means— how *climate change is a manifestation of the ground and abyss of human being at the razor's edge.* While many previous religious responses to climate change attempt to view it directly and univocally, an alternative way of encountering this intersection is through an *indirect, allusive* portrayal that both illuminates religion and climate change, while standing apart from them. Of course, a number of things can be used to portray the religious crisis of climate change. The changes in the shoreline of Lake Erie, the decimation of the Sinai Baton Blue butterfly, or the migration patterns of common loons all might serve to uncover traces of the complex hermeneutical interplay between religion and climate change. These all focus on *physical* tipping points. But the razor's edge of which we speak is deeper than this: it is a conceptual tipping point that reflects on *the edge of gaining or losing our human being, our spiritual wholeness, through climate change.* Such conceptual tipping points are the stuff of novels, artworks, and other cultural media; therefore I would like to explore this particular tipping point through Ian McEwan's novel *Solar*.[22]

*Solar* is the story of Michael Beard, a Nobel Prize winning physicist. The novel begins in 2000, when Beard is 53 and has taken on the role of "eminent scientist"—someone who lends his name to institutes but no longer does research. At the beginning of the novel, he is floundering in his fifth marriage to Patrice, after his infidelities have pushed her into the arms of their contractor. Beard is unlikeable, morally ambiguous, and balances between an embrace of fatalism and unsought responsibility. He is certainly an unlikely hero: in our society, the morally compromised do not figure in our plans for salvation.

Beard has been named the scientific director of a new National Center for Renewable Energy. *Solar* is not about the merits of renewable energy. It is not a book about climate change at all—rather, as McEwan noted in 2008, "climate

---

[22]  Ian McEwan, *Solar* (New York, 2010). Hereafter citations will appear as page numbers in the text. McEwan himself might look with askance at a theological treatment of his novel, because of his "growing conviction that religious faith is 'at best morally neutral, and at worst a vile mental distortion.'" David Impastato, "Secular Sabbath," *Commonweal*, 136 (October 23, 2009): p. 15.

change would 'just be the background hum of the book.'"[23] By resisting the urge to moralize on climate change, McEwan meditates on the dynamics at issue in the debate: the relationship between our human failings and desires, our scientific hubris, our voraciousness, and the tenuous balance between the individual and society. Thus the crisis of climate change is portrayed as ever-present, yet it is not focused upon: it is the overwhelming, all-pervading context through which we unwittingly structure the meaning of our lives.

While not directly about global warming, McEwan's novel is fruitful for theological reflection on climate change because it contains a trace of reflexivity. McEwan's writing is not a "thinking about climate change," but *a thinking about the fracture of the human condition as it changes in our climate*. As readers we do not experience climate change, but rather we experience a relationship with those who inhabit its effects and possible solutions. As the "background hum," it is curiously central. Climate change is not discussed; it is ever-present through its absence. Its absence is marked by mitigation and the creation of alternatives: alternative energies, alternative relationships, alternative lives, alternative definitions of the selfhood of Beard. Climate change is not, properly speaking, a here-and-now to which we point; it is an important placeholder for thinking—a "background hum"—which absently signifies a dramatically changing presence in our temporal flow.

Nowhere is this "background hum" more apparent than in Beard's relationship with Tom Aldous. Beard determines the first major project of the Center will be a wind-turbine. Enter Tom Aldous, one of the many post-docs working at Beard's Center. After attempting to get Beard's attention in other ways, Aldous designs a sophisticated and brilliant turbine for the project. While both are gifted physicists, in other respects Aldous is what Beard is not. Aldous is young, passionate about climate change, and monastic in his existence. He is developing an efficient process of artificial photosynthesis that greatly increases our ability to create solar power. Because his work was based on Beard's Nobel Prize-winning work, he seeks Beard out simultaneously to win a mentor and to save the planet.

Beard is threatened by Aldous: Aldous becomes a competitor as a physicist and as a lover. This will be the cause of Aldous' death, for Beard returns home to find Aldous naked after a liaison with Patrice. During this confrontation, Aldous

---

[23] Philip Ball, "A Warming Tale," *Prospect*, 169 (2010): p. 75.

slips and fatally hits his head. Beard impetuously finds a way to frame Patrice's earlier lover Rodney Tarpin. In death, Aldous gives Beard an incredible gift. In his possessions was a folder, marked for Beard. The folder contains the scientific information for an incredible leap in solar energy. With Aldous' death, Beard has come upon a major resolution to the world's energy problem—and there seems to be no one who would suspect that it originated with Aldous, or that Aldous' death was accidental in the presence of Beard.

The second section of the book begins in 2005. Beard is older, has gained more weight, and has a new lover. He also has been forced out of the Center, and taken on a more entrepreneurial position of keeping Aldous' memory alive for his own benefit. We are told Aldous had been forgotten by everyone, save Beard. Late one night, Beard thinks to himself:

> Four years ago, in the rented flat he now irresponsibly owned, stretched out on the stinking sofa, which was still there, smelling no better, he had seen in ways that no one else could the true value of Tom's work, which in turn was built on Beard's, as his was on Einstein's. And since that time he had sweated, he had done and was still doing the hard work. He was securing patents, assembling a consortium; he had progressed the lab work, involved some venture capital; and when it all came together, the world would be a better place. All Beard asked, beyond a reasonable return, was sole attribution. (188)

By 2005, then, Beard has reinvented himself. He has become a scientist again, improving Aldous' work, for Aldous "had been correct in his general assumptions and wrong in certain particulars ..." (214). Beyond his scientific work, Beard became an advocate for alternative energy. But Beard's purpose is still fatally flawed with a self-serving sense of pride and entitlement. He also holds a naïve realist view of the world, which means he is unable to acknowledge the complexity and ambiguity at the heart of religion and climate change. For instance, he becomes mistrustful when a humanities professor explains his reasons for hearing Beard speak: "Well, I'm interested in the forms of narrative that climate science has generated. It's an epic story, of course, with a million authors." Beard registers his suspicion of such concerns, before—without any irony—he embarks on telling an apocalyptic narrative of climate change.

Beard's actions toward the humanities—especially in light of his own objective view of the world—hints at the tipping point between religion and climate change. Certainly climate change is a crushing *scientific* problem, which sets in motion the plot. But Beard's moral failing is not caused by his scientific expertise. In fact, he grows and matures in his scientific view of the world throughout the novel. Instead, what Beard neglects is the question of "the integrity of life." He treats the individual and the social as if they were bifurcated. This shows in his life: Beard precariously balances between his acknowledgment of the primacy of science and his lack of passion over climate change, his intellectual ability and his animalistic self-indulgence, his finitude and the possibility of transcending genius. For Beard, in other words, climate change is fully known through scientific certainty *and thus not known at all.* By limiting climate change to one element of human being— namely our calculative knowing and acting—climate change forms a groundwork of contemporary life. But it thereby becomes a moral absence, finally unknowable as more than data sets and energy use patterns. Beard—and us as well—balance between such presence and absence. This conclusion we draw if climate change is a manifestation of the ground and abyss of human being at the razor's edge.

In the novel's third section the issue of the integrity of life becomes even clearer. In 2009, the promised breakthrough is on the verge of becoming a reality. The solar array, made through pride, along with selfishness and fatalism, unwittingly is poised to become essential in safeguarding our natural goods, and might even usher in a new hope for the integrity of life. And this is no longer simply the result of scientific arrogance: contrary to Beard's wishes, his partner has his child; as a result, he now has a connection with the future.

Is the book—and our present predicament with it—a comedy or a tragedy? Beard's life finally unravels, and with it the improbable hope he embodies. Indeed, in 2009 Beard is old, overweight, and in poor health. He still is morally dubious and still fatalistically prone to giving in to his desires. But he also appears to have grown in his attempts to be a father, a businessman, and a scientist. Is this an implausible catalyst for hope?

The end is a laughable yet just ruin for Beard. Personally, his life is destroyed when his partner in England is called by his lover in New Mexico. Further, his doctor discovers cancer, and he is unwilling to pursue treatment. Professionally, his deception concerning the origin of his work is uncovered. He is accused of fraud, the solar array is shackled with lawsuits, and the patents are now contested. The technological breakthrough is, in sum, both within reach and in an untouchable limbo. Not only is this a legal limbo: Beard's work is physically destroyed after an altercation with the recently released Rodney Tarpin. After all of the work to harness light, it is let loose and its shackles broken. While Beard appears through the novel to grow into a hero of sorts, someone who we can place our hopes of a different future in, the tale ends with our hopes dashed.

Yet Beard and his work *does* represent the possibility of a future that is "otherwise." That is to say, limitations are not the end of *our* story—*our story is one of hope in spite of limitation, and one of imagination born of fallibility.* Although Beard does not ultimately move beyond his own physical, moral, and intellectual fallibility; although he does not acknowledge Aldous' passion and intellect; although he lacks altruism; indeed, although he cannot carry through with his desires for personal betterment, Beard nonetheless portrays how we inhabit the tipping point between a known present and a possible future that resolves itself *within* the complexity of climate change. The novel is a commentary on our own personal and social situation, on the verge of two strikingly different imaginative futures: one that is tragically said, and one that is hoped-for but unsaid. McEwan traces the increasing pressure of personal fallibility in the midst of climate change, and in so doing we are given the contours of the possibility of hope.

Thus McEwan's novel acknowledges the limit that was seen in the previous section: climate change will not be solved by theological thinking that exclusively seeks purified moral transformation or systemic change. But Solar also points toward an alternative frame through which to view the unstable intersection of religion and climate change: a fruitful theological response comes in the midst of our own hope-filled fallibility, and within our morally-corrupt but ever-present imagination. This interplay becomes the lived structure through which we see religion becoming religion, and the alteration of the changing climate. That is to say, McEwan's book is the narrative, the story of the moral tension of the individual and the social. As such a narrative, Solar reveals and particularizes the religious crisis of climate change. Beard's failures are personal failures; he neither exhibits ecological virtues nor virtues in other areas of his personal life. Yet his work brings out possibility and hope. But is it truly this easy? Science still works within the flawed systems that gave rise to Beard's hubris. Certainly there is no logical reason why fallibility makes one unable to alter the structures of society. But this novel alerts us to the existential drama inherent in such a change. The ambiguity of each of us, the inevitable fallibility we each hold, is echoed in the limits of the finite structure of society, placing us within a cycle of individual and systemic failure—and only then, within a cycle of individual and communal hope.

Likewise, the imperfect structures of society are shown in this novel, and they appear destructive of those with passion and imagination. But despite this, such imperfect structures open the possibility for the fallible (as represented by Beard) to become a vessel for our hopeful imagination of the future. That is to say, we must acknowledge the individual blame and lack of responsibility we each carry, and also acknowledge the social structure that hinders any progress toward a more hopeful future. But McEwan also suggests that even in this imperfect place, the hope of an imagination of what might be can emerge, akin to plants pushing through the cracks in a sidewalk. Is this book a tragedy or a comedy? It depends on whether the imagination can thrive in such an unlikely place, or whether the end of the novel signifies the inability to overcome obstructions and to allow more than shallow growth.

## Conclusion

McEwan's novel is a particular illustration of third-way theological thinking of climate change. McEwan offers a parable that frames climate change as the razor's edge of the irreducible interplay between *fallibility* and *imagination*. To learn from this tale, I would like to suggest, we must take up the juxtaposition of fallibility and the imagination in order to respond to the one-sided limitations of seeing climate change as merely a social or an individual problem.

Structural responsibility for climate change deals with transformations such as correcting markets and establishing justice. But this tends to neglect the lived experience within those structures, and the abilities of individuals and communities to undertake such a transformation. For example, "fixing the market" usually is *based* on market principles. However, this limits the possibility of confronting the structural problems inherent in the market. *Imagination* is the possibility of "thinking otherwise," of providing a basis for overcoming the limitations of individual and social blame. As exposed by *Solar*, imagination can emerge even within the imperfection of individuals, presenting something that is unexpected. Climate change thus is a question of imagination, defined by the unexpected yet possible. Of course, insofar as our imagination is anchored by fallibility, so too are our responses.

A similar dynamic occurs in the one-sided emphasis on individual responsibility, which focuses on individual wellbeing and transformation. Personal transformation is defined through personal freedom. But our aspirations are anchored in our own finitude and self-contradiction. Thus, "Those in the West (especially) who seek to live low-carbon domestic lifestyles—low-energy light bulbs, locally sourced food, driving hybrid cars—and yet who holiday two or three times a year at destinations at the end of an international or intercontinental flight, reveal the psychological tension which this clash of values can lead to."[24] Not only does our fallibility present discernible limits to the possibility of individual transformation; fallibility also becomes the location for a transcendence of imagination. At the site of imagination, the possibility of the otherwise transcends our finite frames of being.

The interplay of fallibility and imagination is not simply a particular *diagnosis* of the failures of a bifurcated religious response to climate change. It is also a changing site of the depth between religion and climate change. This is a theological claim, insofar as it desires to think of God in the space of identity and difference; God is the transforming saturation that moves apart from the individual and the social. Finding God in a changing climate, at the ground and abyss of the razor's edge, happens indirectly; cultural works (including works in the humanities, arts, and sciences) and natural locales beckon us to seek a deeper interpretation. For instance, we have used *Solar* as one promising site for discovery. McEwan's novel opens the possibility of seeking the *depth* that is the overplus of human freedom imaginatively transcending the limits of social structures and human failings, and at the same time our flights of fantasy begin tethered and sculpted by the humility of fallibility. We have moved from the limits of individual and social responsibility, to the theological tensions in religious crisis of climate change, and finally to a spiritual climate residing at the interplay between fallibility and imagination. In this movement, theological thinking approaches climate change and religion

---

[24]   Hulme, *Why We Disagree About Climate Change*, p. 171.

through the *ontological* tension of imagination and fallibility, and in so doing overturns the *ethical* tension of individual and social blame and responsibility.

## Selected Bibliography

Hulme, Mike, *Why We Disagree About Climate Change* (Cambridge: Cambridge University Press, 2009).

Klemm, David E. and William Klink, "Constructing and Testing Theological Models," *Zygon*, 38 (2003): pp. 495–528.

Klemm, David E. and William Schweiker, *Religion and the Human Future* (Malden: Blackwell, 2008).

McEwan, Ian, *Solar* (New York: Doubleday, 2010).

## Chapter 8

# Hegel Beyond the Ideal of Idealism

### Andrew W. Hass

If we are to think about a return of Hegel in today's world—and Hegel has always been returning, in one form or another, since he himself began writing as a seminarian student at Tübingen in the late 1700s—then we must think about this "return" as a "beyond." Even though a return is generally considered mutually exclusive with a going beyond, we must understand, at least for Hegel, that they are one and the same. To return to Hegel today is to go beyond Hegel. But to fulfill a thing by surpassing it, to embrace a thing by negating it, is *precisely Hegel*. That is, we best serve Hegel, we best work Hegel, when we out-Hegel Hegel. And did not Hegel announce this himself when, in the Preface to the *Elements of the Philosophy of Right*, he gave us that famous image of the bird whose glaring eyes come alive only after the sun has fallen: "the owl of Minerva begins its flight only with the onset of dusk"?[1]

German Idealism might have long since had its day. And the Hegelian "ideal" of that idealism, that a certain absolutization of a progressive march of history finds itself manifest in the Western culminations of the advanced modern Spirit, is also a hope now left behind. So why does Hegel return to us now? And why today, of all times, when progressive marches of history have led, and continue to lead, to such catastrophe, to such regressive attempts at how the world ought to be, and how we ought to think the world to be? Perhaps we can say it is precisely because our progressions have become regressions that Hegel returns, but now a Hegel who is outstripped by his own internal mechanism. For Hegel invoked Minerva's owl in a paragraph that began this way: "A further word on the subject of *issuing instructions* on how the world ought to be: philosophy, at any rate, always comes

---

[1]  G.W.F. Hegel, *Elements of the Philosophy of Right*, ed. Allen Wood, trans. H.B. Nisbet (Cambridge: Cambridge University Press, 1991), p. 23.

too late to perform this function."[2] If philosophy is always a step behind the ethical imperative, if the ethical life is already actualized before philosophy can set its own agenda upon it—and this from a book whose idealism will go on to set just such an agenda—then philosophy (as it is formed by Hegel, or as it informed by Hegel) will always have to *return back* to find itself. But in doing so it will in fact undo itself, go beyond itself as a doctrine of positive contrast to what has gone before. Instead its coloration will be "grey in grey," as Hegel says,[3] neither white nor black, and not even a grey mixture of both, as in a convenient act of sublation between two extremes, but a grey in a grey, a sublation of a sublation, one that effects a disappearance, but at the same time brings out the colour all the more. Hegel returns, even at the point of ethical uncertainty, or even at this point of ethical actuality that carries so much uncertainty, because Hegel is our first modern philosopher who understood the absolute need and the absolute desire to negate himself.

The return of Hegel today, in certain circles of theology, philosophy and theory, is predicated on this negation. Or since, according to Hegel, "philosophy forms a circle," the return of negation today is predicated on Hegel.[4] Hegel becomes both predicator and predicated, both subject and object, in a new return to the idea of a negation that had marked so much of the twentieth century and now harbors in the thought of so many recent Continental thinkers—Badiou, Jean-Luc Nancy, Žižek, Agamben, even Vattimo, to name just the prominent—all of whom might, for better or for worse, be regarded as post-postmodern. What bearings do we give this new territory beyond the postmodern, if Hegelian negation is so central to its concerns? How do we determine or delimit negation? Is it simply, as Derrida suggested, that Marx continues to haunt the Western intellectual terrain, and so too, by way of Marx, an inverted Hegel? Certainly the Continent continues to wrestle with Marx, as Jacob did with the angel at the ford of Jabbok, whether in real or spectral terms. But it is more than Hegel by way of Marx. If postmodernism was the political gesture to limit, in the name of theory, the hegemony of powers that resulted from modernity's aggrandizement of Subject and Object, and the eventual antagonisms that ensued between them, extreme as they eventually became, then

---

[2]   Ibid.
[3]   Ibid.
[4]   Ibid., p. 26.

beyond postmodernism we find the attempt to re-address those antagonisms, not by way of concord and reconciliation, but by way of the negation of either side. *Neither* Subject nor Object: hence Hegel. But hence also ethics. For if philosophy comes too late to issue instructions on how the world ought to be, as postmodern theory came too late in the twentieth century, then what comes after theory must address this problem, the problem of the forever after, the "ideal" now in its most pejorative sense—that which takes us beyond the actual, beyond the here and the now, that which is wished for, but never seems possible to attain.

Much of this recent return to Hegel, then, ushers in a more ethical drive, but does so by way of a reconfiguration (we cannot yet say reconciliation, nor even sublation) of opposites: Vattimo's secularised Christianity[5] or Žižek's perverse Christianity, for instance;[6] Nancy's community of "being singular plural";[7] or Agamben's permanent state of exception.[8] Even on the American side of the Atlantic, David Klemm and William Schweiker's "theological humanism," though it is decidedly *not* Hegelian, that is to say, does not operate from a negative impulse, nevertheless attempts an ethical position of integrity, or *integritism*, that reconfigures, by means of what it calls "third-way thinking," classic modern binaries: theology and humanism; confessionalism and critique; religion and politics; the Christian and the pagan; theory and praxis.[9] And in the "death of God" theology of Thomas Altizer, the *coincidentia oppositorum* is ubiquitous, in what we might call a "radical absolute," here a decidedly Hegelian notion of an absolute that must be wholly and unequivocally *rooted* in the present material

---

[5] See Gianni Vattimo, *Belief*, trans. Luca D'Isanto and David Webb (Stanford: Stanford University Press, 1999).

[6] See for example *The Puppet and the Dwarf: The Perverse Core of Christianity* (Cambridge, MA: MIT Press, 2003).

[7] See Jean-Luc Nancy, *Being Singular Plural*, trans. Robert D. Richardson and Anne E. O'Byrne (Stanford: Stanford University Press, 1999).

[8] See Giorgio Agamben, *State of Exception*, trans. Kevin Attell (Chicago: Chicago University Press, 2005), or *Homer Sacer: Sovereign Power and Bare Life*, trans. Daniel Heller-Roazen (Stanford: Stanford University Press, 1999).

[9] David Klemm and William Schweiker, *Religion and the Human Future* (Oxford: Wiley-Blackwell, 2008). For the idea of third-way thinking, see especially pp. 57ff. Though this kind of language invokes Hegelian dialectics, it cannot rightly be called Hegelian insofar as what drives or compels the coming together or confrontation of both poles of the dialectic is not a negativity or contradiction, nor even a negation of negation, but rather a "freedom towards integrity."

state, and which issues an imperative to theology to be nothing else.[10] All these reconfigurations are indeed political, each in their own way. But they are also thereby unavoidably ethical in responding to a philosophy that has come too late to the political realities of late modern extremism.

But by returning to Hegel, how can negation furnish the grounds for what "ought to be" in the world? Especially when, if Hegel is right, it would have to return to that "ought" as something already actualized? How can an ought be actualized? The task here is a steep hill. And, as is often the case with Hegel, one is never quite sure whether one is going up the hill or down it. But either way, traversal is only possible if we see negation not in terms of annihilation, but it terms of an active, creative, generative force. Negation must be seen in terms of bringing something into existence. The question we now have before us is whether it can bring into existence the "ought."

There are two customary places one might take as initial ports of call for any question of what "ought to be" in Hegel. The first is the *Phenomenology of Spirit* in its section on Spirit, which follows the section on Reason and precedes the sections on Religion and Absolute Knowing. There, Spirit is understood first as the ethical order of culture, before in its self-certainty it becomes morality. The moral view of the world that then develops follows on from Kantian duty, at least in postulating a duty that is not found in Nature itself, and yet must be harmonized with Nature. But the harmonizing is not, as it is in Kant, with a mere category of a universal "as if"; it is with actual Nature as the thing in itself. *Pure* morality, however, cannot ever be actualized in itself: "There is no *moral, perfect, actual* self-consciousness," Hegel states. There is only a sought after unity of duty and reality, "but as a *beyond* of its reality, yet a beyond that ought to be actual."[11] In the *Phenomenology*, the Kantian ethics of "as if" still govern the conditions of the ethical sphere.

---

[10] The theological notion of a *coincidentia oppositorum* is rife throughout all of Altizer's writings in numerous forms: God and Evil (Satan), life and death, genesis and apocalypse, self and non-self, yea-saying and nay-saying, etc. Hegel too populates all of Altizer's work, but see especially *The Genesis of God: A Theological Genealogy* (Louisville: Westminster/John Knox Press, 1993) and *Godhead and the Nothing* (New York: SUNY Press, 2003).

[11] G.W.F. Hegel, *Phenomenology of Spirit*, trans. A.V. Miller (Oxford: Oxford University Press, 1977), p. 373, §613 and §614.

The second port of call is, of course, the *Philosophy of Right*. This, the last of Hegel's planned monographs, published in 1820, before he gave over to major revisions and lecture annotations, provides a more direct sense of what Hegel meant as "morality" and "ethical life." And ethics here is even more politically bound up with our social and state structures, and ultimately with world history itself. That is, ethical life in Hegel (*Sittlichkeit*) becomes objective rationality in the form of state laws and social institutions.[12] So whereas the *Phenomenology* looks back to Kant, the *Philosophy of Right* is an elaboration of the third part of Hegel's *Encyclopaedia*, first devised in 1817. More exactly it is an elaboration of the second part of that text, "Objective Mind," before "Absolute Mind" takes over through art, revealed religion and philosophy. That is to say, it is the elaboration of part of the system in its encyclopaedic form, encompassing both subjective and objective sides, as it moves from logic, through nature, to mind (as soul, consciousness and psychology), and then to the objective realities of law, morality and social ethics, before finally reaching its apex in the absolute spheres of art, religion and philosophy. It thus lends itself to a systematized Hegelianism at its most complete and most advanced stage beyond Kant. But for that very reason we ought not to take it as the definitive view any more than we should the *Phenomenology*, if we are still under the compulsion to go beyond Hegel. Instead, we should return to Hegel's most complete and most advanced understanding of negation, as this comes to us in the *Science of Logic* of 1812, which stands equidistant between the *Phenomenology* and the *Encyclopaedia*. It is true that the *Encyclopaedia* is an elaboration and extension of the *Science of Logic*. But perhaps we should hold to this thought: that any *beyond* is not to be construed by means of the circumscribing nature of systematic elaboration. If the *beyond* is within, it is only so as that initial hole made by the displacement of water from the stone that is dropped, before its widening concentric circles take us further and further from the evacuated center. That center is the *Science of Logic*.

The *Logic* is in reverse to the Encyclopaedia's *Philosophy of Mind*. Rather than moving from the subjective to the objective (from individual soul/consciousness/psychology to social law/morality/ethics), it moves from the objective to the subjective (from being and essence to concept/notion [*Begriff*]). In the opening

---

[12]    As stated clearly at the beginning of Part III, "Ethical Life," in *Philosophy of Right*, §144–145 (pp. 189–190), which is then worked out in the remainder of the text.

section, the triadic movement is from Being (*Sein*) to Determinate Being (*Dasein*) to Being-for-self (*Fürsichsein*). While in the first movement Being gains its determinateness through a dialectical process of pure being, pure nothing and pure becoming, the process begins again in a modulated form in the second: determinate being as such, *Dasein*, leads to finitude, and then on to infinitude. This then moves to Being-for-self. Negation operates fundamentally at each level of these triadic movements. Now, at the center of the second process, whereby Being has become determinate, beyond its pure state, at the coordinates of the "*da*" of the *Dasein*, and where it then moves from finitude to infinitude, we find, like a strange alien descended from another galaxy, the figure of the "ought." What is an ought—any ought—doing here, or doing *there* (*da*), and how can it possibly relate to the logic of Being in all its developing determinateness?

Hegel is here working out Being as determined by its finite character. To make something distinct from something else, a limit must be imposed. The pure state has no limit; but determination imposes limit, and limit marks out distinctness. But *what* in determination does the imposing? What brings limitation? Hegel's answer is: negation. To render the pure state no longer, it must be negated as pure. Only then can its opposite, distinctness, arise. We have said "imposing," but negation should be better seen as Hegel wants us to see it, as "generating." And this for two reasons: negation is not an extraneous force, but comes from within; and what is done away with also, by that very move, produces something else. The negated pure state, without determination or distinction, brings into existence the limit of the finite state. And it is only in that state of finitude that we can say, determinatively, that some-thing exists, and exists *da*—"there."

But the finitude of Being, for all its singular distinction, carries with it a "sadness." The finite "in its limit both *is* and *is not*."[13] It *is*, by virtue of its newfound status as determinate; it *is not*, by virtue of the *other* that is created by the generation of the limit. By putting a boundary down, we now have two sides, and thus we bring into existence all the binary terms that we use to define these two sides: subjective/objective, inside/outside, within/beyond, self/other, etc. As the *Logic* shows, it is sometimes difficult to distinguish between the two when the limit is placed upon Being itself: "Something has its determinate being *outside* (or,

---

[13]  G.W.F. Hegel, *Science of Logic*, trans. A.V. Miller (New York: Humanity Books, 1969), p. 127.

as it is also put, on the *inside*) of its limit; similarly, the other, too, because it is something, is outside it. Limit is the *middle between* the two of them in which they cease to be. They have their determinate being *beyond* each other and *beyond* their limit; the limit as the non-being of each is the other of both."[14]

The sadness arises then in the awareness that, in all these movements operating towards and beyond determinate being, non-being constitutes a thing's nature and being. For what is the other of Being as determined *within itself*? It can only be non-Being. "Finite things *are*, but their relation to themselves is that they are *negatively* self-related and in this very self-relation send themselves away beyond themselves, beyond their being."[15] Or, more poignantly, and in a manner that Heidegger will later pick up, "the being as such of finite things is to have the germ of decease of being-within-self: the hour of their birth is the hour of their death."[16]

Now, it is precisely from this *coincidentia oppositorum* at the heart of Being that the ought makes its entry. The self-limitation of Being creates an internal division, by generating an externality within inwardness. But in order for these opposites to co-reside and to co-ordinate, they must continue to cancel each other out, so that the external is negated by the inwardness, as much as the inwardness is negated by the external. Both cease to be, while both cease ceasing to be, simultaneously. The best way to grasp this is by the self-generative nature of negation: for negation to bring something into existence, it must keep generating *itself*—negation of negation, which of course is affirmation, a productive positing of what has been negated. The limit is this very positing in its productivity, but it is also a productive positing of negation, which brings the limit to its existence. Hegel thus calls the relation to one's own limit a positive or posited negation, a relation that must therefore also, in its self, transcend the limit by negating the limit, for the limit is both the negation and the negation of the negation. This double relation, as the *in-itself* of Being's double nature as being and non-being, Hegel then calls the *ought*.[17]

The chief characteristic of the ought is that it is "to be." When something "ought to be," its "to be" is still only in its infinitive form. We can see this in

---

[14]   Ibid.

[15]   Ibid., p. 129.

[16]   Ibid.

[17]   Ibid., p. 132.

two ways. One is negatively: it has yet to be determined finitely as an "is," and therefore it is beyond the here and now. The compulsion to come to pass has *not yet* been made manifest as arrival. Thus in its being it has a limitation: it cannot realize itself. The second is positively: as an ought, something is precisely "raised above its limitation," for the ought incurs going beyond that something, beyond its limitation as a finite "is." Hegel says that these two ways are inseparable. What "is" is not what "ought to be"; but also, it is precisely in making what "ought to be" what "is" that the "ought to be" finds its meaning, its purpose. In Hegel's terms, what determines the "ought to be" within itself is the "is"; and yet that "is" is negatively related to it, since it "is not" (it only ought to be). The very structure of "ought" is a transcendence of itself towards an "is," but that "is" negates it from within. It thus both *is* and *is not*. And so it becomes a constituent feature of Being, which is caught in its own ought as the self-transcending limit of its own limitation.[18]

In all the vertiginous motions of these contradictory comings and goings, the ought is what, eventually, leads us towards the infinity ("to be") of our Being, the transcending of our limitation. But this is only possible, Hegel says, because of the negation at its heart: the breaking apart or sundering that negation engenders of the sameness, the *diremption* of identity into being and non-being, into self and other, into the "is" and the "ought to be," is also what turns on itself, as the negation of negation, and brings new identity between being and non-being, between self and other, between the "is" and the "ought to be." Infinity, says Hegel, is nothing else than this generated *other* within. But it is also, thereby, the restored relation of the self to its other.[19] And it is in this transition between the two states, the transition towards this restoration of the self-identical in opposites, this *becoming*, where we find what Hegel calls the "ideal" or the "ideality" of idealism. This

---

[18]    Hegel, in the *Zusätze* (Remark) on this passage of the "ought," unfolds the matter in relation to the question of possibility: "'You can, because you ought' – this expression, which is supposed to mean a great deal, is implied in the notion of ought. For the ought implies that one is superior to the limitation; in it the limit is sublated and the in-itself of the ought is thus an identical self-relation, and hence the abstraction of 'can'. But conversely, it is equally correct that: 'you cannot, just because you ought.' For in the ought, the limitation as limitation is equally implied; the said formalism of possibility has, in the limitation, a reality, a qualitative otherness opposed to it and the relation of each to the other is a contradiction, and thus a 'cannot', or rather an impossibility." Ibid., p. 133.

[19]    Ibid., pp. 137–138.

"ideal," as we can see, is always beyond, but that beyond is also here and now. And the consummation of these two opposing sides in reconciliation, in sublation of one another through the ought to the infinite, is finally the Being-for-self, the *Fürsichsein* that ends the first section of the *Logic*.

Now, if we are to go beyond the esotericism of all such Hegelian logic, and actualize the ought again in the here and now, beyond pure ontology towards the ethical,[20] and beyond the ideal of idealism, while retaining the negative impulse that generates a new ideal, precisely how might we possibly do this? How could we possibly move into the possible, and to beyond the possible back to the actual?

At this stage, we can only be suggestive, and perhaps draw out some considerations for a certain kind of ethics of negation along the following contours.

The first contour is the most obvious, the least new, and thus perhaps the least convincing. We can understand the negative impulse in the critical sense of an ongoing critical theory of the kind that gains its culmination in a work like Adorno's *Negative Dialectics*. There have been many attempts to go beyond the critical,[21] and beyond the critical theory of the Frankfurt School in particular, even as Habermas continues as the last lingering voice of that tradition. And perhaps we can endorse those surpassing attempts when the conditions for Marx's *Ideologiekritik* have in fact been supplanted by Habermas' work, and yet when Habermas' work, especially on communicative rationality, has itself been supplanted by a postmodernity that Habermas fully comprehends yet finally refuses to embrace. But does this necessarily mean we have done away with critical theory entirely as an emancipatory discourse, or at the very least as a hermeneutics of suspicion? I suspect not. I suspect, in fact I am convinced, that there is still a role to play for this critical gesture in unmasking forces and systems that parade themselves as incontrovertible realities, truths or imperatives.[22] But the negative impulse of this kind of critical theory is admittedly limited, for the

---

[20]   On the ought as ontological in Hegel's *Logic*, see Stephen Houlgate, *The Opening of Hegel's Logic* (West Lafayette: Purdue University Press, 2006), pp. 391–393.

[21]   Even the early Hegel saw himself in this light, by going beyond the critical philosophy of Kant, under the rubric of speculative philosophy. But of course critique, and critical theory, took on a new meaning, and a new directive, with Marx and the Marxian tradition.

[22]   One might think of the present state of the university in the West, and its increasing regimentation as a systems driver for economic activity: what seems patently evident is the need now, more than ever, for critical voices from within to challenge the narrative of

"ought" tends to be supplanted by the powers of resistance and unmasking, where the "is" is denuded for what it really is more than for what it ought to be. Important as critique, suspicion, resistance, and what continues to go these days under the name of deconstruction are, they have not supplied the kind of potency that takes us beyond to the "ought to be."[23]

Let us then, secondly, follow more closely in the direction of the ought, but by going back to Hegel's sense of ought as the internal other of Being. One of the most difficult challenges in any ethics of modernity, and more acutely in any ethics of postmodernity or post-postmodernity, is how one constructs the self in relation to the ought. This is not simply the facile understanding of "what the self ought to do." It is more, what do we understand of the self that is supposed to carry this ought—an understanding of an ought already operating upon an ought: the ought that *ought to be*, ontologically, part of the modern self. Here the discourse of "self-interest" has come into play, not necessarily as an ethics centered upon the self and for which all ethical decisions and actions are made in relation to promoting that self's best interest, but as a self that is coherently constituted as a sound and reliable site upon which to construct an ought. It might be suggested that virtually all modern ethics begin with this assumption of self-interest, and even Hegel himself seems to be in conformity, with his "Being-for-self" (*Fürsichsein*), the third term sublated between *Sein* and *Dasein*. But as we have just seen, Hegel's self-interest is more etymologically literal in that the "interest" of the self sits between its two opposing sides of existence, its being and non-being, its pure self and its other. This is precisely what *Fürsichsein* expresses. And in that between state, a state of transition, where we have located the ought as the coming other, there operates negation as the fundamental generative force that allows for the transition and allows the self to come into its own, as it were, to be self-interested, but through its opposite. That is to say, the self, and any self-interest, is predicated only on negativity, on what it is not. Even the later Hegel of the *Philosophy of*

---

corporatization, managerialism and market-driven knowledge. This is but one example, close to home.

[23]   Again, following the previous example, we in the Humanities might all be in general agreement that the university is being led along the wrong path, but in the intransigent economic conditions of the present day, how many of us within the academy have advanced an alternative of what ought to be, practically and definitively, the right path?

*Right* retains this fundamental premise: "'I' determines itself in so far as it is the self-reference of negativity."[24]

The implications for such negative self-referencing would be profound. If the ought of the self is always its internal other, then what impels the self beyond the limitation of itself is its own negation, *otherness* as such. This drive not only punctures "self-interest" in the base sense of "self-centeredness"; it also punctures any sense of the "self" as a stable and whole being capable of carrying out the ought in any self-containing or self-mastering manner. The other must necessarily define the self as part of its ethical aspect. Hegel keeps returning to the late stages of modernity (the liquid stages of modernity, as Zygmunt Bauman describes them[25]) because he became the one modern philosopher to articulate fully, even "systematically," the diremped self that requires the other for its being. This idea we can see later worked out in the late twentieth-century work of Levinas and Ricoeur, most famously.[26] But when engendered through the negation of self, the other must go beyond even these thinkers in finding a way for self-interest to be forever blocked by its own internal mechanisms and for any interest to be thoroughly and completely shared with the other. Here Julia Kristeva comes closer to the mark, with her notions of the abjected self as "neither subject nor object."[27] If there is an integrity at work in such an *inter*-ested self, it is towards a (w)hole whose oral expression betrays its inner ambiguity and contradiction: the self as

---

[24]   *Philosophy of Right*, p. 41, §7. Emmanuel Levinas' titled volume *Entre Nous* has this same sense of "interest" in mind for the self, as its subtitle shows: *Essais sur le penser-à-l'autre (Thinking-of-the-Other*—trans. Michael B. Smith and Barbara Harshav [New York: Columbia University Press, 1998]). He offers a similar understanding to Hegel's quote here in the essay "A Man-God?": "To unsay one's identity is a matter of the *I*" (p. 60).

[25]   See *Liquid Modernity* (Oxford: Blackwell, 2000). Julia Kristeva, in her *Revolution in Poetic Language*, says that "negativity is the liquefying and dissolving agent that does not destroy but rather reactivates new organizations and, in that sense, affirms"—trans. Margaret Waller (New York: Columbia University Press, 1982), p. 109.

[26]   The entire corpus of Levinas is driven by the call of the Other upon us. For Ricoeur, the title alone of *Soi-même comme un autre* (*Oneself as Another*—trans. Kathleen Blamey [Chicago: Chicago University Press, 1990]) shows the intention of the author throughout his 10 studies.

[27]   See the beginning of her essay on abjection, *The Powers of Horror*, trans. Leon S. Roudiez (New York: Columbia University Press, 1982), pp. 1–6. Kristeva's understanding of the importance of Hegel's negation is evident from the early texts, especially *Revolution in Poetic Language* (orig. 1974).

other, or the other as self, is built upon a hole, which its opposite must necessarily fill in order to be made whole.

The idea of giving up the self for the sake of the self is of course not new. "He that findeth his life shall lose it: and he that loseth his life for my sake shall find it."[28] Or more recently, Yeats' Crazy Jane says to the Bishop: "For nothing can be sole or whole / That has not been rent."[29] But if we were to work out an ethics from such self-negation, then we would have to begin from the premise that there is no such thing as "self-interest" in the common sense of this term. Any interest would always be beyond itself. I do not pretend that the refinement of such an ethics and its implementation on all levels of our social life would be an easy matter to realize, for self-interest is at the heart of our conception of liberal democracy. But it is apparent that it would completely alter our presuppositions about, first, the ought of the "ought to be," second, how we would go about insisting on the ought, and third, for whose sake we would insist on it. And it is also apparent that any altered presupposition would be theological in nature: we cannot begin from a place of wholeness, because wholeness is beyond us, here and now.

The final contour to trace out briefly is perhaps the most radical. It returns us to the generative function of negation. If negation brings something new into being, even in its most interior chambers, then we cannot avoid the creative nature of the ought. The ought, we remember, breaks with the self's limitation by going beyond to an infinite. Infinity here is not the *ad infinitum* of endless succession, what Hegel famously calls "bad infinity," or less famously "spurious infinity,"[30] but more a circular kind of infinity, which loops back upon itself to be unified again with the finite (the "in-" prefix used in all its functions: as a privative, as directing an inward motion, as an intensive, etc.). This circle creates a space—much like the artificer's circle—out of which creation arises, or creation is made possible. And one can argue that all of Hegel's writings, including the system that becomes known as Hegelianism, are imbued with this kind of poetical character in which negation is continually re-creating, or re-inscribing, the site from which any supposed third term arises, or any dialectical movement is maintained. This infinity of course is most poetical in *Phenomenology of Spirit*, but it appears throughout

---

[28]    Matthew 10:39 (KJV).

[29]    William Butler Yeats, "Crazy Jane Talks to the Bishop."

[30]    *Science of Logic*, p. 150.

the Hegelian corpus, even as a far as the *Philosophy of Right*: "infinity as self-referring negativity, *this ultimate source of all activity, life, and consciousness.*"[31] If the ought itself is a creative source, then we cannot but help rethink ethics from an understanding of art, an art of negation, which not only disinters Nietzsche, but more, places the artist back into the responsibility of an ethical domain, no longer as the singular Nietzschean *Übermensch*, but as the social creature she always was, now bound to dirempting herself by means, we might say, of the demands—the ought—of her art. Here Giorgio Agamben and Jean-Luc Nancy have come closest to theorizing the generative *poesis* of Hegelian negation. In Agamben's *The Man Without Content*, the artist becomes, negatively, the person of the title, the one "who has no other identity than a perpetual emerging out of the nothingness of expression and no other ground than this incomprehensible station on this side of himself."[32] In Nancy, art gains, positively, a new sense, or sensibility, of "sense"—a unity or identity of sensation (the finite stuff of art) with meaning and understanding (infinity or ideality that art strives for beyond its materiality)— "sense" in all its senses.[33] To *make sense*, then, would be the supreme task of the artist. And this making would have to make a space for nothing, in order to allow the other to come forth from within (within the self, as the self). Art would thus have to make sense of the ought and in multiple senses: it would have to actualize the ought in the material world of our senses; it would have to give meaning to the ought; it would thus have to *make the ought* as the hermeneutically interpreted other; and the ought would have to make it as the other that compels creation.

In combining the dirempted self with this creative ought, we might say, finally, that both self and other would be displaced, would be re-created and would be *sublated*, into a "we": neither subject nor object, but a plurality, even within the singular. This of course would be to follow Nancy's path of "being singular plural."[34] But it also suggests that any art is also displaced from the singularity of the artist and must move outwards towards the social in a more inclusive hermeneutics of

---

[31]   *Philosophy of Right*, pp. 41–42, §7 (Remark).

[32]   Giorgio Agamben, *The Man Without Content*, trans. Georgia Albert (Stanford: Stanford University Press, 1999), p. 55.

[33]   See especially Nancy's *Hegel: The Restlessness of the Negative*, trans. Jason Smith and Steven Miller (Minneapolis: Minnesota University Press, 2002); and *The Muses*, trans. Peggy Kamuf (Stanford: Stanford University Press, 1996).

[34]   See fn. 8 above.

neither subject nor object. As Nancy says of Hegel's famous quote on art: "The 'end of art' is always the beginning of its plurality."[35] In following these pluralities we would also displace the concept, and the highly developed discourse, of human rights, upon which modernity, and all its present politics, are so fundamentally grounded. In this sense, Hegel's own concept of "right," as articulated in his last full work, is exceeded and gone beyond. For it is no longer that personal right and its accompanying subjective freedom are consummated in the institutions of the State—an idea that has worried many prior to the twentieth century, and repulsed most during and after the twentieth century. It is that "right" succumbs to the "ought"—not as the imperative norms of morality or the sovereign politics of *Sittlichkeit*, but as personal freedoms that are limited by the other towards a new possibility, freedoms, that is, made possible by the necessity of a certain poetry of negation: or, and this amounts to the same thing, as the affirmation of an ideal beyond the self-interested claim of "rights," and towards a re-creation of the self as "we." This is not the ideal of idealism, the "we" of absolutized *Geist*, the spirit of philosophy. It is the ideal of the real "we" actualized in reality, recreated in the here and now, an ideal that, as even Klemm and Schweiker claim, "points to reality and how we can and ought to inhabit the world."[36]

The tracing of such contours leaves out, of course, the detailing of any specific features. The ethical landscape is always a troublesome one to detail insofar as the topography keeps changing. I only suggest they may help to give a general shape to an ethics of negation, and by ethics here I have had Ricoeur's definition in mind all along: an optative mode of living well in distinction to an imperative mode of obligation.[37] Hegel's ought, as reconceived, is ultimately to be seen in the optative mood, where desire and future hope go beyond the obligatory laws and customs as encrusted in the present systems of our beliefs and institutions. But then, as Nancy has pointed out, Hegel's system is always driven by the optative mood: "Self-consciousness is essentially desire, because it is consciousness *of self* as and out of its consciousness *of the other*."[38] But this drive is also, in the most Hegelian fashion, towards the indicative, towards the here and now. And it is the optative

---

[35]  "Why are There Several Art Forms?", in *The Muses*, p. 37.

[36]  Klemm and Schweiker, *Religion and the Human Future*, p. 54.

[37]  *Oneself as Another*, p. 330.

[38]  *Hegel: The Restlessness of the Negative*, p. 60.

as indicative, the "may it be" as both "ought" and "is," Hegel as himself beyond himself, that we now need to think on and act on most acutely, and most creatively.

## Selected Bibliography

Agamben, Giorgio. *The Man Without Content*. Trans. Georgia Albert. Stanford: Stanford University Press, 1999.

Hegel, G.W.F. *Elements of the Philosophy of Right*. Ed. Allen Wood. Trans. H.B. Nisbet. Cambridge: Cambridge University Press, 1991.

Hegel, G.W.F. *Science of Logic*. Trans. A.V. Miller. New York: Humanity Books, 1969.

Nancy, Jean-Luc. *Hegel: The Restlessness of the Negative*. Trans. Jason Smith and Steven Miller. Minneapolis: Minnesota University Press, 2002.

Ricoeur, Paul. *Oneself as Another*. Trans. Kathleen Blamey. Chicago: Chicago University Press, 1990.

# Chapter 9

# The Mystery of Catholicism

Thomas J. J. Altizer

Nothing is a greater mystery than the Roman Catholic Church, by far the most enormous and most powerful religious body in the history of the world, and the most catholic or universal body in history, comprising more peoples and more traditions than any other world body, and the Catholic Church is truly unique in this universality. Moreover, Catholicism is genuinely unique in so fully integrating reason and revelation, nature and grace, time and eternity, liturgy and praxis, and freedom and hierarchy. But it is Catholic freedom that is most baffling to the non-Catholic, a freedom realized in a truly hierarchical world, a world that Dostoyevsky could justly know as the world of the Grand Inquisitor; inquisitors who were the first to banish freedom so as to make order possible, an order that is a holy order even in its banishment of freedom. Yes this is a paradoxical banishment, one suppressing and granting freedom simultaneously, and its very suppression of freedom can be understood as a realization of freedom, for in the Middle Ages Catholicism created an absolutely new freedom, and one that ultimately transformed the world.

One of the many ironies of Catholicism is that the very modernity which is the deepest enemy of Catholicism was created by Catholicism itself. Even Aquinas played a decisive role in this creation, but it is Dante who most openly embodies it, that Dante who can be understood as the most revolutionary seer in history, and yet a Dante who is the ultimately Catholic poet. Dante is the poet of that Church, which is Church and Empire at once, and in the Middle Ages Catholicism fully and decisively gave itself to creating the Church as Empire, thereby creating the seeds of modern totalitarianism, and inducing whole peoples to identify the Catholic Church as the Antichrist. Certainly no religious body has ever even approached the overwhelming power of the Catholic Church, a power that innumerable Catholics can know as a demonic power, just as it is the Catholic Acton who can know that absolute power corrupts absolutely, but nonetheless such power is truly power, and can even fall under Nietzsche's understanding of the Will to Power. Here, lies the ultimate mystery of Catholicism, a Catholicism that is wholly natural and wholly gracious simultaneously, wholly of this world and wholly other-worldly at once and altogether, at once absolutely here and now and absolutely transcendent.

The great master of Catholic power is the most powerful of all Popes, Pius IX, whose most astute move was the proclamation of the dogma of the Immaculate Conception in 1854, as for the first time a dogma was proclaimed by the Pope apart from a Church Council, thus making possible the proclamation of the dogma of the Infallibility of the Pope (1869–70), the most Catholic of all dogmas, and a dogma creating a truly new and absolute ecclesiastical authority. But only a wholly new vacuum or void made this proclamation possible, one voiding all absolute authority, a voiding created by what the originally Catholic Heidegger knows as the onto-theological event of the death of God, a death making possible and even occasioning the First Vatican Council, as for the first time a Church Council met in an ultimately Godless world, creating dogmas that could only be real in such a world. This is above all true of the Infallibility of the Pope, and even Newman profoundly opposed this dogma, as did most Catholic intellectuals, leading to a dangerous schism in the Church that was healed only in a time of ultimate crisis, in which the Church was shaken to its deepest foundations.

The truth is that Pius IX risked all in his proclamation of the dogma of Infallibility. This may well be the most solitary solemn decision ever made by a Pope, and it defined the modern Papacy, and perhaps even defined the modern Catholic Church, a Church which came into existence with the advent of a universal atheism in the French Revolution. All too significantly Eastern Orthodox thinkers such as Dostoyevsky can know Catholicism as the creator of atheism, an atheism perhaps inseparable from an ultimate worldliness, and an atheism unique to the post-Classical Western world. Now what most defines Catholicism as opposed to all other religious bodies is a uniquely Catholic realism, a realism first embodied conceptually in Aquinas, whose philosophy inevitably became the official philosophy of the Catholic Church, an Aquinas who was a primary spokesman for the Papacy, as in *De regimine principum*, where he declares that all Christian monarchs owe the same submission to the Pope as they do to Christ Himself, and that the Pope possesses both spiritual and temporal sovereignty.

Catholic realism is truly distinctive in its very comprehensiveness, one comprehending every domain whatsoever, and here a genuine integration occurs, creating the very universality of Catholicism. Nevertheless, this is a realism that is a deep mystery, and even a mystery to Catholicism itself, apparently never explored in its depth by Catholic theology, as though it is a genuinely forbidden topic. Yet it is absolutely primal in great Catholic literature and art, and above all manifest in Dante and Joyce, that Dante who created what the modern sensibility and world knows as *mimesis*, and one reaching its fulfillment in *Finnegans Wake*, just as it is Joyce and Dante who created the greatest Catholic epics, which are themselves the most realistic of all epics. This realism is truly Catholic, even if it is unexplored theologically, and in Dante and Joyce it is an historical realism, with no parallel whatsoever in the ancient world, for an absolutely new world is born in the *Inferno*, and consummated in the *Wake*. This is a world creating an absolutely new freedom, one not even anticipated in the ancient world, except insofar as this occurred in Augustine, the Church Father who had the greatest impact upon Catholicism, and who can even be known as the creator of Catholicism, or the creator of a Catholicism which is independent of Eastern Orthodoxy.

This is most purely manifest in the dogma of Predestination, an Augustinian creation wholly alien to Eastern Orthodoxy, but deeply affirmed by every major Western theologian, and even affirmed to make freedom possible, that is, the freedom which is only known to the West. For this is a depth of freedom only possible through a prevenient or eternal grace, one simply unknown apart from that grace, or unknown in its actuality, an actuality embodied in the freedom of the will. But will itself was first discovered by Augustine, and has never been realized apart from an Augustinian ground. Hence freedom can be known as the great gift of Catholicism to the world, even if a Catholic freedom is unreal apart from Predestination, although a post-Augustinian Catholicism could only realize this through the Reformation, but a Reformation that finally renewed Catholicism itself in the Counter-Reformation, thereby making possible what we know as the modern Catholic mind and sensibility.

This is a sensibility deeply moulded by the Eucharist, a uniquely Christian Eucharist or feast realizing the Real Presence, a presence that is the consequence of millions of years of history, and of sacrificial cults throughout the world, but one nonetheless unique as a consequence of the Crucifixion, and of a crucifixion which is the crucifixion of God. While Catholic theology has never dared affirm this, only knowing the Crucifixion as the crucifixion of the Humanity and not the Divinity of Christ,[1] this is a decisive reason why the Eucharist is such a profound mystery in Catholicism, and why the body of the Eucharist is so elusive as the Body of Christ. Indeed, in all of the vast body of Catholic literature only once is the Eucharist purely and comprehensively enacted, and that is in *Finnegans Wake*, whose profound Catholicism is challenged only by the *Commedia*, even if this is an underground Catholicism, and one inseparable from the onto-theological event of the death of God.

The very first pages of the *Wake* to be written, 380–382, became the conclusion of Book II, chapter 3, which is both the central or axial chapter of the whole book, and also the most difficult and complex section of this dream or night epic. Now the cosmic mass is a dream mass, but it is the Eucharist nonetheless, and a Eucharistic feast, a feast culminating in the cosmic consumption of H.C.E. or Here Comes Everybody. The virtually literal center of the earliest writing in the *Wake* is a divine acceptance of eucharistic death—*I've a terrible errible lot todue todie todue tooterribleday*—a death that is the center not only of a cosmic Holy Week, but which is re-enacted again and again throughout the course of the epic. If the universal humanity of the *Wake* is both a legendary Ireland and a contemporary Dublin pub, and H.C.E. is both a local innkeeper and the most glorious and divine king of our archaic past, then the action and the speech of the *Wake* are divine and human simultaneously, a simultaneity which is present in a mystery play or drama that is the universal history of humanity. While everything is the same in this eternal recurrence or return, it is the "seim anew" (215.23), and the "mystery repeats itself todate" (294.28).

The fall, condemnation, and crucifixion of H.C.E. is the dominant epic action of the *Wake*, and it is repeated again and again, even as the Host is ever broken in the mass. And just as the liturgical acts and action of the mass culminate in communion, so fall and death culminate in a festival or orgiastic communion in this apocalyptic epic, a communion whose very blasphemy, and scatological blasphemy, undergoes a constant ritual repetition in the text. But lying at the center

---

[1]    *Summa Theologica* III. 46, 8.

of the epic, even as the breaking of the Host lies at the center of the mass, is the execution or crucifixion of "Haar Faagher," an execution which becomes most dramatic and most scatological in the television skit by the comics Butt and Taff of "How Buckley Shot the Russian General." This occurs in the axial chapter of the *Wake*, and it culminates in that tavern orgy which is a cosmic repetition of an Easter which is Good Friday, an Easter or Resurrection which is an ecstatic consumption of the crucified Body of God. Yet this cosmic Easter is possible only as a consequence of the breaking of the Host.

After the announcement of this primal event, H.C.E. is accused of the crime, he pleads guilty, and goes on to associate or link himself with the executioner:

> I am, I like to think, by their sacreleigion of diamond cap diamond, confessedly in my barren gentilhomme to the manhor bourne till ladiest day as panthoposopher, to have splet for groont a peer of bellows like Bacchulus shake a rousing guttural at any old cerpaintime by peaching (allsoe we are not amusical) the warry warst against myself in the defile as a lieberretter sebaiscopal of these mispeschyites of the first virginal water who, without the auction of biasement frm my part, with gladyst tone ahquickyessed in it, overhowe and underwhere, the tottly tolly poppy flussy conny dollymaukins! (365.3–12)

Indeed, the death of God is the self-sacrifice of God, and not only is the executed the executioner, but the condemned one is the eternal Judge, and nothing whatsoever distinguishes guilt and condemnation or crime and execution, because Victim and Judge and Host and Creator are one. While these primordial and apocalyptic motifs are only indirectly and elusively present in Christian Scripture, they are directly and immediately present in the eucharistic liturgy, a liturgy revolving around the breaking of that Host and Victim who is God Himself. True, these primal motifs are dismembered and disguised in Christian theology, but they are present with an immediate power in the Eucharist, and that power can only be recovered or renewed by reversing or inverting the given or manifest form and language of both liturgy and catechism, of both Scripture and Tradition, an inversion and reversal enacted in the *Wake*.

Now the awe and sublimity of the mass passes into a comic ribaldry, but a ribaldry and even a scatological ribaldry which is absolutely essential to this epic project of inverting and reversing the mass, and the language of the Roman rite becomes the very opposite of itself in *Finnegans Wake*, but nothing else could effect a resurrection of the liturgy, or a contemporary awakening of the Christian God. The Easter celebration of Book Four opens with that Sanctus which is the great prayer of consecration in the canon of the mass—*Sandhyas! Sandhyas! Sandhyas!*—chanted in Sanskrit since East and West are now one. And an elusive motif of the *Wake* now becomes decoded, this is the Augustinian phrase, *securus judicat orbis terrarum*, which converted John Henry Newman, and that is the center and leitmotif of his *Apologia Pro Vita* (1864). This phrase, in various transpositions, appears again and again in the *Wake*, offering yet another Catholic ground of Joyce's vision, and one which was not decisively articulated until the composition of this epic. This is the theological ground which states the very essence of Catholic authority: that the judgment of the whole world cannot be wrong. Not until *Finnegans Wake* does a Catholic work appear which realizes both the universal and the cosmic identity of the *orbis terrarum*. Now *securus judicat* becomes *securus jubilends* (593.13), as an external and exterior authority passes into a *missa jubilaea*, a cosmic and apocalyptic mass.

Just as the *Paradiso* culminates in a visionary voyage into the depths of "Infinite Goodness," depths wherein an interiorly resurrected Dante sees the scattered limbs or leaves of the universe bound by love "in one single volume" (XXXIII, 86), so *Finnegans Wake* culminates in Anna Livia Plurabelle's final soliloquy with the cosmic dispersal of her body or leaves:

> So. Avelal. My leaves have drifted from me. All. But one clings still. I'll bear it
> on me. It reminds me of. Lff! So soft this morning. ours, Yes. (628.6–9)

But as opposed to the final "Yes" of *Ulysses*, this "Yes" is followed by a summons to the divine Father and Creator.

> Carry me along taddy, like you done through the toy fair. If I seen him bearing
> down on me now under widespread wings like he'd come from Arkangels, I sink
> I'd die down over his feet, humbly, dumbly, only to washup. Yes, tid. There's
> where. First. (628.9–13)

Going far beyond Molly Bloom, A.L.P. or Anna Livia Plurabelle is the underground Catholic Mother of God, a dark but ultimate source of grace, and one ultimately distinguished from the Orthodox Mother of God insofar as she is totally incarnate, and totally incarnate as flesh or Flesh itself. Now even if Catholic theology has never developed a full doctrine of the Incarnation, this is certainly realized in Catholic art and literature, and in *Ulysses* and *Finnegans Wake* this occurs through the incarnation of both Jesus and Mary.

In one sense it is very difficult to distinguish the Catholic Mother of God from the Orthodox Mother of God, but in another sense there is an overwhelming distinction between them. Not only is the Catholic Mother of God far more intimately present, but she is also primal in Catholicism as she is not in Orthodoxy, a process beginning in the High Middle Ages when the Gothic cathedrals were erected as sanctuaries and embodiments of the divine Mother, and for the first time in Christian history worship and devotion were far more fully directed to the Mother of God than to the Son of God. Thus, the Annunciation replaced the Nativity as the primary Christian icon, a transformation that is fulfilled in the *Commedia*. However, in the *Commedia* Mary is most embodied or incarnate as Beatrice, the one and only source of salvation for Dante, who can know either the Son of God or the Mother of God only through Beatrice. Beatrice is first unveiled in canto XXXI of the *Purgatorio*, which is the most intimate canto of the *Commedia*, and the only one in which Dante evokes his own name. Here, Beatrice makes manifest that *quia* or "thatness" which is her own center, a *quia* that is the very heart of the real, and which is given us even in the absence of a total understanding which would have precluded the necessity of the Incarnation.[2] Finally, *quia* is unspeakable but it is indubitably real, and real as a present and intimate actuality.

Perhaps this is the point at which we are closest to the essence of Catholicism, one wholly conjoining nature and grace. Dante can even know perception itself as a realization of compassion, the theme of Virgil's discourse on love in the canto XVIII of the *Purgatorio*. And, despite appearances to the contrary, this is no less true of Joyce, who enacts the absolutely common as a wholly prosaic redemption, or as Joy itself, a Joy in full continuity with the Joy of the *Commedia*, even if the heavenly Joy of the *Commedia* becomes the earthly Joy of *Ulysses* and *Finnegans Wake*. But this, too, is the essence of Catholicism, even if alien to all Catholic

---

[2]  *Purgatorio*, III, 37.

canons and catechisms, catechisms and canons which are alien to the glories of Catholic art and literature, and even alien to that *quia* which is the very heart of Catholicism. Catholicism can claim to be the most realistic of all ways, the one most embodying "thatness" itself, as celebrated in its great poets and artists, and as enacted in the Eucharist itself, and a uniquely Catholic Eucharist, wherein the Real Presence is the presence of the absolutely incarnate Christ.

Commonly the Real Presence is thought of as a supernatural or other-worldly presence, but precisely the opposite is true, for it is the ultimate presence of the world itself, or of that world which is a consequence of the Incarnation. Here, *quia* itself is all important, that *quia* or "thatness" which is the real itself, but one known in Catholicism as not being simply inseparable from grace, but finally indistinguishable from grace. So that to know *quia* is to realize grace, and to realize a prevenient and eternal grace, a realization only possible through Predestination, and precisely thereby only possible through freedom. Once again this is an ultimate paradox in the inseparability of freedom and Predestination, but this concretely occurs in a eucharistic consecration, one that is not only eternally predestined, but impossible apart from the absolutely free sacrifice of Christ, or the absolutely free sacrifice of God. Yet Catholicism can know the world itself as a consequence of that sacrifice, hence the world itself is a new world or new aeon, and it is only paganism that can know the world as old aeon or old creation.

Such an "old world" is not a truly actual world, not a world in which "thatness" is manifest, but far rather a truly passive or inactual world, a world in which freedom is impossible, and death or an eternal death is all in all. Certainly, Catholicism is absolutely inseparable from damnation and hell, as every Catholic knows, even if that knowledge is now unspeakable, and even as a Catholic redemption is meaningless apart from a redemption from damnation. This is damnation itself which most purely illuminates an "old world." And this is an ultimately passive condition precluding the possibility of "thatness," a "thatness" inseparable from a pure actuality, and a pure actuality that is nature and grace at once, as known by Catholicism alone. Is this the true mystery of Catholicism? A mystery that is the very opposite of the common identity of Catholicism, the opposite of absolute hierarchy and absolute order, or an absolute order that is not a wholly natural order, an ultimate "thatness" that is the very Body of Christ, or the very Body of God.

## Selected Bibliography

Dante, *The Divine Comedy*.

Joyce, James, *Finnegans Wake* (London: Faber & Faber, 1939).

# Chapter 10

# The Artist and the Mind of God

David Jasper

However, if we do discover a complete theory, it should in time be understandable in broad principle by everyone, not just a few scientists. Then we shall all, philosophers, scientists and just ordinary people, be able to take part in the discussion of the question of why it is that we and the universe exist. If we find the answer to that, it would be the ultimate triumph of human reason – for then we would know the mind of God.

(Stephen Hawking, *A Brief History of Time*)

But if all of us, and it would have to be universal for no debate could remain, were truly to know the mind of God, then indeed we should know everything and therefore nothing: for we would not be in a state of knowing but of pure being beyond all consciousness. It has been rightly observed of the scientific mind that "most major scientific theories rebuff common sense. They call on evidence beyond the reach of our senses and overturn the observable world. They disturb assumed relationships and shift what has been substantial into metaphor."[1] At the furthest reaches of the human mind, science and poetry meet, and beyond that there is indeed—*nothing*, perhaps the mind of God; one doubts it, one can but have faith. In his *Biographia Literaria* (1817), the poet and thinker Samuel Taylor Coleridge, against the background of scripture but drawing on his intellectual immersion in, among others, Kant and Schelling and German philosophy, describes the Primary Imagination as "the living Power and prime Agent of all human Perception, and as a repetition in the finite mind of the eternal act of creation in the infinite I AM."[2] If this indeed be the case, then the poet is at once and at the same time the most holy and the most profane of human beings, being at one, in the finite mind, with the

---

[1]  Gillian Beer, *Darwin's Plots* (London: Routledge & Kegan Paul, 1983), p. 3.

[2]  S.T. Coleridge, *Biographia Literaria* (1817). *The Collected Works*, Vol. 7, Part 1. Edited by James Engell and W. Jackson Bate (Princeton: Princeton University Press, 1983), p. 304.

mind and creative activity of God, and thereby trespassing, with ultimate daring, upon territory that is God's alone:

> Weave a circle round him thrice.
> And close your eyes with holy dread,
> For he on honey-dew hath fed,
> And drunk the milk of Paradise.[3]

Coleridge's contemporary, the madman and genius, William Blake, who walked among the fires of hell, delighted with the enjoyments of Genius, which to Angels look like torments and insanity,[4] associated the "poetic genius" with the Creator God without remainder, and in this the poet participates in this most Christocentric of all our poets. Isaiah, Blake's fellow poet, speaks to him:

> I saw no God, nor heard any, in a finite organical perception; but my sense discover'd the infinite in every thing, and as I was then perswaded, & remain confirm'd, that the voice of honest indignation is the voice of God, I cared not for consequences, but wrote.[5]

But few would willingly burn with Blake in the fires of hell. At the very most we might allow ourselves to be led, as the poet Virgil led Dante, as observers on the edge of the incomprehensible and prepared to contemplate the possibility that these poets among us, at the risk of their souls, might dare impossibly to think the unthinkable and to touch upon the region that can be known only in the mind of God. It was the breath of this region that Coleridge experienced when he encountered, in his own way, the aesthetics of incomprehensibility in German Romantic thought after the Kant of the Third Critique. In the region of such aesthetics Novalis, the student of Schiller and friend of Friedrich Schlegel, describes how "Everything

---

[3]    S.T. Coleridge, *Kubla Khan* (1798).

[4]    William Blake, *The Marriage of Heaven and Hell* (c.1790–93). *Complete Writings*. Edited by Geoffrey Keynes (Oxford: Oxford University Press, 1966), p. 150.

[5]    Ibid., "A Memorable Fancy", p. 153.

Visible cleaves to the Invisible – the Audible to the Inaudible – the Palpable to the Impalpable. Perhaps the Thinkable to the Unthinkable."[6]

Now let us change our tone for a moment. The primary sources of Christian theology—Judaism and Hellenism—both contain strong elements of the iconoclastic.[7] The fear of idolatry gives rise to the smashing of images, but there is a deeper, less well articulated fear also; the fear of ambivalence and of touching with the senses that which can only be profoundly unknowable. And yet, in spite of this fear, theology remains fascinated and inspired by the language of the artist and poet, aware of its deep commitment to that realm of thinking which knows the final inadequacy of the propositional frame of mind. In his "Letter on Humanism" (1947), Martin Heidegger provocatively argues for the "multidimensionality of the realm peculiar to thinking. The rigor of thinking, in contrast to that of the sciences, does not consist merely in an artificial, that is, technical-theoretical exactness of concepts. It lies in the fact that speaking remains purely in the realm of Being, and lets the simplicity of its manifold dimensions rule."[8] Such simplicity, however, is infinitely complex, available only in Heidegger's challenge to what "understanding," "knowing" or "thinking" finally mean.[9] At its heart in poetry is precisely the capacity to think not through and towards some hidden or obscure meaning, but rather a wisdom which is characterized by a "letting the unsayable be not said."[10]

We can suggest an example of precisely such knowing presented in Heidegger's reading of the first lines of the German Romantic poet Friedrich Hölderlin's Hymn "Germania."[11] Stated propositionally the poet here speaks of the disappearance and absence of the gods.

---

[6] Novalis, "Studies in the Visual Arts", quoted in Kathleen Wheeler (ed.), *German Aesthetic and Literary Criticism: The Romantic Ironists and Goethe* (Cambridge: Cambridge University Press, 1984), p. 14.

[7] George Pattison, *Art, Modernity and Faith: Restoring the Image* (London: Macmillan, 1991), pp. 10–11.

[8] Martin Heidegger, "Letter on Humanism", reprinted in Lawrence Cahoone (ed.), *From Modernism to Postmodernism: An Anthology* (Oxford: Blackwell, 1996), p. 276.

[9] Heidegger, *What is Called Thinking?* Trans. J. Glenn Gray (New York: Harper & Row, 1968).

[10] Quoted in Timothy Clark, *Martin Heidegger* (London: Routledge, 2002), p. 118.

[11] Heidegger, *Elucidations of Hölderlin's Poetry*. Trans. Keith Hoeller (New York: Humanity Books, 2000).

> Not them, the blessed, who once appeared,
>
> Those images of gods in the ancient land,
>
> Them, it is true, I may not now invoke ...[12]

But actually the flight and absence of the gods in the poem precisely open up a space in which "knowing" becomes possible—the gods for the first time actually known through their unknowability.

In the first instance I want to deliberately separate the epistemological foundations of such poetic "thinking" in the modern world from anything specifically religious or theological, though the connection will later, by implication, be reasserted. But to start with we need to link it with the intellectual tradition of what Coleridge calls the "clerisy," and what in a once famous and now largely forgotten work entitled *La Trahison de Clercs* (1927)—*The Treason of the Intellectuals*—Julien Benda identifies with the tradition of the "clerks."

> I mean [he writes] that class of men whom I shall call the *clercs*, gathering under that title those whose activity does not in its essence aim at practical goals, and who, finding their satisfaction in the practice of art, of science or of metaphysics (in short in the possession of unworldly wealth), announce in one way or another, "My kingdom is not of this world."

> ... the action of these *clercs* remained above all theoretical. They did not prevent hatreds or slaughter on the part of the laity. But they did prevent the people at large from making a religion out of its aspirations, from thinking itself important in attempting to realize them. *One can say that, thanks to them, humanity has for two thousand years performed evil but honoured goodness. That paradox is the glory of the human race, and the crack through which civilisation was able to slip.*[13]

---

[12]    Friedrich Hölderlin, *Poems and Fragments*. Trans. Michael Hamburger (London: Anvil, 1994), p. 423.

[13]    Julien Benda, *The Treason of the Intellectuals*. Trans. Richard Aldington (New Brunswick: Transaction Publishers, 2009), pp. 43–44. Emphases added.

One might immediately see why such a form of thinking could be associated with someone like Heidegger and his notorious adherence, despite his philosophical importance, to the Nazi Party. More broadly, and in a way no less disturbingly, it finds its nineteenth-century embodiment in such works as Coleridge's *On the Constitution of the Church and State* (1830), and Cardinal Newman's *The Idea of a University* (1873), and in forms of Romantic conservatism, religious and secular, that were opposed to that vocational and science-based approach to the education of the thinking mind which we should generally identify as Utilitarian. Its project begins with an abiding sense of the whole and an organic view of society and the human condition rather than with the individual abstracted from such holistic ways of thought "without which or divided from which," Coleridge remarks in an eerie anticipation of Heidegger's vocabulary, "his Being cannot even be thought."[14] In the nineteenth century, such thinking was located in what Owen Chadwick has carefully analyzed as the complex and paradoxical relationship between the onset of European secularization and religious faith (a complexity which was, and usually still is, over-simplified in debates between science and religion, often epitomized in the argument between T.H. Huxley and Bishop Samuel Wilberforce). Actually, we should remember, religious understanding has long been accommodated to the task of adjustment, albeit sometimes slow, to new knowledge about the world, and even to new ways of thinking that such knowledge seems to require. The real issue is approached when the question is asked whether the processes of "secular"—and largely scientific—thinking are "inseparable from an actual *reduction* of Christianity" and the mind is thrust "back upon the foundations of religious faith and practice."[15] It is at this point that the language of religion faces its most serious challenge, for once it begins to anticipate the epistemology and forms of the secular in its own defense, then the rift through which, in the words of Benda, civilization has slipped into the world, and whereby humanity continues to do evil yet honors good, is, paradoxically, sealed, religion forgets itself and the poetic language of faith is finally deserted.

---

[14]   S.T. Coleridge, *On the Constitution of the Church and State* (1830). Quoted in John Barrell, Introduction to the Dent edition (London: J.M. Dent, 1972), p. ix.

[15]   Own Chadwick, *The Secularization of the European Mind in the Nineteenth Century* (Cambridge: Cambridge University Press, 1975), p. 16.

We can look at this in two ways. As an admittedly at times rather confused disciple of German idealism, Coleridge drew from Kant the distinction between two ways of knowing in pure and practical reason. *Vernunft* is the higher way, translated by Coleridge as "reason," "through which truth could be directly apprehended, [and which] freed men from total dependence on naturalistically conditioned knowledge."[16] *Verstand*, on the other hand, called by Coleridge "understanding," is the lower faculty, a form of cognition that draws merely from phenomena.

But, and this is the second way, engagement purely with the former and higher way of knowing must necessarily be in a contemplative mode, taking us back to the ancient Christian prioritizing of the *vita contemplativa* over the *vita activa* which has its biblical origins in the story of Martha and Mary (Luke 10: 38–42) and in later Christianity in the contemplative traditions of monasticism which tend to emphasize "being" over "doing." Or, as a poet whose experience turned him against the religion of his fathers, wrote of his poems on World War I (the poet is Wilfred Owen): "these elegies are to this generation in no sense consolatory. They may be to the next. All a poet can do today is warn. *That is why the True Poets must be truthful.*"[17]

And so here is the dilemma, or the contradiction: thanks to the "clerks" humanity does evil but honors good. Poets and artists do nothing, their inutility at the very heart of the current onslaught on the humanities in universities as unproductive and unprofitable. And so why does Coleridge, himself a poet, fear the poets, and yet defend the clerisy? Plato would banish the poets from his Republic, yet their vision is close to the heart of Newman's "idea" of a university—an idea for which we now in our own time must fight. But we have not properly addressed the real rub of Benda's contradiction—that it is *thanks* to the "clerks" (or to the poets, or to those whose kingdom is not of this world) that humanity does evil—yet honors good. A clue to the heart of this dilemma, it may be suggested, lies in the perpetual dilemma in Christianity over the nature of art and the poetic. Without the church Western art is almost inconceivable, and yet it is precisely the church which has

---

[16]    Ben Knights, *The Idea of the Clerisy in the Nineteenth Century* (Cambridge: Cambridge University Press, 1978), p. 20.

[17]    Wilfred Own, Preface to *War Poems*. Edited by C. Day Lewis (London: Chatto & Windus, 1963), p. 31. Emphases added.

so often deliberately smashed beautiful objects or broken the hearts of poets like Gerard Manley Hopkins, nothing if not a religious man. St. Augustine in *The City of God* suggests that material things

> Offer their forms to the perception of our senses, those forms which give loveliness to the structure of this visible world ... We apprehend them by our bodily senses, but it is not by our bodily senses that we form a judgement on them. For we have another sense, far more important than any bodily sense, the sense of the inner man, by which we apprehend what is just and what is unjust, the just by means of the "idea" which is presented to the intellect, the unjust by the absence of it. The working of this sense has nothing to do with the mechanism of eye, ear, smell, taste or touch. It is through this sense that I am assured of my existence.[18]

In another work, the *Confessions*, Augustine writes with fine artistry of the dilemma for him:

> I have learnt to love you late, Beauty at once so ancient and so new! ... You were within me, and I was in the world outside myself. I searched for you outside myself and, disfigured as I was, I fell upon the lovely things of your creation ... The beautiful things of this world kept me far from you and yet, if they had not been in you, they would have had no being at all.[19]

Art and the language of poetry may then be signs of the beauty of the divine—but merely to fix our gaze on or give our attention to them is to fail to attend to the "idea" which is presented in them to us. And so even we may, perhaps, come to see without seeing, or know without knowing.

In what sense, then, may the poet be said to know the mind of God? Not, certainly, as Stephen Hawking might have us think, in the triumph of human reason. Rather it is in the extraordinary capacity of the human mind to think in

---

[18]   St. Augustine, *The City of God*. Trans. Henry Bettenson (Harmondsworth: Penguin, 1972), p. 462.

[19]   St. Augustine, *The Confessions*. Trans. R.S. Pine-Coffin (Harmondsworth: Penguin, 1961), pp. 231–232.

words beyond words, to hear and enact an impossibility through a medium that can dare to allow in words the unsayable to remain unsaid. Elsewhere I have written of Kant's memorable words in the *Critique of Practical Reason*[20]: "Two things flood the mind with ever increasing wonder and awe, the more often and the more intensely it concerns itself with them: the starry heavens above me and the moral law within me." But, as Arthur C. Danto has pointed out, what is even more awesome than the starry heavens and the moral law is the fact that Kant is aware of them; "that his consciousness can reach into the universe, both outer and inner, and is open to that which is, in itself, unpictureable and even unintelligible."

In exploring further this "consciousness" I would wish to move beyond the limits of the debate as set by Tina Beattie when she turns to "the power of narrative and story-telling to shape our lives" in her published debate with the New Atheists such as Dawkins and Hitchens.[21] For in Beattie's arguments the sense remains very much of the tone of those misguided nineteenth-century arguments between science and religion, and from them art (and therefore religion) emerge as too innocent in their championship of freedom against "every destructive and oppressive force."[22] The matter is actually more complex, more recessed, more ambivalent than that seems to suggest. For art and religion are both two-edged swords, and it is their deep love for and profound suspicion of one another that is the key to the mystery. Other words than suspicion come to mind—unease, contradiction, perhaps multiplicity—which drive the language of poetry and its way of knowing, its epistemology.

In his "Stanzas from the Grande Chartreuse" written in 1855, Matthew Arnold famously wrote, with gospel overtones written ironically into his language, of the nineteenth-century dilemma of faith:

> Wandering between two worlds, one dead,
> The other powerless to be born,
> With nowhere yet to rest my head,
> Like these, on earth I wait forlorn.

---

[20]    David Jasper, *The Sacred Body: Asceticism in Religion, Literature, Art and Culture* (Waco: Baylor University Press, 2009), p. xii.

[21]    Tina Beattie, *The New Atheists: The Twilight of Reason and the War on Religion* (London: Darton, Longman and Todd, 2007).

[22]    Ibid., p. 163.

The "these" refer to the men of faith who have inhabited the Grande Chartreuse, the monks of whose forebears, the Desert Fathers of Egypt, it was once said that "while dwelling on earth in this manner they live as true citizens of heaven."[23] What is driven apart in the dislocated language and culture of the Victorian Age, caught between the seemingly unreconcilable opposites of idealism and utilitarianism, science and religion, faith and materialistic unbelief, is the capacity of poetry to inhabit two (and perhaps more) worlds simultaneously, and thus to move us beyond Arnold's despair (though as a poet he knows this even while he remains abandoned on the darkling plain of martial ignorance).[24] The poetic imagination, as a repetition in the finite mind of the infinite I AM, lies at the very heart of the identity of the sacred community which sings the Sanctus simultaneously with the whole company of the faithful both in heaven and here on earth. And it is the identity and Being of this community which is sustained by a Knowing that is at the same time an unknowing—a contradiction, or, as Blake would have better described it, a "contrary," without which there is no progression. As with the monks of old, their worlds inaccessible to Arnold, the true poets do nothing, but in their contemplation human life is a possibility, or, as it is said in the *Historia Monachorum*, the *Lives of the Desert Fathers*, "through them too human life is preserved and honoured by God."

The key to "thinking" this in the nineteenth century lies in the dynamic form of idealism which we first find expressed in the writings of Coleridge. It is dynamic because it begins with a theory of mind and the world as process, sustained, for Coleridge, by the creative power of God.[25] Coleridge takes the step which Kant had failed to take to the transcendental conclusion—that all is mediated through the oneness of God, "the eternal identity of Allness and Oneness." In this oneness all is related and we come to God in the contemplation of the interdependence of all particulars, and thus we may perceive, however dimly, the one in the many. For

---

[23]    *The Lives of the Desert Fathers*. Trans. Norman Russell (Kalamazoo: Cistercian Publications, 1981), p. 50.

[24]    I refer to "Dover Beach":

"And we are here as on a darkling plain

Swept with confused alarms of struggle and flight,

Where ignorant armies clash by night."

[25]    Knights, *The Idea of Clerisy*, p. 43.

Coleridge the reality is the One in which alone the particulars can be understood. In a letter to James Gillman he wrote:

> The sum of all … is; that in all things alike, great and small; you must seek the *reality* not in any imaginary *elements* … All of which considered as other than elementary relations … Are mere fictions … The Alphabet of Physics no less of Metaphysics, of Physiology no less than of Psychology, is an Alphabet of *Relations*.[26]

Such thinking extends to the community in which the particulars are only perceived and known in the unity of the whole, and it is through poetry alone that this unity can begin to be articulated. Coleridge best describes this in his explanation of the "symbol"—which closely echoes the sense of the sacramental in both its materiality and its particularity. In his "Lay Sermon" of 1816 entitled *The Statesman's Manual*, Coleridge writes: "A Symbol … is characterized by a translucence of the Special in the Individual or of the General in the Especial or of the Universal in the General. Above all by the translucence of the Eternal through and in the Temporal. It always partakes of the Reality which it renders intelligible; and while it enunciates the whole, abides itself as a living part in that Unity, of which it is the representative."[27]

Thus in the symbol, which is known only through a community which is itself symbolic, the eternal is glimpsed through the temporal in an impossible act of knowing which is possible only through the participation of the "being" of the community. In this act of making, or *poeisis*, language renders intelligible that which is beyond comprehension, and it links Coleridge's symbolic, or better sacramental poetics with Heidegger's sense of what it means to "dwell poetically on the earth as a mortal."[28] James C. Edwards has described such Heideggerian dwelling thus:

---

[26]   Samuel Taylor Coleridge, *The Collected Letters*. Edited by E.L. Griggs (Oxford: Clarendon Press, 1956–1971), Vol. IV, p. 688.

[27]   Samuel Taylor Coleridge, *Lay Sermons. The Collected Works*, Vol. 6. Edited by R.J. White (Princeton: Princeton University Press, 1972), p. 30.

[28]   See, Martin Heidegger, "Being, Dwelling, Thinking", in *Basic Writings*. Revised Edition, edited by David Farrell Krell. (London: Routledge, 1993), pp. 344–363.

> To dwell poetically on the earth is to live in awareness of the godhead, the
> clearing, the blank but lightening sky. It is to live so as to measure oneself against
> that Nothing – that No-thing – that grants the possibility of the presence of and
> the Being of the things that there are. Within that clearing, as Heidegger puts it,
> brightness wars with darkness. There we struggle with particular ignorances and
> incapacities to bring forth truth.[29]

The triumph of reason is to respond to the provocation that what we usually call
thinking is merely a protection and therefore a bare maintaining of the status quo,
the thinking of what the poet describes as "*O curvae in terram animae et celestium
inanes*"—"Minds turned to the world and heedless of the heavens."[30] Rarely, in
science or religion, do we encounter thought that is only truly thinking when it
measures itself against its own impossibility. Such thinking alone facilitates a
dwelling poetically as a mortal, and allows a non-appropriative understanding of
the poetic and a kind of paradoxical knowing in which the sacred is already at
work within the poetic act, that is an act of pure stillness, an act of Being.[31]

In *Biographia Literaria*, Coleridge, with a reference back to Theseus in *A
Midsummer Night's Dream*,[32] describes his purpose in contributing to the *Lyrical
Ballads* as to "procure for these shadows of imagination that willing suspension of
disbelief for the moment, which constitutes poetic faith."[33] He is not playing games
here, whereby we might be prepared to believe, for the moment, in the fictional
world of the poem, play or novel. His purpose is much more serious, being about
that move from the reasonable into a deeper rationality that sustains contradictions
which require a renewed sense of wholeness and our place in it not as individuals
living alone, "in the sea of life enisled,"[34] but as an organic community into which
the poet, "diffuses a tone, and a spirit of unity, that blends, and (as it were) *fuses*,
each into each, by that synthetic and magical power, to which we have exclusively

---

[29]   James C. Edwards, *The Plain Sense of Things: The Fate of Religion in an Age of
Normal Nihilism* (University Park: Penn State University Press, 1997), p. 184.

[30]   Benda, *The Treason of the Intellectuals*, p. 43.

[31]   See further, Clark, *Martin Heidegger*, p. 120.

[32]   "The best in this kind are but shadows; and the worst are no worse, if imagination
amend them." Act 5, Sc. I, 211–212.

[33]   *Biographia Literaria*, Part 2, p. 6.

[34]   Matthew Arnold, "To Marguerite".

appropriated the name of imagination."[35] Only then, at this point, can we move on from words as merely instruments of technology and language as a poor means of reference to recover a sense of words as living things endued afresh with the sense of the sacred and a capacity ever to say more than they appear to say.

Those who have might been fortunate enough to experience the recent production of *King Lear* with Derek Jacobi, and its ability to reduce a theater to utter silence, will have known again the power of language to engender an extraordinary sense of wholeness, a necessary reminder in a world that is always moving on. As Marshall McLuhan expressed it:

> *King Lear* is a kind of elaborate case history of people translating themselves out of a world of roles into the new world of jobs. This is a process of stripping and denudation which does not occur instantly except in artistic vision. But Shakespeare saw that it had happened in his time. He was not talking about the future. However, the older world of roles had lingered on as a ghost.[36]

*King Lear* tragically follows a change from an inclusive to an exclusive sense of the world, from Cordelia's "being" with Lear—a form of poetic dwelling—that adds up to "nothing"—"nothing will come of nothing"—in a world of emergent "shrill and expansive individualism"[37] which results finally only in mutual destructiveness. More moving even than the death of Lear is the crucial scene when the aged king and Cordelia are led in by Edmund as prisoners in which Lear—envisaging a community with Cordelia which, even in prison, is not of this world, a way of being and knowing that is finally impervious to the "poor rogues" at court—speaks to Cordelia of their impending captivity. His vision is of an impossible world of mutual blessing and forgiveness in which in perfect unity they

> take upon's the mystery of things,
> As if we were God's spies: and we'll wear out,
> In a wall'd prison, pacts and sects of great ones

---

[35]  *Biographia Literaria*, Part 2, p. 16.

[36]  Marshall McLuhan, *The Gutenberg Galaxy* (Toronto: University of Toronto Press, 1962), p. 14.

[37]  Ibid., p. 15.

That ebb and flow by th' moon.

Upon such sacrifices, my Cordelia,

The Gods themselves throw incense. Have I caught thee?

He that parts us shall bring a brand from heaven,

And fire us hence like foxes. Wipe thine eyes;

The good years shall devour them, flesh and fell,

Ere they shall make us weep: we'll see 'em starv'd first.

Come.[38]

Of course, it is a vision that is never realized, nor could it possibly be, for the world must go on. In a short while Cordelia lies dead in her father's arms—a new *pieta*—and his heart breaks, never quite convinced of her earthly parting from him. But then the world must go on, sadder and wiser, as Edgar concludes the play.

The weight of this sad time we must obey;

Speak what we feel, not what we ought to say.

The oldest hath borne most: we that are young

Shall never see so much, nor live so long.[39]

In *King Lear*, what E.H. Gombrich in his book *Art and Illusion* (1960) calls the illusion of the third dimension is effected in the art of the stage in the illusory fall of Gloucester from the cliff. But in Lear's vision of the mystery of things, the third dimension is surpassed and transcended as he imagines looking down on the world—"as if we were God's spies."

The tragedy of *King Lear* marks a shift between two worlds, and it is a shift which drives Lear to madness and others to murderous conflict. But the way of knowing which we have been reflecting upon, the vision of dwelling poetically on earth as a mortal, is touched upon in the identity of the sacred community which is the community centered upon the sacrament in which finite and infinite touch and voices can be raised for a moment in harmony with heaven in the singing of the Sanctus. This is a community of poetic voices that pays a heavy price for its necessary contradictions in this world and always has done, for its

---

[38]   *King Lear*, Act 5, Sc. III, 16–26.

[39]   Ibid., Act 5, Sc. III, 322–325.

passion is salvation. It is from this passion alone that the poet writes, even, as Blanchot has reminded us, one as despairing as Franz Kafka, for "salvation is an enormous preoccupation with him, all the stronger because it is hopeless, and all the more hopeless because it is totally uncompromising."[40] For the poet and sacred community, whose language is an unutterable poetry, alone know the depths of evil at the root of the tragedy of Lear, and, as Terry Eagleton has recently written:

> On the whole, postmodern cultures, despite their fascination with ghouls and vampires, have had little to say of evil. Perhaps this is because the postmodern man or woman – cool, provisional, laid-back and decentred – lacks the depth that true destructiveness requires. For postmodernism there is nothing really to be redeemed. For high modernists like Franz Kafka, Samuel Beckett, or the early T. S. Eliot, there is indeed something to be redeemed, but it has become impossible to say quite what.[41]

Perhaps in the later Eliot, the social critic of *The Idea of a Christian Society*, published in 1939 a few months after the outbreak of World War II, though not altogether in the poet of the *Four Quartets*, this impossible vision becomes caught in a static portrait of a monolithic "Christian world-order," of a society dominated by the church with its "explicit ethical and theological standards."[42] This is quite different from the way of knowing that we have been pursuing which is at once more fragile and contradictory, even given to tragedy, and yet more enduring than anything in its inutility and its manner of contemplation. Such a way of knowing celebrates no ultimate triumph of human reason in its conversations with the divine and is even content to be forgotten by the urgent imperatives of the ever-present world order, knowing of it only that in their being human, human beings are mixed creatures striving for wholeness and integrity.[43]

---

40    Maurice Blanchot, *The Space of Literature*. Trans. Ann Smock (Lincoln: University of Nebraska Press, 1982), p. 57.

41    Terry Eagleton, *On Evil* (New Haven: Yale University Press, 2010), p. 15.

42    T.S. Eliot, "Religion and Literature" (1935), in *Selected Essays*. Third Edition (London: Faber & Faber, 1951), p. 388.

43    See further, David E. Klemm and William Schweiker, *Religion and the Human Future: An Essay on Theological Humanism* (Oxford: Blackwell, 2008).

The novelist J.G. Ballard once wrote a brief story entitled "The Life and Death of God."[44] Here, in a declaration signed by 300 scientists and divines, it is affirmed categorically that "God Exists: Supreme Being Pervades the Universe," an existence proven by the observation of a system of "ultra-microwaves." The consequence is not a cause for joy but it is the utter breakdown of all order in human society. Theology is now become a science of certainty—and nothing in society, politics or religion makes any sense whatsoever. "The term 'deity' was, in any useful sense, meaningless," and it is the United Faith Assembly which proclaims in its Christmas encyclical that *God is Dead* …. It is, in fact, the rebirth of the ultimate contradiction and the resurrection of speech, known, for Christianity in the passion narrative. In the words of the American theologian Thomas J.J. Altizer:

> The real ending of speech is the dawning of resurrection, and the final ending of speech is the dawning of a totally present actuality. That actuality is immediately at hand when it is heard, and it is heard when it is enacted. And it is enacted in the dawning of the actuality of silence, an actuality ending all disembodied and unspoken presence. The speech is truly impossible, and as we hear and enact that impossibility, then even we can say: "It is finished."[45]

## Selected Bibliography

Altizer, Thomas J.J. *The Self-Embodiment of God* (New York: Harper & Row, 1977).

Benda, Julien, *The Treason of the Intellectuals*. Trans. Richard Aldington (New Brunswick: Transaction Publishers, 2009).

Clark, Timothy, *Heidegger* (London: Routledge, 2002).

Knights, Ben, *The Idea of the Clerisy in the Nineteenth Century* (Cambridge: Cambridge University Press, 1978).

---

[44]    J.G. Ballard, *Low-Flying Aircraft and Other Stories* (London: Triad/Panther, 1978), pp. 136–147.

[45]    Thomas J.J. Altizer, *The Self-Embodiment of God* (NewYork: Harper & Row, 1977), p. 96.

# Chapter 11

# Living Up To Death

Pamela Sue Anderson

In my recent work on *Living up to Death*, I have proposed that Ricoeur scholars should move from thinking about Ricoeur's texts to his life as a thinker. In fact, after his death in 2005, Ricoeur's own texts direct readers back to reflection on his active life of thinking.[1] For me, this reflection has involved two tasks. First, I have urged readers to reflect on Ricoeur's Spinozist affirmation of the distinctiveness of human life. Life should express, in Ricoeur's own words, 'the Joy of "yes" in the sadness of the finite'.[2] This is an expression which David Klemm, as will be well-known to his friends, has cited more than once in person, but also in print.[3] As we reflect, life as the joy of 'yes' in the sadness of the finite only becomes more poignant as we grow older and witness the fragility of each of our lives.

Second, I have urged an attentive reading of the posthumously published fragments of Ricoeur's last thoughts on death near the end of his own life.[4] In his unpublished notes written about death (when his wife was dying), and while 'living

---

[1]  Pamela Sue Anderson, 'From Ricoeur to Life: "Living up to Death" with Spinoza, but also with Deleuze', in Todd Mei and David Lewin (eds), *From Ricoeur to Action* (London and New York: Continuum, 2012), pp. 19–32.

[2]  See Paul Ricoeur, *Fallible Man*, trans. C. Kelbley with an introduction by Walter J. Lowe (New York: Fordham University Press, 1986), p. 140. Compare Benedict de Spinoza, *Ethics*, ed. and trans. G.H.R. Parkinson (Oxford: Oxford University Press, 2000), pp. 257–259.

[3]  This phrase from Ricoeur's *Fallible Man* is quoted by David Klemm, 'Searching for a Heart of Gold: A Ricoeurian Meditation on Moral Striving and the Power of Religious Discourse', in John Wall, William Schweiker and W. David Hall (eds), *Paul Ricoeur and Contemporary Moral Thought* (New York: Routledge, 2002), p. 103; cf. Ricoeur, *Fallible Man*, p. 140.

[4]  For the posthumously published fragments of Ricoeur's thoughts near and at the end of his own life, see Paul Ricoeur, *Living Up To Death*, trans. D. Pellauer (Chicago: University of Chicago Press, 2009), pp. 11–22; cf. Anderson, 'From Ricoeur to Life', pp. 21, 25–28.

up to death' (when he was approaching his own death), Ricoeur demonstrates clearly that a philosophy of life cannot be merely reflection upon 'an abstract idea' of finitude. Instead the philosopher must seek simultaneously 'the concrete core' of living and the abstract dimension of thinking up to death.

For this chapter, I have chosen for my subtitle to appropriate the title of one of David Klemm's own essays on Ricoeur, 'Searching for the Heart of Gold: A Ricoeurian Meditation on Moral Striving and the Power of Religious Discourse',[5] in order to reflect hermeneutically on what it is we are actually searching for in living up to death. When Ricoeur reflects on dying as the sadness of the finite, he claims that finitude goes towards a 'limit beginning from the inside' and 'not toward a boundary that our gaze can cross'.[6] Here we recognise a Kantian understanding of moving towards a 'limit' (*Schranken*), but the question is whether Ricoeur's own self-description as post-Hegelian Kantian also allows for a Spinozist understanding of living within Kant's 'unmoveable boundaries' (*unveraendliche Grenzen*).[7]

Arguably, in *Living Up To Death*, Ricoeur gives a highly distinctive Spinozist dimension to his post-Hegelian philosophy. Yet with this, Ricoeur's thinking begins to appear 'un-Kantian' insofar as he ignores, if not rejects, the Kantian postulate of immortality. Can Ricoeur 'have it both ways'? On the one hand, there is his necessarily obscure thought of 'being toward the end or for the end, from within', when finitude for the person who is dying remains 'a gaze that *forbids* itself *a bird's eye view, one from above, on a boundary whose two sides could be looked at – from above*'.[8] On the other hand, Ricoeur describes the concrete core of death's mark on our finitude as 'the anticipated agony of the dying person looked at from the person who witnesses and survives that death'.[9] Both the *passion* of dying and the *anticipated agony* of those who will witness (his) death take Ricoeur in the direction of Spinoza.

---

[5]   Klemm, 'Searching for a Heart of Gold', pp. 97–116.

[6]   Ricoeur, *Living Up To Death*, pp. 11–12.

[7]   Pamela Sue Anderson, 'Metaphors of Spatial Location: Understanding Post-Kantian Space', in Roxana Baiasu, Graham Bird and A.W. Moore (eds), *Kantian Metaphysics Today: New Essays on Time and Space* (New York: Palgrave Macmillan, 2012), pp. 167–192.

[8]   Ricoeur, *Living Up To Death*, p. 11, italics added.

[9]   Ricoeur, *Living Up To Death*, pp. 12–14.

After having defended Ricoeur's post-Hegelian Kantianism in my own early writings, it was initially surprising (to me at least) to find the prominence of Spinoza in Ricoeur's thinking about this life, especially before his own death, and his anticipation of life after death. Given his own place of birth in France and his suffering of personal losses in two world wars, Ricoeur does fit into a French twentieth-century tradition which re-interpreted Spinoza, in particular, to think about life, not death, and 'the primordial power that Spinoza ... name[s] "God"'.[10] Ricoeur himself is explicit in praising Spinoza's *Ethics* for thinking life.

The inspirational role of a Spinozist sense of life is clear in the last of his published Gifford Lectures, 'What Ontology in View?'.[11] With reference to Sylvain Zac, Ricoeur defends the conviction that 'all Spinozist themes can be centered around the notion of life'.[12] He also cautions that

> We should not, however, forget that the passage from inadequate ideas, which we form about ourselves and about things, to adequate ideas signifies for us the possibility of being truly *active*. In this sense, the power to act can be said to be increased by the retreat of passivity tied to inadequate ideas (cf. [Spinoza,] *Ethics*, bk. 3, prop. 1, proof and corollary). This conquest of activity under the aegis of adequate ideas makes the work as a whole an *ethics*. Thus there is a close connection between the internal dynamism worthy of the name of life and the power of the intelligence, which governs the passage from inadequate to adequate ideas. In this sense, we are powerful when we understand adequately our, as it were, horizontal and external dependence with respect to all things, and our vertical and immanent dependence with respect to the primordial power that Spinoza continues to name 'God'.[13]

A careful reading of *Oneself as Another*, but also of Ricoeur's earlier work on a philosophy of the will, demonstrates that Spinoza's *Ethics* had a profound, enduring impact upon Ricoeur's characteristically twentieth-century French

---

[10]  Paul Ricoeur, *Oneself as Another*, trans. K. Blamey (Chicago: University of Chicago Press, 1992), p. 316.

[11]  Ricoeur, *Oneself as Another*, pp. 298, 315–317.

[12]  Sylvain Zac, *L'Idée de vie dans la philosophie de Spinoza* (Paris: PUF, 1963), pp. 15–16; cf. Ricoeur, *Oneself as Another*, p. 315.

[13]  Ricoeur, *Oneself as Another*, pp. 316; cf. *Fallible Man*, p. 140.

philosophy. In turn it is Spinoza together with Kant informing Ricoeur's *Fallible Man* that is evident in David Klemm's philosophical theology. In fact Klemm witnesses to the significance of Ricoeur's distinctively 'religious' philosophy in 'On Searching for the Heart of Gold', especially the Ricoeurian 'moral striving' and 'power of religious discourse' within this life. 'Life', as seen in (the block quotation from) Ricoeur, includes the assumption of a Spinozist 'power' in moving from 'inadequate' to 'adequate' ideas. It also includes the power to 'understand adequately' the location of thinking within a social-political reality such as life after the Second World War in France. My argument in the present chapter is about Ricoeur giving a highly significant reading of Spinoza after Kant. In recent years I have followed Ricoeur's own writings carefully back to Spinoza's *Ethics*, but also back to other neo-Kantians. From reading Ricoeur's texts and their connection to the life of French philosophy, it quickly becomes clear that other neo-Kantian philosophers in twentieth-century France turn to Spinoza.

For example, the French early twentieth-century, neo-Kantian philosopher Jean Nabert draws upon Spinoza's conception of *conatus*, in order to understand life in terms of activity and passivity. Ricoeur frequently mentions 'the desire to be' and 'the effort to exist' as phrases drawn from Spinoza, but also explicitly admits the guidance he received from Nabert's neo-Kantianism which directed Ricoeur to these Spinozist ideas.[14] For another example, although Ricoeur does not mention Gilles Deleuze, Deleuze is a major twentieth-century French philosopher who wrote extensively on Spinoza and life.[15]

Directly and indirectly Ricoeur – even after his death – pushes his readers into new dialogues with a great range of French and other European philosophers.[16]

---

[14]   For more background on Ricoeur's debt to Jean Nabert, see Ricoeur's postscript and prefaces in the following: Philippe Capelle (ed.), *Jean Nabert et la question du divin*, Postface de Paul Ricoeur (Paris: Les Éditions du Cerf, 2003); Jean Nabert, *Éléments pour une éthique*, Préface de Paul Ricoeur (Paris: Aubier, 1992); and Nabert, *L'Expérience intérieure de la liberté*, Préface de Paul Ricoeur (Paris: PUF, 1994), respectively. For Ricoeur's own early lectures on Spinoza in Paris, see the Archives, *Fonds Ricoeur*, Paris, at www.fondsricoeur.fr.

[15]   Gilles Deleuze, *Expressionism in Philosophy: Spinoza*, trans. M. Joughin (New York: Zone Books, 1992).

[16]   For Ricoeur's possible differences to other European twentieth-century philosophers such as Heidegger and Derrida on death, see Christina Howells, *Mortal Subjects: Passions of the Soul in Late Twentieth-Century French Thought* (Cambridge: Polity Press, 2012), pp. 89–93.

Ricoeur in living and thinking sought to understand life and those who wrote about living. Now, from our vantage point in the twenty-first century, we can see how Ricoeur's Spinozist account of the interaction between living and thinking resonates with the provocative claim that 'Only life explains the thinker'.[17] But the converse claim is also true for Ricoeur. In brief, not only would Ricoeur himself agree that certain reciprocal relations between living and thinking must be acknowledged as true, but that his life's work demonstrates the converse: that the thinker explains life.

This reciprocal relation makes more sense when it is understood in terms of Ricoeur's post-Hegelian Kantian philosophy. Rather than an incompatibility between Spinoza's *Ethics* and Kant's postulate of immortality, Ricoeur as a post-Hegelian thinker who explains life and whose life explains him as a thinker brings the two rationalist philosophers, Spinoza and Kant, together. The very fact that Ricoeur gives priority to living, not death, and to a philosophy of life is Spinozist.[18] But the fact that Ricoeur gives priority to thinking (life, especially human freedom) is equally Kantian.

Domenico Jervolino confirms that an 'active life' is central to Ricoeur's thinking. The Spinozist tones in Jervolino's words about (Ricoeur's) ethics are clear in the following:

> to exist in time, to live historically our liberation as humans, to live by thinking and think by living. To carry out this task of transforming the human desire and effort to exist into an active, responsible human practice ... [this] is what can be called 'ethics'.[19]

Previously I have argued that, following Nabert's appropriation of Spinoza, Ricoeur interprets 'the desire to be' and 'the effort to exist' as a fundamentally

---

[17] Gilles Deleuze, *Spinoza: Practical Philosophy*, trans. Robert Hurley (San Francisco: City Light Books, 1988), p. 14.

[18] For more background on the role of life in Ricoeur's thinking, see Pamela Sue Anderson, 'Ricoeur and Women's Studies: On the Affirmation of Life and a Confidence in the Power to Act', in Scott Davidson (ed.), *Ricoeur Across the Disciplines* (New York: Continuum, 2010), pp. 142–143.

[19] Domenico Jervolino, 'The Depth and the Breadth of Paul Ricoeur's Philosophy', in Edwin Hahn (ed.), *The Philosophy of Paul Ricoeur* (Chicago: Open Court, 1995), p. 538.

human 'cognitive-conative capability'.[20] So cognition and conation characterise Ricoeur's conception of a fundamentally human capability, making possible *two distinct powers* of acting and of suffering.[21] Moreover, Ricoeur makes a 'connection between the phenomenology of the acting and suffering self' and 'the actual and potential ground against which selfhood stands out' on the basis of Spinoza's *conatus*.[22] This means that power is not merely potential, or actual doing in everyday life, it is productive ontologically. In other words, it is crucially empowering life. The effort to exist is an always unsatisfied desire; but the desire to be gives power in the sense of productivity to the subject in acting but also in individual suffering. The priority which Ricoeur gives to *conatus* is crucial to his descriptions of 'the ethical;' and this means that neither Aristotle nor Kant is sufficient for Ricoeur's ethics.

With a Spinozist conception of *conatus*, ensuring that a line of continuity runs through the relation of activity (*potentia*), as an actual (human) power and of the productivity (*potestas*) (of humans) to be affected, Ricoeur renders the human subject capable of expressing her own nature and not merely reacting to the nature of another. For a Spinozist, increasing activity is an expression of (human) freedom.[23] So, the point to bear in mind, with Ricoeur, is that the relation of actual power (*potentia*), plus productive capacity (*potestas*), constitutes a fundamental condition of *conatus* for each human life. I am less clear that Ricoeur's idea of human freedom can be anything but Kantian; more work would need to be done on Spinoza's conception of freedom in relation to 'life', but also to Kantian autonomy to see whether Ricoeur discovers a link between these two rationalists.

A critical passage from *Living Up To Death* shows that Ricoeur never gives up living and thinking, even struggling to go beyond – as he says (below) – 'the make-believe death' which is merely an abstract idea. A summary of Ricoeur's Spinozist position on 'living up to death' appears as follows:

---

20    Pamela Sue Anderson, 'On Loss of Confidence: Dissymmetry, Doubt, Deprivation in the Power to Act and (the Power) to Suffer,' in Joseph Carlisle, James C. Carter and Daniel Whistler (eds), *Moral Powers, Fragile Beliefs: Essays in Moral and Religious Philosophy* (London: Continuum, 2011), pp. 84, 85–89.

21    Ricoeur, *Oneself as Another*, pp. 315–317.

22    Ricoeur, *Oneself as Another*, p. 315.

23    *Spinoza: Practical Philosophy*, pp. 97–99.

The idea that I must die one day, I do not know when, or how, carries too flimsy a certitude ... for my desire to take hold of ... (distinguishing the two phrases): a desire to be, an effort to exist. I am well aware of everything that has been written and said about anxiety about one day no longer existing. But, if the path has to be taken up again of an accepted finitude, it is after the struggle with the make-believe death ...

Dying as an event: passing ending, finishing: In one way, my dying tomorrow is on the same side as my being-already-dead tomorrow. On the side of the future perfect tense. What we call a dying person is one only for those who attend his agony, who maybe help him in his agony – ...

To think of myself as one of these dying people is to imagine myself as the dying person I shall be for those who attend my dying. Nevertheless the difference between these two make-believe situations is large. To be present at a death is more precise, more poignant than simply surviving ... But, in the end, it is still for me an internalized anticipation, the most terrifying one, that of the dying person I shall be for those who attend my death. Well! I am saying that it is the anticipation of this agony that constitutes the concrete core of the 'fear of death'.[24]

From this, it is relevant equally to remember the extent to which Ricoeur's life had been marked by traumatic deaths (his father in the First World War; his mother not long after his birth; his sister and only sibling as a young adult before his marriage; one of his sons to suicide; his wife; friends and other contemporaries in the Second World War and so on). And yet, remember the extent to which his philosophical thinking always aimed to celebrate living.

Here is where I return to paraphrase the expression about life which Klemm is so fond of citing, from Ricoeur's *Fallible Man*, it is 'the Joy of "yes" in the sadness of the finite'.[25] As stated at the outset, *Fallible Man* acknowledges the sadness running through the passionate dimensions of human life which we have equally found in Ricoeur's own life and in his thinking life. In fact, Ricoeur's

---

[24] *Living Up To Death*, p. 13.
[25] Ricoeur, *Fallible Man*, p. 140; cf. Spinoza, *Ethics*, pp. 257–259.

post-Hegelian Kantian philosophy in this gem of a book actually moves through different stages which roughly follow Kant's three *Critiques* of human knowing, acting and feeling. In this way, Ricoeur both confronts the conative extremes of sadness-joy and finds cognitive coherence in a Kantian architectonic. The structure of *Fallible Man* reflects the manner in which Ricoeur reads Kant, and yet his Kantian subject can never completely transcend its passionate life. So Ricoeur rereads Kant to sketch his architectonic of human life, culminating in the human capacity for self-affection. Crucial to self-affectivity is the role of both activity and passivity, in the phenomenology of acting and suffering. As mentioned already, in Ricoeur's later *Oneself as Another*, he returns to metaphysical questions about life, its powers in acting and suffering, its being and nonbeing; he addresses life's active and passive emotions. In retrospect, we now can recognise what is latent in *Fallible Man*: Ricoeur's desire to transform a (Spinozist) *conative* power in the effort to exist and the desire to be. This conative power becomes crucial to Ricoeur's description of a conative-cognitive capability which, in his *Reflections on the Just*, will also suffer a dis-abling (cognitive) loss due to the injustice we afflict upon one another.[26] In this light, fear of death is not the only (conative-cognitive) experience of suffering to which human life remains vulnerable.

Not only does Ricoeur describe the distinctiveness of human life as 'the Joy of "yes" in the sadness of the finite',[27] but he recalls Spinoza's definition of sadness as a passion which moves the soul in the direction of a lesser perfection.[28] Ricoeur extends Spinoza's *Ethics* to understand the most extreme forms of sadness which afflict the capable subject. I cannot do justice to the rich uniqueness of Ricoeur's last writings on human capability, of acting and suffering. Yet we can continue to read Ricoeur in dialogue with other philosophers who turn to Spinoza in order to believe in this life, its passions and its possibilities.

To conclude, I have urged that we attend to the posthumously published fragments of Ricoeur's last thoughts on death near the end of his own life, while recalling his long trajectory of post-Hegelian Kantian philosophy, including his neo-Kantian Spinozist thinking and ethical striving in this life. As a tribute to

---

[26]   Ricoeur, 'Autonomy and Vulnerability', *Reflections on The Just*, trans. D. Pellauer (Chicago: University of Chicago Press, 2007), pp. 75–77.

[27]   Ricoeur, *Fallible Man*, p. 140; also see pp. 106 and 139.

[28]   Spinoza, *Ethics*, pp. 257–259.

David Klemm, I have also chosen to pay careful attention to Ricoeur's early claim that 'life is the joy of "yes" in the sadness of the finite'. The saying of a joyful 'yes' even in the face of an all-too finite life is an expression which in fact reminds me of Klemm's own writings on Ricoeur. In 'Searching for the Heart of Gold: A Ricoeurian Meditation on Moral Striving and the Power of Religious Discourse',[29] Klemm urges us to follow Ricoeur in bringing his ethics together with religion; this is a union of disciplines which is sought by Klemm and was sought not only by Ricoeur and Kant, but by Spinoza.

Crucially, Klemm also asks us 'for theological reasons to provide a deeper analysis of religious feeling in relation to dialectical thinking than Ricoeur does'.[30] I present a sample of Klemm's own thinking in the 'deeper analysis' here:

> Immediate self-consciousness is not necessarily religious. It becomes so precisely with the felt insight that the self's positing itself as being posited is itself posited by the absolute ground and goal of all human thinking – that is, what Schleiermacher calls the Whence of the feeling of absolute dependence or 'God'. What does Schleiermacher mean by 'religious feeling' so described? Ricoeur has the best answer. It is precisely the lived feeling – psychological and empirical – of the Joy of Yes in the Sadness of the finite. The felt element of joy arises from the free activity of self-positing; the felt element of sadness arises from the sheer contingent givenness of being-posited. The felt element of the Yes – the affirmation and love of life – grounds both joy and sadness. The Yes is the felt capacity to embrace both the joyful and the sorrowful. In its absence the self oscillates between joy and sadness – seeking joy, fleeing sadness. Together they constitute the feeling of the love of life, gratitude for the goodness of finite being. There is nothing arbitrary about this religious feeling; it expresses the dialectically conceived essence of the self. When it is aroused by religious discourse, we humans receive the religious power that can change the heart.[31]

I am not sure if there is anything greater that we can learn about human life than to search confidently for a 'heart of gold'. This is the heart changed to the gold that

---

29    Klemm, 'Searching for a Heart of Gold', pp. 97–116.
30    Klemm, 'Searching for a Heart of Gold', p. 113.
31    Klemm, 'Searching for a Heart of Gold', p. 114.

is glimpsed in the living of thinkers like Ricoeur and Klemm. Klemm continues to teach us how to reflect hermeneutically on living up to death and on moral striving and the power that names 'God'.

## Selected Bibliography

Todd Mei and David Lewin (eds), *From Ricoeur to Action* (London and New York: Continuum, 2012).

Paul Ricoeur, *Fallible Man*. Trans. C. Kelbley (New York: Fordham University Press, 1986).

Paul Ricoeur, *Oneself as Another*. Trans. K. Blamey (Chicago: Chicago University Press, 1992).

Paul Ricoeur, *Living Up To Death*. Trans. D. Pellauer (Chicago: Chicago University Press, 2009).

John Wall, William Schweiker and W. David Hall (eds), *Paul Ricoeur and Contemporary Moral Thought* (New York: Routledge, 2002).

# Chapter 12

# Historical Consciousness and Freedom

Dale S. Wright

This chapter seeks articulation of the most recent development in the history of historical consciousness—emergence of reflexivity—a self-conscious awareness of our own human envelopment within history. This recent historical development can best be understood and appreciated within the larger context of other dimensions of historical consciousness. For this reason we begin with an overarching hypothesis about the gradual emergence of historical consciousness within human history. This hypothesis is that there are at this point in human history, and in human consciousness, three—perhaps four—forms or levels of historical awareness and that each embodies a distinct form of human freedom. The hypothesis begins with the thought that human beings became historical, and historically conscious, when their grammar developed tense or time, and when story telling emerged in the midst of language use. This development would have come to its most telling form in archaic mythology. When myths began to tell stories about creation—where we came from, who we are, and what we are to do—these narratives about the beginning of time initiate historical consciousness.

Accordingly, in *The Sacred and the Profane*, Mircia Eliade claimed that, "myth relates a sacred history, that is, a primordial event that took place at the beginning of time, *ab initio* … myth proclaims the appearance of a new cosmic situation or of a primordial event. Hence it is always the recital of a creation; it tells how something was accomplished, began to be."[1] Although in that work and elsewhere Eliade contrasts historical thinking with mythical thinking, no one was clearer on the degree to which mythic thinking begins the process of historicizing human culture by placing current or future cultural practices in relation to a past and primordial order of time. This first form of historical consciousness is basically

---

[1]    Mircia Eliade, *The Sacred and the Profane* (New York: Harper & Row, 1959), p. 95.

synonymous with the breakthrough to linguistically articulated communal identity and the development of particular traditions of human thinking. The kinds of human freedom made possible by that development are so monumental that I won't attempt to address them here, but they encompass all the forms of cultural freedom that language using, story-telling creatures demonstrate in their lives and that other primates do not.

A possible second form of historical consciousness may have emerged in the Axial Age of the further development of written culture, but here I only pose a question I am in no position to answer right now: this is whether the first written histories—the historical books of the Hebrew Bible, the Greek and Chinese histories written before the common era—Heroditus and Ssu-ma Chien—whether these constitute a textuality-generated breakthrough in historical consciousness, or whether the advent of historical writing simply begins a gradual process of transformation from the mythical sense of the eternal return of the same to the nineteenth-century, critical-historical and evolutionary sense of the eternal proliferation of difference. Does the emergence of history writing constitute a breakthrough to a new historical sensibility or is it simply that mythology in literate cultures gradually takes on more historical specificity by virtue of being written but that its essential structure is still myth—stories that, while different, are meant to reveal what is structurally true for all time, the eternal nature of things? That and many other questions I leave open for further reflection in order to proceed to the focus of this chapter.

By the turn of the eighteenth into the nineteenth century in Europe, a new form of historical awareness emerged when interpreters of sacred and classic texts began to realize that changes in language, culture, and worldview might mean that our way of understanding the transmitted teachings of Jesus or Socrates may not coincide with their author's original intentions. History, we realized, impels change—significant structural change—and in order to understand the past, our readings would require a new kind of methodical, critical questioning to account for changes wrought by the passage of time. Schleiermacher, as is widely known, was the most thoughtful theoretician of this new historical understanding. His revival and systematic transformation of the classical art of hermeneutics rests on the thought that, especially in historical inquiry, if we proceed on the assumption that understanding occurs naturally, that assumption will inevitably yield misunderstanding because the passage of time propels social/cultural differentiation, transformations in language and worldview that open a crevasse of distance between text and interpreter.

For Schleiermacher, then, what the text seems to say to us *cannot* be what it originally meant to say. Its original meaning, therefore, is recoverable only through a rigorous science of history that methodically reconstructs the cultural and linguistic patterns of past societies. The new discipline of historical understanding would demand that interpreters extricate themselves from the entanglements of the present so that their own views don't prejudice or distort human meanings that derive from altogether different cultural worlds. The form of freedom that corresponds to modern historical consciousness is the freedom of change—the freedom to acknowledge and to cultivate change, the freedom to value change and to seek it intentionally. Therefore, modern historical awareness brings to light the freedoms associated with innovation, with imagination and human creativity, that is, the forms of freedom brought to conceptual articulation for the first time in the Romantic movement.

Finally, a third (or fourth) dimension. As we moved through the nineteenth century and into the twentieth, it began to seem that any thinking about humanity or any aspect of human culture that *isn't* historically attuned is necessarily naïve. History isn't just one discipline among others, but a fundamental dimension of all disciplines. Although Hegel and Nietzsche are the prophets of this new historical awareness, Heidegger is its thinker, based on his claim that the human mode of being is itself historical through and through just by virtue of the truth that the meaning of being is time. Rather than "having a history," Heidegger asks what it means that human beings *are* historical? Heidegger's reflexive orientation within historical consciousness constitutes the most recent and most sophisticated turn in the sequence of our overarching hypothesis, and this is where the remainder of this chapter dwells.

In Division II of Martin Heidegger's monumental *Being and Time*, where he is working out his early conception of "authentic historicality," Heidegger claims that "what is primarily historical is Dasein, human being-in-the-world itself. That which is secondarily historical ... is what we encounter within-the-world,"[2] that

---

[2]  Martin Heidegger, *Being and Time* (New York: Harper & Row, 1962), p. 433.

which is "historical by reason of belonging to the world."[3] "World" in this setting means not the totality of objectively existing entities, but rather the referential context of human significance, the web of cultural meanings that render what we are doing intelligible. For the most part, historians today and in the past track what Heidegger calls the "secondarily historical," that is human artifacts, institutions, and activities that reflect a past world of human culture. An ancient Chinese gravestone is historical, as are Stonehenge and the marble caryatides of the Acropolis, but the million-year-old stones found along a mountain stream are not because, although they have been shaped by an extensive past of development and decomposition, they become historical only when they are marked by their involvement in a human cultural world. Gravestones are historical by virtue of their cultural grounding in the myths and rituals that give meaning to death.

Correlatively, the myths and rituals that render these stones historical are themselves historical, indeed, even more primordially so. Social institutions such as marriage are historical not just in the sense that they develop over time and are therefore different in different epochs, but in the further, more basic sense that those who participate in them understand who they are through the myths and rituals that ground these institutions. This background of understanding makes particular forms of life intelligible, and their meanings are inscribed upon the lives of participants as they carry them out in socially sanctioned practices, customs, and rituals. Therefore, following Heidegger's lead, we would say that the objective history of how a human society has developed is subordinate to a more fundamental historical understanding that establishes that culture in the first place by grounding social norms and customs in sacred history. These narratives function less to explain why things are this way than to *make* them this way by inscribing their intentions and purposes onto all dimensions of cultural life.

So even though the societies chronicled in Eliade's many pre-literate cultures did not record history or think historically in the developmental sense, they were in fact deeply historical in this more basic sense. Their mythical histories functioned not primarily to explain a cultural world but rather to create and sustain such a world. Participants in them lived the lives they lived by identifying with stories about how things were founded *in ille tempore*—in the beginning—and this proto-historical identity structures their self-understanding. That we modern historians

---

[3]    Ibid., p. 433.

would develop the capacity to trace the historical evolution of this identity is secondary to the more basic historical capacity to ground cultural purposes in sacred history. My point here is that Heidegger's realization that human beings *are* historical—that our being is historical, without a fixed nature—constitutes a further breakthrough in historical consciousness, one that results from and empowers a new level of reflexive awareness.

While nineteenth-century historical consciousness is marked by the startling realization that we modern human beings live in cultural worlds that are fundamentally different from those of our ancestors, with the emergence of the level of reflexive historical consciousness in the twentieth century we have begun to notice structural practices that help make us historical, practices that, while not eternal, are certainly enduring. One of the insights generating Alasdair MacIntyre's work is the realization that the kinds of "narrative identity" that ethnographers like Eliade found in ancient and pre-literate cultures are no less functional in our lives. Hence, MacIntyre's "central thesis" in *After Virtue* says: "Man is in his actions and practices, as well as in his fictions, essentially a story telling animal. He is not essentially, but becomes through history, a teller of stories that aspire to truth. But the key question for men is not about their own authorship; I can only answer the question 'What am I to do?' if I can answer the prior question 'Of what story or stories do I find myself a part?'"[4] "Hence there is no way to give us an understanding of any society, including our own, except through the stock of stories which constitute its initial dramatic resource. Mythology, in its original sense, is at the heart of things."[5] Hence, human identity *is* historical in the sense that narratives about who we are, what we're doing, and why, constitute the background or meaning of everything we do.

Not only is the identity of the self a function of interpretive self-fashioning through the rituals and narratives of one's culture, any individual action or experience is intelligible only in relation to these overarching historical structures. Although our actions can be singled out and abstracted from their larger narrative contexts for particular interpretive purposes, they can only be identified as meaningful actions in the first place in relation to that larger, historical background. What

---

[4] Alasdair MacIntyre, *After Virtue: A Study in Moral Theory* (Notre Dame: University of Notre Dame Press, 1981), p. 216.

[5] Ibid., p. 216.

MacIntyre calls the "primary intention" of an action—its very reason for being— is its relation to a story or stories that fill out this background of significance. What you are doing right now in the activity of reading, for example, makes sense only in relation to now internalized narratives about literacy, textuality, and the quest for higher knowledge.

Heidegger's account of the way actions are grounded in social meaning is in important respects similar to MacIntyre's, but carried out to an astonishing level of hermeneutical subtlety. There, self-understanding isn't a set of beliefs about oneself but rather an ability to be, a know-how, a skill drawn from the cultural world into which one has been initiated and socialized. We learn to do what one typically does or ought to do in all of our worldly involvements. What we do is intelligible to us and to others only in light of social norms, customs, and institutions—a cultural world, the always present backdrop of significance that supports meaning. Self-understanding, for Heidegger, is a "reflection back" from this world through the activities in which we are engaged. Each of us is *Das Man*, the anyone, the oneself, understood in the same third person terms that we understand others. We learn and take over the intentions that are available or possible for us in our particular cultural setting, and we see ourselves as anyone else who does that. Only because our actions are understood by ourselves and by others as conforming to a general type do they count as purposeful behaviors that can be judged successful or not. Human identity, therefore, is a kind of engaged anonymity, an active participation in pre-given cultural meanings.

Although we gain our particular historical identity by means of identification with the non-individualized cultural norm, for the early Heidegger, becoming "I myself" as opposed to just "anyone" requires some degree of disruption and transformation of this identity. So it is at this point in *Being and Time* that Heidegger begins to provide ontological grounding to human freedom and to a form of "authentic historicality" that will put this freedom to transformative use. By human freedom here I mean Heidegger's understanding of authentic existence—a partial surfacing of individuated awareness out of the anonymity of *Das Man*, an awareness that is evoked by the liminal experiences of the mood of anxiety, the understanding of one's own mortality, and the discourse or call of conscience. That account in *Being and Time* of the emergence of "I myself" out of the "anyone" of social involvement is, for Heidegger, the appearance of accountability and freedom. My focus here, however, will be on what Heidegger calls "authentic historicality" rather than more generally on "authentic existence." But the two are closely aligned, and the key issue in both is time. As Heidegger puts it: "The concept of authentic historicality is just a more complete working out of temporality."[6]

We are historical insofar as our existence is timed, that is, structured by past, present, and future. *Dasein*—human being-in-the-cultural/linguistic world of active engagement—is a being who is an issue for itself. We are open questions for ourselves, questions that require our own answers. Because we have no fixed nature something crucial is always at stake for us in our efforts to be. We are, Heidegger claims, the care that we take in attempting to answer these questions for ourselves in practice. As a function of this care, we project ahead in life, always taking a stand that expresses our effort to come to grips with our being here. Heidegger calls this forward movement and future-directedness, *existence*. Existing is standing out beyond or ahead of ourselves and aiming at an answer to our questioning by projecting possibilities. Our future is not a quantity of time yet to come but rather a condition of possibility for our caring.

In projecting ahead, however, Heidegger claims that we circle back to appropriate and carry forth what has been. What has been is an always moving but pre-given setting, a situation and set of possibilities into which we are thrown. Finding ourselves born into a particular context and form of life, we confront our lives as open-ended tasks, responding to our given heritage in living out our lives. Past, present, and future are ontologically or structurally presupposed in every aspect of the care we take in life—and all three temporal ecstasies coalesce or come together in all of our actions.

In Heidegger's view our awareness of history is activated and comes alive only to the extent that our sense of time becomes, in Heidegger's sense, authentic—that is, really our own—the timing of our own existence set within the character of our particular moment in history, this in contrast to a general, shared sense of clock time or quantities of time, or the generalized time of anyone. When authentically timed, we pull back from our dispersal into the possibilities available to anyone, and make resolute commitments to the defining possibilities of our particular situation and historical moment both individually and communally. Authentic

---

[6] *Being and Time*, p. 433.

historicality consists in retrieving and repeating possibilities bequeathed to us by our heritage and taking a resolute stand on those that best align with our own lives and the life of our community.

So, what does this mean for the practice of history, for historiography, the disciplined study of history? It means that all historical interpretation proceeds directly from the historian's own historicity—the historian's own belonging to history and embeddedness in it. Being themselves historical, historians always interpret the historical objects they study on the basis of a pre-reflective understanding of being that has taken shape within the historian's own concrete situation and in relation to his or her own past and future. In the same way that human temporality projects a future, the historian's work begins with the projection of possibilities. In the course of choosing which historical events are worth the labor of historiographical work, the historian anticipates either explicitly or implicitly what our past has now made possible and where our current history is going. Any such choice of topics presupposes a decision about our future, our past and present.

Moreover, these selections are inevitably normative or evaluative—they take a position on values in the very selection of subject matter, and in the orientation or perspective adopted toward the work. In choosing what to study, the historian must take his or her bearings from a normative judgment about the current demands of our time and community based on a vision of our current situation and its future possibilities. Historiographical works that emerge from a true or revealing vision of our future help bring that future about. In rethinking the past, they project an understanding of what might truly be of value, what could be achieved in our time, and read the past for its possible contribution to that ideal future. Just as an authentic individual thoughtfully retrieves the past in order to project a future, the historian gathers up the resources of his or her tradition, orchestrating them in such a way as to disclose their current insight or value to the community.

Doing this effectively necessarily entails critical thought, thinking that submits common and flattened interpretations of the tradition to the test of critical evaluation in order to insure that they don't devalue and deplete the rich reservoir of possibilities history provides. Historical work that is reflexively aware, therefore, cannot be treated at arm's length, as a task of forming representations about an object of study in isolation from its repercussions for the future of our world.

Instead, a self-aware historiography emerges from our indebtedness to tradition, our belonging to it as its media of disclosure and advancement. From this reflexive point of view, the ideal of historical study is a quest for a tradition's or humanity's latent possibilities, possibilities whose time for actualization (*kairos*) may have come.

Heidegger spent the rest of his life developing and extending this phenomenological reading of human historicity. And in the massive wake of his insights, so did others. Hans-Georg Gadamer's lifelong efforts to clarify authentic historicity constitute a parallel achievement.[7] What Gadamer brings to historical study is an impressive articulation of the reflexive dimension of historical understanding, a dimension of understanding that had been largely invisible to academic historians working out of the fruitful but not always appropriate model of natural science. Reorienting historical thought in this way made it possible for historians to realize that their own immediate participation in cultural traditions is crucial, not simply as another topic for historical investigation but as the necessary condition for the very possibility of historical understanding in the first place. If the historian's present situation constitutes the ground of the entire process of understanding, attempting to set that ground aside in order to grasp an object of understanding objectively obscures one fundamental dimension of the full event of understanding. Rather than conceive of the function of the past as supplying the objects of historical interpretation, Gadamer shows how the past, in the form of tradition, constitutes the ground we always stand upon when we seek to understand historically. Rather than cutting us off from the past, as earlier historical method supposed, the historian's finite embeddedness in a particular history is recognized as what opens history up to us, its enabling condition.

Given this point of departure, Gadamer claims that authentic historical understanding is not best conceived as the reconstruction of the past but rather as its mediation into the present on behalf of the future—an act of translation. So conceived, the effort to grasp the past "in itself" misunderstands the meaning and the point of historical understanding. "To understand a text does not mean primarily to reason one's way back into the past, but to have a present involvement in what is said."[8] The image of historical thinking that Gadamer develops points away from

---

[7]    Hans Georg Gadamer, *Truth and Method* (New York: Seabury Press, 1975).

[8]    Ibid., p. 353.

the application of a method of study by an historian whose own subjectivity has been set aside to an image that emphasizes the ways that history encompasses both the subjectivity of the historian and the historical objects of study. More than an act of subjectivity, historical understanding is an event of transmission in which past and present are mediated on behalf of what might come to be.

Extending these grounds, Gadamer was able to re-conceive the stark opposition that modernity had drawn between tradition, representing the weight of the past, and current inquiry, which rejects the past in order to bring new understanding into being. The image of historians freeing themselves from past acts of understanding in their quest for current understanding fails to recognize that it is precisely this past that gave rise to and made possible the perspective from which new realizations might emerge. It fails to appreciate that every new act of historical understanding is an extension of tradition, and the historian only the most recent bearer of the tradition's extended continuity. Taking that perspective helps account for the necessity and inevitability of repeated, ongoing efforts to achieve critical understanding. It renders naïve the idea of the so-called "definitive study," the intellectual work that aspires to foreclose all further reflection. What emerges in every new historical situation are new points of departure from whose perspective history reopens the past.

The present vantage point from which both past and future are interpreted is itself another particular moment in the flow of history, a moment that will at some point be subsumed in subsequent events of understanding. Hence, historical understanding is itself historical, a productive event in the movement of history, and the past that it seeks to understand appears as always in process and transformation. The past that the historian studies, therefore, is not a static object of investigation, but an inexhaustible and always changing source of possibilities. Gadamer treats these possibilities that are disclosed in ongoing historical inquiry as facets of meaning already there in the tradition even if hidden or latent, rather than as unilateral productions of the historian's subjectivity. Every distinct act of understanding the tradition is itself a moment in the life of that tradition.

But rather than understand our being historical—this immersion in history— as a denial of freedom, as many modern interpreters certainly have, Gadamer's work shows how our historical consciousness is the very source of our freedom. Indeed, human freedom is precisely what history is disclosing to and through us,

which is to say that awareness of our immersion in the larger proc[
has itself become a form of freedom. More comprehensive av
greater freedom in every sphere of life, including the reflexive di
understanding. A significant dimension of this freedom occurs in the process of
coming to understand historical change and difference. Being faced with cultural
assumptions quite other than the historian's own brings not just the other's way
of being human into view but one's own as well. Confrontation with the other's
"horizons," as Gadamer calls them, brings to awareness ways of understanding
so deep-seated in our own mental practices that they are presupposed rather than
known and chosen. When reflexively attentive, our own being who we are is
disclosed to us in the act of historical understanding, and the difference between
the horizons of our own understanding and the horizons of the other who we
seek to understand establishes the possibility that new possibilities might come
to awareness.

Gadamer calls this awareness "effective history," a sense of one's own
historicity and finitude so potent that it forges an openness to transformation and
depth.[9] Lacking a sense of "effective history" we fail to see both who we are and
what might be possible for us here and now. As Gadamer puts it: "Reflection on
a given pre-understanding brings before me something that otherwise happens
'behind my back.'"[10] And what happens "behind my back" is not something
that I am free to consider. Occurring "behind my back," it can't be a matter of
deliberation in relation to possible alternatives. It simply structures the way I
understand without my recognition or awareness. Acknowledging and cultivating
the reflexive dimension of historical understanding, therefore, transforms some
of our presuppositions into conscious suppositions, opening questions and the
freedom of deliberation where previously only closure existed. For that reason, it
seems to me that deepening our awareness of our own historicity in reflexive self-
disclosure both makes possible and *is* the emergence of greater human freedom.

In conclusion it is worth pausing to reflect on models of reflexive historical
understanding in contemporary culture. There are many. Robert Bellah's work
on American culture from the perspective of his earlier work on Japanese culture

---

[9] Ibid., p. 305.

[10] Hans-Georg Gadamer, *Philosophical Hermeneutics* (Berkeley: University of
California Press, 1976), p. xviii.

is exemplary, as is Charles Taylor's effort to trace the roots and meaning of modernity on behalf of that very modernity. And Alaisdair MacIntyre's work is a model of "authentic historicity." MacIntyre reads Western intellectual history as a direct challenge to contemporary culture. He aspires to show all of us what damage is currently being done "behind our backs." There is a prophetic character to MacIntyre's exhortations and warnings in *After Virtue*—our current state of life precludes our seeing who we are and the severely distorted or fallen condition of contemporary moral reflection. In the Introduction to *After Virtue*, MacIntyre claims that our moral language and therefore our capacity for moral deliberation are in a tragic state of disorder, a state now so pervasive that we have lost the perspective from which we might be able to see it for what it is and to pass judgment on our cultural condition. Philosophy, he writes, is impotent to help us through this because only an *historical* analysis of how we got here can bring our cultural condition to awareness. At that point, MacIntyre writes:

> Suppose it were the case that the catastrophe of which my hypothesis speaks had occurred before, or largely before, the founding of academic history, so that the moral and other evaluative presuppositions of academic history derived from the forms of the disorder which it brought about. Suppose, that is, that the standpoint of academic history is such that from its value-neutral viewpoint moral disorder must remain largely invisible. All that the historian will be allowed to perceive by the canons and categories of his discipline will be one morality succeeding another: 17th century Puritanism, 18th century hedonism, the Victorian work-ethic, and so on … For the forms of the academic curriculum would turn out to be among the symptoms of the disaster whose occurrence the curriculum does not acknowledge.[11]

Suppose, in other words, that our practices of historiography are so imbued with our state of moral disability that historians can neither recognize the problem nor see the point of proposing solutions.

MacIntyre then proceeds to mine his own Western tradition of thought both for a narrative account of how this happened and for resources powerful enough to both envision the predicament and to begin to get us out of it. His reflections

---

[11]  MacIntyre, *After Virtue*, p. 4.

on Aristotle's ethics and teleology have already substantially altered the character of ethical reflection in Western thought. I remind you of this example only to demonstrate the pattern of historical understanding expressed here—that authentic historical study works its way through and out of standard, flattened interpretations of the tradition, drawing on latent possibilities in that tradition in order to envision alternatives capable of altering our future. MacIntyre's work is exemplary in this way. Whether readers are in agreement with his diagnosis or not, the power and contemporary resonance of his cultural challenge demonstrates the centrality and importance of this reflexive dimension of historical understanding and the possibilities for freedom that it enacts.

## Selected Bibliography

Eliade, Mircia, *The Sacred and the Profane: The Nature of Religion* (1959).

Gadamer, Hans Georg, *Truth and Method* (New York: Seabury Press, 1975).

Gadamer, Hans Georg, *Philosophical Hermeneutics* (Berkeley: University of California Press, 1976).

MacIntyre, Alasdair, *After Virtue: A Study in Moral Theology* (Notre Dame: University of Notre Dame Press, 1981).

Chapter 13

# Divine Lordship, Divine Motherhood

Julia A. Lamm

## Introduction

This chapter is part of a larger project on Julian of Norwich's doctrine of grace. I shall focus here on how Julian's rather odd juxtaposition of two entrenched and seemingly incompatible social roles—motherhood and lordship—serves in fact to dislodge dominant social and political ideals from their moorings. Julian combines them in such a way as to reinvent them utterly: she holds forth a new ideal, one that calls for an almost complete realignment of the feudal system and of ecclesial authority.

In relation to the nobility, including bishops, this ideal stands as a thoroughgoing critique, no less powerful for being indirect. Julian holds forth an ideal of the exercise of authority that stands in such vivid contrast to the reality on the ground in Norwich that the chasm almost speaks for itself: a significant turning is required. In relation to townsfolk and peasants, she offers an ideal not by way of contrast but by words of comfort: they do not have to strive to become what they are not; they have only to realize they are already enclosed in God and that God, in the incarnation, has identified completely with them; their toiling in the fields and their ragged clothing are not justified punishment for the fall but are the very conditions Christ himself freely took on—before the fall—out of great love and with great dignity.

Julian's pursuit of this particular ideal is radical in that, even more than calling for justice or basic decency, it calls for a social, political, and religious trans-valuation: a reordering of roles, attitudes, affections, and ideas; a reassessment of the dignity and value of lower status roles and individuals; and a reconfiguration of what the church is.

Yet it is not this new ideal itself that I will examine here, but how she arrived at it. My hope is that Julian will provide us with a helpful case study for the topic we are examining together: theological reflection, the pursuit of ideals, and the integrity of life. For, as I shall argue, Julian's reinterpretation of lordship and motherhood, and especially her juxtaposition of the two, turns on a very theological point—namely, on a distinction she draws in her doctrine of grace. Before I get to that argument, however, let me say a few words of introduction to Julian, her world, and her text.

## Julian in Context

We know relatively little about Julian of Norwich. We do not even know her birth name. We know she was born in 1342–3, because she tells us that in May 1373, when she was "thirty and a half years old" and "on the point of death" and receiving last rites, she received 16 "showings," a Middle English term for revelations. The showings began with, and remained rooted in, concrete visions of Christ's body during crucifixion. Julian did not die from that illness in 1373; she would live for at least four more decades. And during that entire time, she—unlike many medieval visionaries and mystics—remained focused on her original 16 visions. She became an anchoress attached to the Church of St. Julian in Norwich, and there, enclosed in her cell in the center of town, she prayed, studied, gave spiritual advice, and reflected further on her 16 showings. Julian wrote at least two versions of her book, *Showings*—the first version (commonly referred to as the "short text"); and a substantially revised version (the "long text"), written more than 20 years after she received her 16 showings.[1] Julian's *Showings* is the first text in the English language written by a woman, insofar as we know.

The more general context of fourteenth-century Christian Europe and why it was in crisis is well known: the Black Plague, the Avignon Papacy (1309–78),

---

[1]    See the recent critical edition, *The Writings of Julian of Norwich: A Vision Showed to a Devout Woman and a Revelation of Love*, edited by by Nicholas Watson and Jacqueline Jenkins (University Park: Pennsylvania State University Press, 2005). The best known and probably most widely circulated Modern English translation is *Julian of Norwich: Showings*, edited by Edmund Colledge, OSA and James Walsh, SJ (New York and Ramsey, Toronto: Paulist Press, 1978). Quotations shall first be given in the Middle English (Watson and Jenkins) in order to convey the power of Julian's writing; for longer quotations and for shorter passages that may prove difficult, the Modern English (Colledge and Walsh) translation shall then be given.

the beginning of the Western Schism in the church (1378–1417). Nevertheless, it may be helpful to relate these more concretely to Julian's life. The plague reached Norwich by January 1349; in 1362, it returned in a particularly bad form that targeted children; another severe form occurred in 1369, the same year that saw a terrible famine. In 1381, the Peasants' Revolt (aka Wat Tyler's Rebellion, or the Great Rising) was a defining point in English social and political history. It was a revolt against new tax laws, but went so far as to call for an end to serfdom. It was also tied up with religious reform, many of its leaders having been associated with John Wycliffe (ca. 1328–84) and the heretical Lollard movement. It reached Norwich in June and was brutally suppressed by the nobility, both secular and ecclesial, led by the bishop of Norwich, Henry le Despenser (ca. 1341–1406). The leader of the local revolt, Geoffrey Litster, was drawn, hanged, and quartered, with Despenser in attendance. Despenser also had a reputation for vigilance against any signs of "Lollardy" or religious dissent. In 1383, he led a disastrous crusade to Flanders, against a supporter of the "anti-pope," Clement VII. He was reviled for his brutality. The simple point here is that crises in the larger church were not remote but were instead concrete realities affecting everyday life in Norwich.

The Peasants' Revolt and its suppression in Norwich occurred after Julian had received her showings (and probably after she had written the short text[2]) but *before* she had written the long text. It is hard to read Julian's additions to the long text as unrelated to this state of affairs.

## The Problematic and Thesis

The long text of *Showings* is longer, in part, because it includes three major additions: Julian's description of God as mother, one of the things for which she is most well known; a parable of a lord and servant, which is in part a reinterpretation of the fall; and a secondary "revelation of love." All three of these additions provided Julian with hermeneutical keys for arriving at a deeper understanding of her original 16 showings. Indeed, the significance of each of these is evidenced by

---

[2] For the issue of dating the two versions of *Showings*, see Nicholas Watson, "The Composition of Julian of Norwich's *Revelation of Love*," *Speculum* 68 (1993): 637–83. Watson challenges the conventional assumption that the short text was written soon after 1373, arguing instead that it was not begun until 1382 at the earliest.

the fact that, although all three occur in the latter part of the long text, each has a proleptic influence on the earlier chapters. For example, she records her secondary revelation of love in the last chapter of the long text:

> And fro the time that it was shewde, I desyerde oftentimes to witte what was oure lords mening. And fifteen yere after and mor, I was answered in gostly understonding, seyeng thus: "What, woldest thou wit thy lordes mening in this thing? Wit it wele, love was his mening. Who shewed it the? Love. What shewid he the? Love. Wherfore shewed he it the? For love. Holde the therin, thou shalt wit more in the same."[3]

> [And from the time that it was revealed, I desired many times to know in what was our Lord's meaning. And fifteen years after and more, I was answered in spiritual understanding, and it was said: What, do you wish to know your Lord's meaning in this thing? Know it well, love was his meaning. Who reveals it to you? Love. What did he reveal to you? Love. Why does he reveal it to you? For love. Remain in this, and you will know more of the same.[4]]

She carries this back to the very beginning of the long text, which she opens with the words, "This is a revelation of love."[5]

Julian's incorporation of the other two major additions into the long text, however, is not as seamless and arguably presents a problem for interpretation. The parable and the description of God as mother are both introduced at about the same place: in the latter half of her exposition of the fourteenth showing (between chapters 48 and 63). Yet they do not appear to stand in any kind of organic or coherent relation to each other. On the contrary, their respective introductions into the text seem jarring because of the odd juxtaposition of competing imageries.

Julian's first mention of God as mother appears towards the end of chapter 48. At first it appears as though the parable, which is self-contained and constitutes the entirety of chapter 51, interrupts the beginning of her discussion of God as mother, as though the parable were rather arbitrarily inserted in the middle of

---

[3]  Ch. 86, Watson and Jenkins, 379.
[4]  Colledge and Walsh, 342.
[5]  Ch. 1, Watson and Jenkins, 123; Colledge and Walsh, 175.

that other discussion, since she opens chapter 52 with another reference God as mother. But then, in the latter half of 52, she turns back to the parable, expounding and applying its meaning, and continuing to do so for the next couple of chapters, until, in the middle of chapter 54 (ll. 17ff.), she returns to the theme of God as mother, which she then proceeds to develop through chapter 63. In short, these two major thematic and substantive additions to *Showings* appear to be inter-spliced in a less than artful way. They seem entirely unrelated.

Yet, as I have already suggested, they are related, and intricately so, since the divine motherhood redefines what it is to be lord, and the divine lordship raises the status of motherhood. In Julian's mind, the two are, in fact, inseparable.

## Mercy and Grace

### *Motherhood Redefines the Lordship*

To support my claim that the juxtaposition is neither accidental nor arbitrary but serves a purpose, let me draw your attention to a passage immediately following her first reference to God (in this case, the Holy Spirit) as mother.

> For I behelde the properte of mercy, and I behelde the properte of grace, which have two maner of working in one love. Mercy is a pitteful properte, which longeth to moderhode in tender love. And grace is a wurshipful properte, which longeth to ryal lordshippe in the same love. Mercy werketh—keping, suffering, quicking, and heling—and all is of tendernesse of love. And grace werketh with mercy: raising, rewarding (endlessly overpassing that oure loving and our traveyle deserveth), spreding abrode, and shewing the hye, plentuouse largesse of Goddes ryal lordshippe in his mervelouse curtesy. And this is of the habundance of love. For grace werketh oure dredful failing into plentuouse and endlesse solace, and grace werketh oure shameful falling into hye, wurshippeful rising, and grace werketh oure sorrowful dying into holy, blissful life.[6]

---

[6]   Ch. 48, Watson and Jenkins, 267/269, emphases added.

[For I contemplated the property of mercy, and I contemplated the property of grace, which have two ways of operating in one love. *Mercy is a compassionate property, which belongs to motherhood in tender love; and grace is an honourable property, which belongs to royal dominion in the same love.* Mercy works, protecting, enduring, vivifying and healing, and it is all of the tenderness of love; and grace works with mercy, raising, rewarding, endlessly exceeding what our love and labour deserve, distributing and displaying the vast plenty and generosity of God's royal dominion in his wonderful courtesy. And this is from the abundance of love, for grace transforms our dreadful failing into plentiful and endless solace; and grace transforms our shameful falling into high and honourable rising; and grace transforms our sorrowful dying into holy, blessed life.[7]]

Up until this point in the text, "mercy and grace" had appeared as a couplet, in a fairly familiar and conventional manner.[8] Here, for the first time explicitly, she begins to tease out mercy from grace—not to de-couple them entirely, but to draw some interesting distinctions. In so doing, she begins to develop yet another novel aspect in her doctrine of grace.

Mercy, she says, belongs to the divine motherhood, and its movement is downward, its tone compassionate. Grace belongs to royal dominion, or divine lordship, and its movement is upward, its tone joyful. She explains that they are held together in one love. This (mercy and grace, compassion and bliss, condescension and raising) becomes for Julian a shorthand for the holding together of motherhood and lordship—two roles, categories, and concepts normally occupying very different spheres of activity and behavior and signifying very different structures of authority. Moreover, this shorthand method of referring to the "union" of motherhood and lordship, developed for the first time in chapter 48, runs throughout the rest of the text and, more to the point, is used frequently in the parable of the lord and servant.

This, I argue, is an important point, because while others have read the parable as a political statement, they have not recognized the intricate interweaving of the parable with the understanding of God as mother, and so, I would suggest, they

---

[7]    Colledge and Walsh, 262–3, emphases added.

[8]    See, for example, Chap. 40 (lines 3, 12–13, 35–6); 41 (line 16); 42 (lines 17–18, 53); 45 (lines 7–8).

have missed the full power of Julian's critique and of the new ideal she holds forth. Almost all descriptions of the lord (who represents God the Father) in the parable include images drawn either directly from what she has just said about divine mercy in chapter 48 or from what she later says about God as mother. In other words, the understanding of divine motherhood informs just about every aspect of her understanding—her radical understanding, I might add—of lordship.

> The lorde sitteth solempnely in rest and in pees. The servant stondeth before his lorde reverently, redy to do his lordes wille. The lorde loketh upon his servant *full lovely and swetly, and mekely* he sendeth him into a certaine place to do his will.[9]

> [The lord sits in state, in rest and in peace. The servant stands before his lord, respectfully, ready to do his lord's will. The lord looks on his servant *very lovingly and sweetly and mildly*. He sends him to a certain place to do his will.[10]]

> And right thus continuantly his loveing lorde full tenderly beholdeth him ... full mekly and mildely, with gret rewth and pitte ...[11]

> [And all this time his loving lord looks on him most tenderly ... very meekly and mildly, with great compassion and pity ...[12]]

Not only the lord's demeanor, but also his physical appearance, is described in terms of these markers of motherhood:

> His eyen were blake, mos fair and semely, shewing *full of lovely pitte*, and *within him an hey ward, long and brode, all full* of endlesse hevens.[13]

---

[9]   Ch. 51, Watson and Jenkins, 273, 75, emphases added.
[10]   Colledge and Walsh, 267, emphases added.
[11]   Ch. 51, Watson and Jenkins, 275.
[12]   Colledge and Walsh, 268.
[13]   Ch. 51, Watson and Jenkins, 279, emphases added.

[... his eyes were black, most beautiful and seemly, revealing all his *loving pity*, and *within him there was a secure place of refuge, long and broad, all full* of endless heavenliness ...[14]]

Here Julian describes a womb-like "place of refuge" or keeping within the lord. This is one of many references to the lord enclosing us in himself, of the lord protecting his servants. This particular reference also hearkens back to the "fair, delectable place" (the tenth showing, chapter 24)—Christ's side-wound—into which he led her understanding; it is described as a place large enough for all humankind. Such imagery of enclosure is central to her worldview: while present in the short text, its development in the long text it is very much tied to the notion of God as mother.

Let us continue looking at her description of royal lordship in terms of markers of motherhood. Julian writes:

And the *lovely loking* that he loked on his servant continually—and namely in his falling—methought it might melt oure hartes for love and brest them on two for joy.

This fair loking shewed of a semely medelur, which was marvelous to beholde. That one was *rewth and pitte*, that other joy and blisse.[15]

[And the *loving regard* which he kept constantly on his servant, and especially when he fell, it seemed to me that it could melt our hearts for love and break them in two for joy. This *lovely regard* had in it a beautiful mingling which was wonderful to see. Part was *compassion and pity*,[16] part was joy and bliss.[17]]

She comes at this point to the theme of anger (I shall say something more about this in a bit), insisting again that

---

[14]   Colledge and Walsh, 271, emphases added.
[15]   Ch. 51, Watson and Jenkins, 279, emphases added.
[16]   That is to say, mercy and motherhood.
[17]   Colledge and Walsh, 271, emphases added.

… only paine blameth and ponisheth, and oure curteyse lorde comforteth and socurreth. And ever he is to the soule in glad chere, loving and longing to bring us to his blisse.[18]

[… only pain blames and punishes, and our courteous Lord comforts and succours, and always he is kindly disposed to the soul, loving and long to bring us to his bliss.[19]]

Having already made the point that God knows no anger, Julian now makes it clear that a lord should not be angry with a servant. The phrase "courteous Lord" is one she uses frequently in her *Showings*, often juxtaposing it to "homely," meaning familial and familiar. In other words, through another unexpected juxtaposition, she redefines rules of courtesy.

For example, in the sixth showing, where Christ thanks her for her service, she adds a banquet scene to the long text:

… I saw our lorde God as a lorde in his owne house, which lorde hath called alle his derewurthy frendes to a solempne fest. Than I saw the lorde taking no place in his awne house, but I saw him ryally reigne in his house, and all fulfilleth it with joy and mirth, himselfe endlesly to glad and solace his derewurthy frendes, fulle homely and fulle curtesly, with mervelous melody of endelesse love, in his awne fair blissed chere. Which glorious chere of the godhede fulfilleth alle heven of joy and blisse.[20]

[I saw our Lord God as a lord in his own house, who has called all his friends to a splendid feast. Then I did not see him seated anywhere in his own house; but I saw him reign in his house as a king and fill it all full of joy and mirth, gladdening and consoling his dear friends with himself, very familiarly and courteously, with wonderful melody in endless love in his own fair blissful

---

[18]   Ch. 51, Watson and Jenkins, 279.
[19]   Colledge and Walsh, 271.
[20]   Chap. 14, Watson and Jenkins, 173.

countenance, which glorious countenance fills all heaven full of the joy and bliss of the divinity].[21]

Paula Barker, building on the work of Marian Reynolds, argues (I quote at length),

> courtesy was the cardinal virtue of the aristocratic social ethic ... [Reynolds] observed that "homeliness", on the other hand, pertained to the lower social sphere. The word normally meant "familiar" or "intimate". Julian uses it to speak of the nearness and tenderness of God and of God's service to each person. Reynolds concluded that "there appears to be no literary precedent for Julian's coupling of the concept of homeliness with that of courtesy; the words belong to different worlds ..." In other words, Julian's use of these two terms was original. Her juxtaposition of them would have been startling to her contemporaries. Therefore, this was an effective way for her to express the conjunction of two dispositions in God that was so startling to her.[22]

As we have seen, for Julian the proper work of royal dominion is grace. In her development of her doctrine of grace, and in the way she uses the very word *grace*, it is clear that its social associations (with nobility, courtly manners, and feudal structure) are much in her mind. In particular, her frequent use of the phrase "good lord" points to the power a lord had in feudal society to change dramatically the status and circumstances of any vassal—for good—but without the qualifier of "good" a lord can clearly change the status for ill.[23]

---

[21]　　Chap. 14, Colledge and Walsh, 203.

[22]　　Paula S. Datsko Barker, "The Motherhood of God in Julian of Norwich's Theology," *Downside Review* 100 (1982): 295–6. See Anna Maria Reynolds, C.P.,"Courtesy and Homeliness in the Revelations of Julian of Norwich," *Fourteenth Century English Mystics Newsletter* 5 (1979): 12–20. Mary Olson argues the same basic point, citing Reynolds but not Barker, in "God's Inappropriate Grace: Images of Courtesy in Julian of Norwich's Showings," *Mystics Quarterly* 20 (1994): 47–59.

[23]　　See Alexandra Barratt, "Lordship, Service and Worship in Julian of Norwich," in E.A. Jones (ed.), *The Medieval Mystical Tradition in England*, Exeter Symposium VII (Cambridge: D.S. Brewer, 2004), p. 177.

## *The Lordship Raises Motherhood to a Higher Status*

Nicholas Watson has argued that, in her use of the terms substance and sensuality, Julian "accepts the social models which define proper female activity, but does so in a way which fundamentally shifts (in some respects even inverts) those models by resisting both the passivity and the low prestige traditionally associated with them."[24] The same can be said for Julian's employment of the "social models" of motherhood and royal lordship. Her intimate linking of mercy (as motherly activity) and grace (as royal activity) not only redefines royal dominion in terms of motherhood, but also makes the raises the status of motherhood, making it co-equal with the fatherhood and with the lordship.

Let us look very briefly at how Julian begins with certain stereotypes of motherhood and familial hierarchies, but then stretches and challenges them, to the point where gendered differences almost collapse. In chapter 58, for instance, she assigns gender-specific roles to each person of the Trinity: fatherhood to the first person of the trinity ("the high might of the trinite is oure fader"), motherhood to the second person ("the depe wisdom of the trinite"), and love and lordship to the third person.[25] She then proceeds, in that same chapter, to explore the meaning of the incarnation in terms of motherhood, a motif in Christianity certainly not new to Julian.[26] Then, in the next chapter, she makes the astounding (and novel) claim, "As verely as God is oure fader, as verely God is oure moder."[27] At this point, she revisits the gender specific divine activities she had entertained in the previous chapter; these are transformed by her insight into the equivalency of the motherhood and fatherhood. Note how startling the words Christ speak to hear sound in the use of the neuter pronoun "it" (rather than in the use of the male pronoun, as Colledge and Walsh render it in their translation):

And that shewde he in all, and namely in theyse swete wordes there he seyth: "I it am." That is to sey: "I it am, the might and the goodnes of faderhode. I it am,

---

[24]   Nicholas Watson, "'Yf wommen be double naturelly': Remaking 'Woman' in Julian of Norwich's *Revelation of Love*," *Exemplaria* 8/1 (1996): 7.

[25]   Ch. 58, Watson and Jenkins, 307. See Colledge and Walsh, p. 294.

[26]   See Caroline Walker Bynum, *Jesus as Mother: Studies in the Spirituality of the High Middle Ages* (Berkeley and London: University of California Press, 1982).

[27]   Ch. 59, Watson and Jenkins, 309. See Colledge and Walsh, p. 295.

the wisdom and the kindnes of moderhode. I it am, the light and the grace that
is all blessed love. I it am, the trinite. I it am, the unite. I it am, the hye sovereyn
goodnesse of all manner thing. I it am that maketh the to love. I it am that makith
the to long. I it am, the endlesse fulfilling of all true desyers." For ther the soule
is hyest, nobliest, and wurshipfullest, ther it is lowest, mekest, and mildest. And
of this substantial grounde, we have all oure vertuse in oure sensualite by gift of
kind, and by helping and speding of *mercy and grace*, withoute which we may
not profite.[28]

[... and he revealed that in everything, and especially in these sweet words where
he says: I am he; that is to say: I am he, the power and goodness of fatherhood;
I am he, the wisdom and lovingness of motherhood; I am he, the light and the
grace which is all blessed love; I am he, the Trinity; I am he, the unity; I am he,
the great supreme goodness of every kind of thing; I am he who makes you to
love; I am he who makes you to long; I am he, the endless fulfilling of all true
desires. For where the soul is highest, noblest, most honourable, still it is lowest,
meekest and mildest.][29]

Shortly thereafter, Julian repeats the phrase "as verely as God is oure fader, as
verely God is oure mother."[30]

Her identification of the divine fatherhood and divine motherhood is no
simile, no metaphor. This is, of course, another example of how motherhood
of God has redefined fatherhood, and both in turn have redefined lordship, but
it also serves to raise the status of motherhood by exporting typically female
properties and activities to typically male spheres of authority and value. In
Julian's theological reflection, the motherhood begins as, in Watson's words, "the
principle of self-emptying (kenosis) within the godhead itself ... which brings
about the Incarnation."[31] Whereas Watson sees this self-emptying occurring in the
second person of the trinity (God the Son), Julian's shorthand of mercy and grace

---

[28]   Ch. 59, Watson and Jenkins, 309, 311, emphases added.
[29]   Colledge and Walsh, 295–6.
[30]   Ch. 59, Watson and Jenkins, 311.
[31]   Watson, "'Yf wommen be double naturelly'," 26.

underscores that it also takes place in God the Father.[32] This is further supported by the fact that, in the parable, the lord is not enthroned: "The place that the lorde sat on was simply on the erth, bareyn and deserte, alone in wildernesse."[33] [The place which the lord sat on was unadorned, on the ground, barren and waste, alone in the wilderness.[34]] Julian also marvels that the lord, who could be waited on by countless servants, "had no servant but one, and him he sent out."[35]

Having identified fatherhood and motherhood, Julian makes at least one more move in the development of her Trinitarian theology, a move that further corroborates that she has raised the status of motherhood through this juxtaposition with lordship. She describes each Person of the Trinity in terms of motherhood:

> I understode thre manner of beholdinges of motherhed in God. The furst is grounde of oure kinde making. The seconde is taking of oure kinde, and ther beginneth the moderhed of grace. The thurde is moderhed in werking, and therin is a forthspreding by the same grace, of length and brede, of high and of depnesse without ende. And alle is one love.[36]

> [I understand three ways of contemplating motherhood in God. The first is the foundation of our nature's creation; the second is his taking of our nature, where the motherhood of grace begins; the third is the motherhood at work. And in that, by the same grace, everything is penetrated, in length and in breadth, in height and in depth without end; and it is all one love.][37]

This last, short sentence echoes what she had said about the properties of mercy and grace: they are "two maner of working in one love."[38]

---

[32] She also extends the motherhood, and principle of kenosis, to the third person of the trinity.
[33] Ch. 51, Watson and Jenkins, 279.
[34] Colledge and Walsh, 271.
[35] Ch. 51, Watson and Jenkins, 281.
[36] Ch. 59, Watson and Jenkins, 311.
[37] Colledge and Walsh, 297.
[38] Ch. 48, Watson and Jenkins, 267.

## Julian's Fierce Struggle

At this point, I could go one of two directions—I could carry the argument forth and examine more thoroughly Julian's pursuit of this new ideal (and there is so much more there—I have only looked at one aspect of it), or I could carry it backward and examine the process of theological reflection that led her to separate out mercy from grace in the first place. I shall do the latter since it helps explain the former.

Julian's juxtaposition of the parable of the lord and servant with her understanding of God as mother serves as her resolution to agonizing tensions that emerged as a result of the thirteenth and fourteenth showings. These tensions have mainly to do with Julian's struggle to come to terms with the apparent contradiction between, on the one hand, what she was "shown" directly by God, "without any meane [intermediary],"[39] and on the other hand, what the church taught. Throughout the entire text of *Showings*, with perhaps one exception, Julian reiterates that she holds and submits to the teachings of the church and that there is no contradiction between her showings and church doctrine. This denial notwithstanding, she is acutely aware, in the chapters leading up to the passages on divine motherhood and the parable, of building tensions (if not contradictions) in particular. I shall touch only very briefly on four of those tensions.

First, in the thirteenth showing, a locutional rather than a visual showing, Julian is so bold as to challenge her Lord, and a dialogue begins:

> And thus in my foly before this time, often I wondred why, by the grete forseeing wisdom of God, the beginning of sinne was not letted. For then thought me that alle shulde have be wele.[40]

> [I often wondered why, through the great prescient wisdom of God, the beginning of sin was not prevented. For then it seemed to me that all would have been well.[41]]

---

[39]   Ch. 4, Watson and Jenkins 135; Colledge and Walsh, 181.
[40]   Ch. 27, Watson and Jenkins, 209.
[41]   Ch. 27, Colledge and Walsh, 224.

Christ answers her, "Sin is behovely, but alle shalle be wele, and alle shalle be wele, and alle maner of thinge shalle be wel."[42]

Second, Christ's words of reassurance that "all will be well"—a refrain throughout the text, one for which Julian is perhaps most well known—leads Julian to question her Lord more. How can all things be well if, according to church teaching, some (many, most?) will be damned?

> And one point of oure faith is that many creatures shall be dampned: as angelis that felle out of heven for pride, which be now fendes, and man in erth that dyeth out of the faith of holy church—that is to sey, tho that be hethen—and also man that hath received cristondom and livesth uncristen life, and so dyeth oute of cherite. All theyse shalle be dampned to helle without ende, as holy church techeth me to beleve. And stonding alle this, methought it was unpossible that alle maner of thing shuld be wele, as oure lorde shewde in this time.

> And as to this, I had no other answere in shewing of oure lorde but this: "That that is unpossible to the is not unpossible to me. I shalle save my worde in alle thing, and I shalle make althing wele."[43]

> [And one article of our faith is that many creatures will be damned, such as the angels who fell out of heaven because of pride, who now are devils, and many men upon earth who die out of the faith of Holy church, that is to say those who are pagans and many who have received baptism and who live unchristian lives and so die out of God's love. All these will be eternally condemned to hell, as Holy Church teaches me to believe.

> And all this being so, it seemed to me that it was impossible that every kind of thing should be well, as our Lord revealed at this time.][44]

---

[42]   Ch. 27; Watson and Jenkins, 209. "Sin is necessary, but all will be well, and all will be well, and every kind of thing will be well" (Colledge and Walsh, 225).

[43]   Ch. 32, Watson and Jenkins, 223.

[44]   Colledge and Walsh, 233.

Julian is clearly incredulous, so incredulous that she asks to see purgatory and hell for herself.

Third, Julian's line of questioning then leads to the conclusion that, because of the "sovereyne frenship of oure curtesse lorde,"[45]

> And notwithstanding alle this, I saw sothfastly that oure lorde was never wroth nor never shall. For he is God, he is good, he is truth, he is love, he is pees ... For I saw truly that it is against the properte of his might to be wroth, and against the properte of his wisdom, and against the properte of his goodnes. God is that goodnesse that may not be wroth, for God is not but goodnes.[46]

> [For I saw truly that our Lord was never angry, and never will be. Because he is God, he is good, he is truth, he is love he is peace ... For I saw truly that it is against the property of his power to be angry, and against the property of his wisdom and against the property of his goodness. God is that goodness which cannot be angry, for God is nothing but goodness.][47]

But, of course, this does not square with what the church preaches or practices—certainly not the church in Norwich, under Henry le Despenser.

Fourth, Julian therefore goes on in chapter 45 to distinguish between two "domes" or judgments: the higher judgment of God, which involves no anger and shows no blame, and the "lower judgment" of holy church, which clearly shows both "blame and wrath."[48] And this brings us back full circle to chapter 48. At the beginning of that chapter she writes:

> For I saw no wrath but on mannes perty, and that forgeveth he in us. For wrath is not elles but a frowerdnes and a contrariousnes to pees and to love.[49]

---

45   Ch. 40, Watson and Jenkins, 243. "the supreme friendship of our courteous Lord" (trans. Colledge and Walsh, 246).

46   Ch. 46, Watson and Jenkins, 263.

47   Colledge and Walsh, 259.

48   Ch. 45, Watson and Jenkins, 261; Colledge and Walsh, 257.

49   Ch. 48, Watson and Jenkins, 267. "For I saw no wrath except on man's side, and he forgives that in us, for wrath is nothing else but a perversity and an opposition to peace and to love" (Colledge and Walsh, 262).

It is precisely at this point, at the climax of these building tensions and the inadequacy of other possible resolutions, that Julian introduces the theme of God as mother and begins to separate out mercy from grace.

This was critical for Julian, because mercy was conventionally understood in terms of divine justice and divine wrath, and it was therefore bound with divine forgiveness and clemency.[50] For Julian, however, if "God is that goodnesse that may not be wroth," and if "oure soule is oned to him, unchangeable goodnesse," then "betwen God and oure soule is neither wrath nor forgevenesse in his sight."[51] So if mercy is not forgiveness, what is it? For Julian, it is "tender love," compassion, and pity.

### The Motherhood Reconfigures the Church

Back when the tensions mentioned above began to mount, Julian had prophesied, "Holy church shalle be shaked in sorow and anguish and tribulation in this worlde as men shaketh a cloth in the winde."[52] ["Holy Church will be shaken in sorrow and anguish and tribulation in this world as men shake a cloth in the wind."[53]] Shortly thereafter, Julian brought together two traditional metaphors for the church: church as mother, and church as the body of Christ (1 Cor. 12: 12). She brings them together, reconfigured through her understanding of Jesus as mother: "For he it is, holy church. He is the grounde, he is the substance, he is the teching, he is the techer, he is the ende, and he is the mede wherfore every kinde soule traveleth."[54]

---

[50]   The *Oxford English Dictionary* defines mercy as "clemency and compassion shown to a person who is in a position of powerlessness or subjection, or to a person with no right or claim to receive kindness; kind and compassionate treatment in a case where severity is merited or expected, esp. in giving legal judgment or passing sentence."

[51]   Ch. 46, Watson and Jenkins, 263. "God is that goodness which cannot be angry, for God is nothing but goodness. Our soul is united to him who is unchangeable goodness. And between God and our soul there is neither wrath nor forgiveness in his sight" (Colledge and Walsh, 259).

[52]   Ch. 28, Watson and Jenkins, 211.

[53]   Colledge and Walsh, 226.

[54]   Ch. 34, Watson and Jenkins, 227.

["... he is that Holy Church. He is the foundation, he is the substance, he is the teacher, he is the end, he is the reward for which every loving soul labors."[55]]

The church is Christ's body; Christ is the church. The body of Christ, however, is that of a mother who encloses us in herself, who feeds us, who holds out her arms to us, who does not get angry and does not judge. The body of Christ is also a porous one, with many points of entry and many places of refuge.[56] At the same time, Christ, Christ's body, and Christ's church are enclosed in us: "Her may we see that us nedeth not gretly to seke ferre out to know sondry kindes, but to holy church, into oure moders brest: that is to say, *into oure owne soule wher oure lord wonneth*."[57] ["Here we can see that we do not need to seek far afield so as to know various natures, but to go to Holy Church, into our Mother's breast, that is to say *into our own soul, where our Lord dwells*."[58]] This stands in sharp relief against her earlier description of the "lower judgment" of the church.

Her redrawing of the church is an extensive one, for—having redefined what it is to be a lord and what it is for the church to be mother—she also redefines what a bishop is. The sixteenth and final showing is one of Christ, as bishop, seated in her soul, which she describes as an endless place of refuge, a blissful kingdom, and a worshipful city: "In middes of that citte sitteth oure lorde Jhesu, very God and very man: a fair person and of large stature, highest bishoppe, solempnest kinge, wurshipfullest lorde. And I saw him clothed solemply in wurshippes. He sitteth in the soule even righte in peas and rest, and he ruleth and yemeth heven and erth and all that is."[59] ["In the midst of that city sits our Lord Jesus, true God and true man, a handsome person and tall, highest bishop, most awesome king, most honourable lord. And I saw him splendidly clad in honours. He sits erect there in the soul, in peace and rest, and he rules and guards everything that is."[60]]

---

[55]   Colledge and Walsh, 236.

[56]   See Julia A. Lamm, "Revelation as Exposure in Julian of Norwich's *Showings*," *Spiritus* 5/1 (2005): 54–78; and Frederick Christian Bauerschmidt, *Julian of Norwich and the Mystical Body Politic of Christ* (Notre Dame and London: University of Notre Dame Press, 1999).

[57]   Ch. 62, Watson and Jenkins, 319, emphases added.

[58]   Colledge and Walsh, 303, emphases added.

[59]   Ch. 68, Watson and Jenkins, 335.

[60]   Colledge and Walsh, 313.

## Metaphysics and Ideals

Julian's understanding of God as mother brings along with it a dismantling of the metaphysical scaffolding that had supported the feudal hierarchies, both secular and ecclesial. According to her vision of the universe, there are endless series of enclosures, so that no one or no thing is any closer to or farther from God than any other person or thing. Once we see this, and see how the imagery of enclosure is so closely linked to her notion of God as mother, we see too how this permeates the entire text, from the first to the last showing. Indeed, as theological author, Julian consciously and deliberately interweaves the metaphysics of enclosure, from the beginning to the end of the text, as she herself explains:

> And oure savioure is oure very moder, in whome we be endlessly borne and never shall come out of him. Plentuously, fully, and swetely was this shewde; and it is spoken of in the furst, wher it saide: "We be all in him beclosed." And he is beclosed in us; and that is spoken of in the sixteenth shewing, where he seyth: "He sitteth in oure soule." For it is his liking to reigne in oure understanding blissefully, and sitte in oure soule restfully, and to wonne in oure soule endlesly, us all werking into him.[61]

> [… our saviour is our true Mother, in whom we are endlessly born and out of whom we shall never come.

> Plenteously, fully and sweetly was this shown; and it is spoken of in the first revelation, where it says that we are all enclosed in him, and he is enclosed in us. And it is spoken of in the sixteenth revelation, where he says that he sits in our soul, for it is his delight to reign blessedly in our understanding, and sit restfully in our soul, and to dwell endlessly in our soul, working us all into him.[62]]

The ideal is not presented as it would be in a neo-Platonic universe—a universe that justified and helped to rationalize the brutal treatment of peasants and dissenters. It is not an elusive goal to which we must ascend and for which we must punish and

---

[61] Ch. 57, Watson and Jenkins, 305.
[62] Colledge and Walsh, 292.

deny ourselves. In fourteenth-century Norwich, most people had already suffered unimaginable sorrow and indignities. For Julian, the mighty must surely empty themselves, but the meek need only come as they are, "naked," and realize that they are already enclosed in God, and God in them.

Julian's criticism of what in Norwich was a cruel and unjust socio-political system could be neither direct nor explicit. She presented it by setting up new ideals, ideals which she believed had been shown to her in 1373 and about which, she also believed, God had given her further instructions for over 20 years, without any intermediary. Her reconstituting of two entrenched social models—lordship and motherhood—took place through lengthy, serious, and sometimes agonizing theological reflection.

**Selected Bibliography**

Julian of Norwich, *The Writings*. Edited by Nicholas Watson and Jacqueline Jenkins (University Park: Pennsylvania State University Press, 2005).

Julian of Norwich, *Showings*. Edited by Edmund Colledge OSA, and James Walsh SJ (New York and Ramsey, Toronto: Paulist Press, 1978).

Walker Bynum, Caroline, *Jesus as Mother: Studies in the Spirituality of the High Middle Ages* (Berkeley: University of California Press, 1982).

# Index